PHYSICAL EDUCATION CURRICULUM ACTIVITIES KIT
FOR GRADES K-6

D1567192

PHYSICAL EDUCATION CURRICULUM ACTIVITIES KIT

FOR GRADES K-6

KEG WHEELER/OTTO H. SPILKER

PARKER PUBLISHING COMPANY
West Nyack, New York 10994

© 1991 by

PARKER PUBLISHING COMPANY

West Nyack, New York

10 9 8 7 6 5

Library of Congress Cataloging-in-Publication Data

Wheeler, Keg (Kenneth B.)
  Physical education curriculum activities kit for grades K–6 / Kenneth "Keg"
Wheeler, Otto H. Spilker.
    p. cm.
  ISBN 0-13-647033-5
    1. Physical education for children. 2. Games. I. Spilker, Otto
H. II. Title.
  GV443.W447 1991
  372.86—dc20
                                                                90-46120
                                                                CIP

ISBN 0-13-647033-5

9 780136 470335

PARKER PUBLISHING COMPANY
West Nyack, NY 10994

A Simon & Schuster Company

On the World Wide Web at http://www.phdirect.com

Printed in the United States of America

About the Authors

Keg Wheeler received his A.B. and M.Ed. degrees from the University of North Carolina at Chapel Hill. He has been involved with education for over 40 years, during which time he taught at several North Carolina schools and universities and was supervisor of health and physical education for the Henderson County (North Carolina) schools. A past president of the North Carolina Alliance of Health, Physical Education, Recreation and Dance, Mr. Wheeler is also the author of *Physical Education for Early Childhood K–3* and *Physical Education for Grades 4–6*, both published by the North Carolina State Department of Public Instruction.

Otto H. Spilker received his B.S. and M.S. degrees from Washington University in St. Louis and his P.E.D. from Indiana University. He has taught at the elementary and high school levels, and at present is a professor of health, physical education, and recreation at Western Carolina University. A published author of articles for several professional publications, including *Coach and Athlete* and *AAHPERD Journal*, Dr. Spilker received the 1976 Honor Award from North Carolina AAHPERD and the 1984 Taft Botner Teaching Award from Western Carolina University, and was the 1986 finalist for the Chancellor's Distinguished Teaching Award.

About This Kit

Physical Education Curriculum Activities Kit for Grades K–6 presents a variety of activities that teach fitness, basic skills, rhythm and dance, tumbling, games, and sports that are appropriate and are in proper sequential order for each grade level from K–6. Each physical education class period should be divided so that a balance between fitness activities and skill teaching is maintained throughout the school year.

A well-planned physical education program will result not only in physical fitness and new skills, but also in a more positive self-image, more desirable social behavior, and the joy of feeling well. The children will also realize the positive impact on their lives that good health produces.

To help you set up an effective physical education program, the *Kit* begins with suggestions on how to set up yearly calendars of activities at the different grade levels and offers sample calendars to follow. These calendars help to ensure proper progressions and sequences of activities for the classroom teacher who is "doing it all" and for the physical educator who is planning for grades K–6. You are also given suggestions for organizing the kindergarten physical education classes as well as the daily class format for all the grades so that there is a balance of activities in each class period.

During the school year, as each activity is being presented, you should constantly encourage child-initiated ideas. Listen to the children's ideas with enthusiasm and compliment them on their thinking. Incorporate as many of these ideas as possible and patiently explain why some of them cannot be used. *Never* make light or embarrass the children for any of their suggestions, no matter how impractical they may seem. You want the children to *think*—this is a vital part of the physical education program. Many of the activities in this kit stem from child-initiated ideas.

Some of the activities suggested in the yearly calendars are given more time than others. You should always feel free to cut short some of the suggested time alloted to certain activities and increase the time allotment on others depending on the class you have at the time. Flexibility of the yearly program depends on common sense and knowledge of the particular class involved. Like children, your classes each year are different; they are never alike. Therefore, adjustments will constantly have to be made (as in other school subjects) in order to make the activities more suitable for a particular class.

Assembling the list of equipment and researching the facilities suggested for the physical education programs in this book are challenges. You may be anxious to begin a program at your school, but you do not have the equipment recommended and your school will not be able to afford to purchase all the items listed at one time. *Very few schools can!* Do not let this stop you. Know that it will take you a few years with available school funds and a good PTA behind you to accumulate slowly the materials and equipment needed to present a sound and varied physical education program. To help you, look for the list of low-budget equipment and facilities following the yearly calendars. This list will help you get your program off the ground and on its way—*now*.

By following the suggestions and using the activities found in *Physical Education Curriculum Activities Kit*, you and your students will have an enjoyable physical education experience!

Keg Wheeler
Otto H. Spilker

Contents

Yearly Calendars for Grades K-6 ══════════════ 1

It is impossible to set up a calendar that could be used in all schools because every school is different. There are differences in *facilities, equipment, philosophy,* and *the needs of the children.* However, to present an idea of what a yearly calendar might look like, we have included sample calendars for grades K–1, 2–3, and 4–6.

We have tried to maintain a balance of fitness and skill activities in this sample program. In these calendars, the "Day" column indicates specific school days. For example, on the 101st day of the K–1 calendar, we suggest that the children run, work on wand routines, and play a simple game if time permits.

Be aware that after carefully designing your yearly calendar, you will encounter unforeseen situations such as bad weather, special programs, meetings, and so on, that will temporarily upset the sequences in some of your activities. Don't let this discourage you. The calendar is flexible in that the "Activity-of-Choice Day" will allow you to make up periods that were lost. By planning your programs ahead, you will come closer to getting most of your activities completed during the year.

The "Activity-of-Choice Day" usually comes on a Friday. There are 33 of them in the K–1 calendar, 34 in the 2–3 calendar, and 30 in the 4–6 calendar. It means just what it says. It can be *your choice* or the children's choice, and can be used to catch up on any activity when days were lost for some reason. Also, in the K–1 calendar, you will need to use two of these days to introduce the children to the routines and safety procedures of rope climbing (see Chapter 11) and pole climbing (see Chapter 12). The days scheduled for rhythms, circuits, parachute, and tug of war are short, so you can use some of the "Activity-of-Choice Days" for more concentration in these areas.

When making up your own yearly calendar, first make a list of the activities you want to cover in your yearly program. Then put all the holidays, workdays, and known special programs into your calendar. This should give you a good picture of the time available. Next, fill in the time slots with the activities you want to cover and give each activity the number of days you think you will need to do a sound job.

Your list of suggested K–1 activities might look something like this:

ACTIVITIES	NUMBER OF DAYS
Orientation	1
Fitness testing	10 (5 in fall; 5 in spring)
Awareness drill (organization)*	3

Running (organization)	1
The bars (organization)	4
Tug of war	5
Tire routines	10
Apparatus	9
Bean bags	9
Balls	9
Hula hoops	6
Wands	6
Carpets (tumbling)	9
Modified relays	6
Circuits	5
Rhythms	10
Parachute	6
Long rope (jumping)	9
Short rope (jumping)	7
"Two Square"	6
Balls (review)	6
"High Net, Low Net"	9
Field day	1
Activity of choice	33
	180 days

*The term *organization* means the number of days needed for the introduction or review of these particular activities. Thereafter, these activities can be a part of the daily routine. For example, "Running" and "The Bars" can also be used during the "Activity-of-Choice Days" for more concentration.

GRADES K-1

In the K–1 calendar, you will find the same activities listed for both years, but be aware that at each grade level the activities will become more sophisticated and challenging—building on the skills the students have developed in their previous physical education classes. For instance, if the students have successfully participated in the preceding K–1 physical education classes, some of the second- and third-graders should be ready to move successfully into soccer, volleyball, four square, regular relays, and so on. How fast they move along depends on how sound a foundation they have developed from previous training. For instance, if a third grade class has never participated in a well planned physical education program it may be wise to start them off from scratch with the "K" schedule and see how they come along. This becomes a real teacher judgment situation.

GRADES 2-3

In the following grades 2–3 activity list, notice that many of the activities have been repeated from K–1. But, as previously explained, the activities should become more sophisticated and challenging each year. For instance, if a child has been exposed to good progressions in the "Balls" activities in grades K–1, then that child should be ready to participate successfully in the "Balls" routines associated with team sports that are appropriate for this age group.

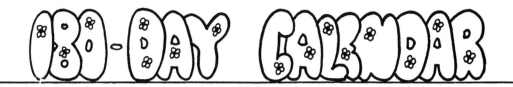

180-DAY CALENDAR

Day	GRADES K-1	
1. INSIDE, ORIENTATION Children's first day (usually a short day)	16. OUTSIDE Run; Tires organization (Chapter 9)	31. OUTSIDE Run; Bars Long rope jumping
2. INSIDE Awareness drill with locomotor skills (Chapter 2)	17. OUTSIDE Run; The bars Tires	32. OUTSIDE Run; Bars Long rope jumping
3. INSIDE Awareness drill with locomotor skills	18. OUTSIDE Run; The bars Tires	33. OUTSIDE Run; Bars Long rope jumping
4. INSIDE Awareness drill with locomotor skills	19. OUTSIDE Run; The bars Tires	34. OUTSIDE Run; Bars Modified relays
5. OUTSIDE Running organization (Chapter 2); Game	20. ACTIVITY OF CHOICE	35. ACTIVITY OF CHOICE
6. OUTSIDE/INSIDE Fitness testing	21. OUTSIDE Run; The bars Tires	36. OUTSIDE Run; Bars; Short rope jumping (Chapter 22)
7. OUTSIDE/INSIDE Fitness testing	22. OUTSIDE Run; The bars Tires	37. OUTSIDE Run; Bars; Short rope jumping
8. OUTSIDE/INSIDE Fitness testing	23. OUTSIDE Run; The bars Tires	38. OUTSIDE Run; Bars Short rope jumping
9. OUTSIDE/INSIDE Fitness testing	24. OUTSIDE Run; The bars Tug of war	39. OUTSIDE Run; Bars Short rope jumping
10. OUTSIDE/INSIDE Fitness testing	25. ACTIVITY OF CHOICE	40. ACTIVITY OF CHOICE
11. OUTSIDE Run; The bars organization (Chapter 3)	26. OUTSIDE Run; Bars; Long rope jumping (Chapter 22)	41. INSIDE Run; Circuit organization (Chapter 16)
12. OUTSIDE Run The bars organization	27. OUTSIDE Run; Bars Long rope jumping	42. INSIDE Run Circuit organization
13. OUTSIDE Run The bars	28. OUTSIDE Run; Bars Long rope jumping	43. INSIDE Run Circuit
14. OUTSIDE Run; The bars; Tug of war (Chapter 14)	29. OUTSIDE Run; Bars Modified relays (Chapter 15)	44. INSIDE Run Rhythms (Chapter 23)
15. ACTIVITY OF CHOICE	30. ACTIVITY OF CHOICE	45. ACTIVITY OF CHOICE

Day   GRADES K-1

46. INSIDE Run; Bean bags Game (Chapter 4)	61. INSIDE Run; Balls (Chapter 6) Game	76. INSIDE Run Hoops (Chapter 5)
47. INSIDE Run Bean bags Game	62. INSIDE Run; Balls Game	77. INSIDE Run; Hoops Game
48. INSIDE Run Bean bags Game	63. INSIDE Run; Balls Game	78. INSIDE Run; Hoops Game
49. INSIDE Run Rhythms (Chapter 23)	64. INSIDE Run Parachute (Chapter 10)	79. INSIDE Run Rhythms
50. ACTIVITY OF CHOICE	65. ACTIVITY OF CHOICE	80. ACTIVITY OF CHOICE
51. INSIDE Run Bean bags Game	66. INSIDE Run; Balls Game	81. INSIDE Run; Hoops Game
52. INSIDE Run Bean bags Game	67. INSIDE Run; Balls Game	82. INSIDE Run; Hoops Game
53. INSIDE Run Bean bags Game	68. INSIDE Run; Balls Game	83. INSIDE Run; Hoops Game
54. INSIDE Run Rhythms	69. INSIDE Run Parachute	84. INSIDE Run Rhythms
55. ACTIVITY OF CHOICE	70. ACTIVITY OF CHOICE	85. ACTIVITY OF CHOICE
56. INSIDE Run Bean bags Game	71. INSIDE Run; Balls Game	86. INSIDE Run; Carpets, Tumbling (Chapter 7)
57. INSIDE Run Bean bags Game	72. INSIDE Run; Balls Game	87. INSIDE Run; Carpets, Tumbling; Game
58. INSIDE Run Bean bags Game	73. INSIDE Run; Balls Game	88. INSIDE Run; Carpets, Tumbling; Game
59. INSIDE Run Rhythms	74. INSIDE Run Parachute	89. INSIDE Run Circuit
60. ACTIVITY OF CHOICE	75. ACTIVITY OF CHOICE	90. ACTIVITY OF CHOICE

Day   GRADES K-1

91. INSIDE Run; Carpets Tumbling; Game	106. INSIDE Run; Wands Game	121. INSIDE Run Apparatus
92. INSIDE Run; Carpets Tumbling; Game	107. INSIDE Run; Wands Game	122. INSIDE Run Apparatus
93. INSIDE Run; Carpets Tumbling; Game	108. INSIDE Run; Wands Game	123. INSIDE Run Apparatus
94. INSIDE Run Rhythms	109. INSIDE Run Circuit	124. INSIDE Run Rhythms
95. ACTIVITY OF CHOICE	110. ACTIVITY OF CHOICE	125. ACTIVITY OF CHOICE
96. INSIDE Run; Carpets Tumbling; Game	111. INSIDE Run Apparatus	126. INSIDE Run Review balls
97. INSIDE Run; Carpets Tumbling; Game	112. INSIDE Run Apparatus	127. INSIDE Run Review balls
98. INSIDE Run; Carpets Tumbling; Game	113. INSIDE Run Apparatus	128. INSIDE Run Review balls
99. INSIDE Run Circuit	114. INSIDE Run Rhythms	129. INSIDE Run Parachute
100. ACTIVITY OF CHOICE	115. ACTIVITY OF CHOICE	130. ACTIVITY OF CHOICE
101. INSIDE Run; Wands (Chapter 8) Game	116. INSIDE Run Apparatus	131. INSIDE Run Review balls
102. INSIDE Run; Wands Game	117. INSIDE Run Apparatus	132. INSIDE Run Review balls
103. INSIDE Run; Wands Game	118. INSIDE Run Apparatus	133. INSIDE Run Review balls
104. INSIDE Run Circuit	119. INSIDE Run Rhythms	134. INSIDE Run Parachute
105. ACTIVITY OF CHOICE	120. ACTIVITY OF CHOICE	135. ACTIVITY OF CHOICE

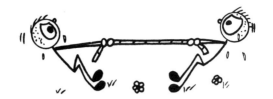

Day	GRADES K-1	
136. INSIDE/OUTSIDE Run; "High Net, Low Net" (Chapter 18); The bars, if outside	151. OUTSIDE Run; "Two Square" The bars	166. OUTSIDE Run; "High Net, Low Net" The bars
137. INSIDE/OUTSIDE Run; "High Net, Low Net" The bars, if outside	152. OUTSIDE Run; "Two Square" The bars	167. OUTSIDE Run; "High Net, Low Net" The bars
138. INSIDE/OUTSIDE Run; "High Net-Low Net" The bars, if outside	153. OUTSIDE Run; "Two Square" The bars	168. OUTSIDE Run; "High Net, Low Net" The bars
139. INSIDE/OUTSIDE Run; Parachute The bars, if outside	154. OUTSIDE Run; Modified relays The bars	169. OUTSIDE Run; Tug of war The bars
140. ACTIVITY OF CHOICE	155. ACTIVITY OF CHOICE	170. ACTIVITY OF CHOICE
141. INSIDE/OUTSIDE Run The bars if outside	156. OUTSIDE Run; Long jump rope The bars	171. OUTSIDE Run; Tires The bars
142. INSIDE/OUTSIDE Run; "High Net, Low Net" The bars, if outside	157. OUTSIDE Run; Long jump rope The bars	172. OUTSIDE Run; Tires The bars
143. INSIDE/OUTSIDE Run The bars, if outside	158. OUTSIDE Run; Long jump rope The bars	173. OUTSIDE Run; Tires The bars
144. INSIDE/OUTSIDE Run; Modified relays The bars, if outside	159. OUTSIDE Run; Tug of war The bars	174. FITNESS TESTING
145. ACTIVITY OF CHOICE	160. ACTIVITY OF CHOICE	175. FITNESS TESTING
146. INSIDE/OUTSIDE Run; "Two Square" (Chapter 13); The bars, if outside	161. OUTSIDE Run; Short jump ropes The bars	176. FITNESS TESTING
147. INSIDE/OUTSIDE Run; "Two Square" The bars, if outside	162. OUTSIDE Run; Short jump ropes The bars	177. FITNESS TESTING
148. INSIDE/OUTSIDE Run; "Two Square" The bars, if outside	163. OUTSIDE Run; Short jump ropes The bars	178. FITNESS TESTING
149. INSIDE/OUTSIDE Run; Modified relays The bars, if outside	164. OUTSIDE Run; Modified relays The bars	179. FIELD DAY
150. ACTIVITY OF CHOICE	165. ACTIVITY OF CHOICE	180. ACTIVITY OF CHOICE

Organization means the number of days needed for the introduction or review of these particular activities. Thereafter, these activities can be a part of the daily routine, such as the bars and running.

As stated before, the activity-of-choice days are for either your choice (makeups, etc.) or for the children's choice. If these days are followed as listed in the 2–3 calendar, the following activities will receive the number of days listed after the activity: tug of war—4 days, circuits—7 days, relays—7 days, tire routines—6 days, active games—8 days, and parachute—2 days plus 4 days scheduled in calendar.

ACTIVITIES	NUMBER OF DAYS
Orientation	1
Awareness drill (organization)	2
Running (organization)	2
Fall fitness testing	4
The bars (organization)	4
Bean bags	4
Balls	12
"Two Square" and "Four Square"	12
Hula hoops	8
Wands	8
Parachute	4
Carpets (tumbling)	12
Gymnastics	12
Rhythms	12
Long jump rope	8
Short jump rope	12
Ball review	8
Volleyball activities	12
"Four Square" review	4
Spring fitness testing	4
Field day	1
Activity-of-choice days	34
	180 days

GRADES 4-6

The 4–6 calendar is also a very basic plan or sequence of activities set up for these grade levels. As previously stated, each of the three years will be based on the present skill level of the class involved in order to maintain a proper sequence of new skills and continuity in the scheduled activities. In other words, begin with your students at whatever skill level they are when you get them and take them as far as you can in each activity. Then, in the following year, the classes' next teacher will, it is hoped, do the same. For example, a good class with good teachers can probably go from playing "Newcomb" in the fourth grade to playing a fair game of volleyball by the sixth grade if proper skill sequences are followed.

The activities listed for grades 4–6 are the same for all three years. But, again, each year the activities will become more advanced and challenging according to the skill level of the

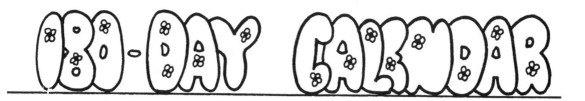

Day   GRADES 2-3

1. ORIENTATION Student's first day (usually a short day)	16. Run The bars Bean bags (Chapter 4)	31. Run The bars Balls
2. Awareness drill (Chapter 2)	17. Run The bars Bean bags	32. Run The bars Balls
3. Awareness drill	18. Run The bars Bean bags	33. Run The bars Balls
4. Running organization (Chapter 2)	19. Run The bars Bean bags	34. Run The bars Balls
5. Running organization	20. ACTIVITY OF CHOICE Run Relays (Chapter 15)	35. ACTIVITY OF CHOICE Run Tire routines
6. Run Fitness testing organization	21. Run The bars Balls (Chapter 6)	36. Run The bars; "Two Square," Grades 2-3 (Chapter 13)
7. Run Fitness testing	22. Run The bars Balls	37. Run The bars "Two Square"
8. Run Fitness testing	23. Run The bars Balls	38. Run The bars "Two Square"
9. Run Fitness testing	24. Run The bars Balls	39. Run The bars "Two Square"
10. ACTIVITY OF CHOICE Run; Tug of war (Chapter 14)	25. ACTIVITY OF CHOICE Run The bars; Active game	40. ACTIVITY OF CHOICE Run Relays
11. Run The bars (Chapter 3)	26. Run The bars Balls	41. Run The bars; "Two Square" (2), "Four square" (3)
12. Run The bars	27. Run The bars Balls	42. Run The bars; "Two Square" (2), "Four Square" (3)
13. Run The bars	28. Run The bars Balls	43. Run The bars; "Two Square" (2), "Four Square" (3)
14. Run The bars	29. Run The bars Balls	44. Run The bars; "Two square" (2), "Four square" (3)
15. ACTIVITY OF CHOICE Run Tire routines (Chapter 9)	30. ACTIVITY OF CHOICE Run Tug of war (Chapter 14)	45. ACTIVITY OF CHOICE Run Circuits (Chapter 16)

Day   GRADES 2-3

46. Run
    The bars
    "Four Square"
	61. Run
	    The bars
	    Wands (Chapter 8)
		76. Run
		    Carpets, tumbling
		    (Chapter 7)

47. Run
    The bars
    "Four Square"
	62. Run
	    The bars
	    Wands
		77. Run
		    Carpets, tumbling

48. Run
    The bars
    "Four Square"
	63. Run
	    The bars
	    Wands
		78. Run
		    Carpets, tumbling

49. Run
    The bars
    "Four Square"
	64. Run
	    The bars
	    Wands
		79. Run
		    Carpets, tumbling

50. ACTIVITY OF CHOICE
    Run
    Active game
	65. ACTIVITY OF CHOICE
	    Run
	    Relays
		80. ACTIVITY OF CHOICE
		    Run
		    Active game

51. Run
    The bars
    Hula hoops (Chapter 5)
	66. Run
	    The bars
	    Wands
		81. Run
		    Carpets, tumbling

52. Run
    The bars
    Hula hoops
	67. Run
	    The bars
	    Wands
		82. Run
		    Carpets, tumbling

53. Run
    The bars
    Hula hoops
	68. Run
	    The bars
	    Wands
		83. Run
		    Carpets, tumbling

54. Run
    The bars
    Hula hoops
	69. Run
	    The bars
	    Wands
		84. Run
		    Carpets, tumbling

55. ACTIVITY OF CHOICE
    Run
    Tug of war
	70. ACTIVITY OF CHOICE
	    Run
	    Active game
		85. ACTIVITY OF CHOICE
		    Run
		    Circuits

56. Run
    The bars
    Hula hoops
	71. Run (Due to cold weather
	    may have to move inside)
	    Parachute (Chapter 10)
		86. Run
		    Carpets, tumbling

57. Run
    The bars
    Hula hoops
	72. Run
	    Parachute
		87. Run
		    Carpets, tumbling

58. Run
    The bars
    Hula hoops
	73. Run
	    Parachute
		88. Run
		    Carpets, tumbling

59. Run
    The bars
    Hula hoops
	74. Run
	    Parachute
		89. Run
		    Carpets, tumbling

60. ACTIVITY OF CHOICE
    Run
    Tire routines
	75. ACTIVITY OF CHOICE
	    Run
	    Circuits
		90. ACTIVITY OF CHOICE
		    Tire routines (indoor)

Day		GRADES 2-3	

91. Run Gymnastics	106. Run Rhythms (Chapter 23)	121. Run Long rope jumping (Chapter 22)
92. Run Gymnastics	107. Run Rhythms	122. Run Long rope jumping
93. Run Gymnastics	108. Run Rhythms	123. Run Long rope jumping
94. Run Gymnastics	109. Run Rhythms	124. Run Long rope jumping
95. ACTIVITY OF CHOICE Run Parachute	110. ACTIVITY OF CHOICE Run Active game	125. ACTIVITY OF CHOICE Run Relays
96. Run Gymnastics	111. Run Rhythms	126. Run (outside weather permitting); The bars Long rope jumping
97. Run Gymnastics	112. Run Rhythms	127. Run The bars Long rope jumping
98. Run Gymnastics	113. Run Rhythms	128. Run The bars Long rope jumping
99. Run Gymnastics	114. Run Rhythms	129. Run The bars Long rope jumping
100. ACTIVITY OF CHOICE Run Relays (indoor)	115. ACTIVITY OF CHOICE Run Tire routines (indoors)	130. ACTIVITY OF CHOICE Run Circuits
101. Run Gymnastics	116. Run Rhythms	131. Run The bars; Short rope jumping (Chapter 22)
102. Run Gymnastics	117. Run Rhythms	132. Run The bars Short rope jumping
103. Run Gymnastics	118. Run Rhythms	133. Run The bars Short rope jumping
104. Run Gymnastics	119. Run Rhythms	134. Run The bars Short rope jumping
105. ACTIVITY OF CHOICE Run Circuits	120. ACTIVITY OF CHOICE Run Parachute	135. ACTIVITY OF CHOICE Run Active game

BEAN BAG PASS
(RELAY)

Day   GRADES 2-3

136. Run The bars Short rope jumping	151. Run The bars; Volleyball activities (Chapter 18)	166. Run; The bars Four square review (Chapter 13)
137. Run The bars Short rope jumping	152. Run The bars Volleyball activities	167. Run The bars Four square review
138. Run The bars Short rope jumping	153. Run The bars Volleyball activities	168. Run The bars Four square review
139. Run The bars Short rope jumping	154. Run The bars Volleyball activities	169. Run The bars Four square review
140. ACTIVITY OF CHOICE Run; The bars Tug of war	155. ACTIVITY OF CHOICE Run The bars; Relays	170. ACTIVITY OF CHOICE Run The bars; Circuits
141. Run The bars Ball review (Chapter 6)	156. Run The bars Volleyball activities	171. Run Fitness testing
142. Run The bars Ball review	157. Run The bars Volleyball activities	172. Run Fitness testing
143. Run The bars Ball review	158. Run The bars Volleyball activities	173. Run Fitness testing
144. Run The bars Ball review	159. Run The bars Volleyball activities	174. Run Fitness testing
145. ACTIVITY OF CHOICE The bars Tire routine	160. ACTIVITY OF CHOICE Run Circuits	175. ACTIVITY OF CHOICE Run Active game
146. Run The bars Ball review	161. Run The bars Volleyball activities	176. FIELD DAY
147. Run The bars Ball review	162. Run The bars Volleyball activities	177. ACTIVITY OF CHOICE (teacher's or children's choice)
148. Run The bars Ball review	163. Run The bars Volleyball activities	178. ACTIVITY OF CHOICE (teacher's or children's choice)
149. Run The bars Ball review	164. Run The bars Volleyball activities	179. ACTIVITY OF CHOICE (teacher's or children's choice)
150. ACTIVITY OF CHOICE Run; The bars Active game	165. ACTIVITY OF CHOICE Run The bars; Relays	180. ACTIVITY OF CHOICE (teacher's or children's choice)

particular class involved. The schedule is flexible enough to allow you to give more or less time for any activity that needs it, and the "Activity-of-Choice Days" allow a good deal of flexibility.

ACTIVITIES	NUMBER OF DAYS
Orientation	1
The bars (organization)	1
Physical fitness test items (practice)	5 (in fall)
Physical fitness testing	4 (in fall)
"Four Square"	9
Soccer	13
Basketball	12
Relays	7
Circuits (organization)	3
Rope jumping	9
Rhythms	14
Gymnastics (tumbling/apparatus)	20
Volleyball	16
Softball	12
Track	11
Physical fitness test items (practice)	4 (in spring)
Physical fitness testing	4 (in spring)
Field day (practice)	2
Field days	2
Activity-of-choice days	31
	180 days

The equipment needed to follow the curriculum presented in the 4–6 calendar includes

30 playground balls (8½")
30 short jump ropes
 6 long ropes
12 cones or gallon milk cartons (see Chapter 26)
 1 tug-of-war rope
 1 parachute
 6 soccer balls (minimum)
 6 volleyballs
 2 homemade volleyball nets (see Chapter 18)
 6 basketballs
 2 movable or permanent basketball goals (for inside)
12 softballs
 2 batting T's (see Chapter 26)
 4 softball bats
 3 tumbling mats (5' × 10' or 6' × 12').
48 old truck tires (with firm casings)

Elementary gymnastic equipment

Horizontal bar
Parallel bar
Horse
Balance beam
1 record player

Outside equipment (see Chapter 26)

Chinning bars
Parallel bars
Vault bars
Horizontal ladder
Climbing poles

Black-top area at least 30′ x 70′

4 "Four Square" courts (see Chapter 26)
1 midline
1 25′ circle
2 fixed basketball goals

FITNESS TESTING FOR GRADES K-6

Give a physical fitness test two times in each school year. The early fall fitness test gives the students an indication of their physical condition after spending two months on summer vacation. Regrettably, during the summer vacation most of the children do not participate in well-planned physical programs that will maintain and improve their strength and stamina. Granted, many are engaged in *recreational* swimming, softball, and baseball, but these recreational activities may do very little to maintain a good level of physical fitness. Also, during this time, the children spend a lot more time sitting and watching movies, TV, and videotapes. The results of this relaxed life-style usually show up on their fall fitness tests with disappointing drops on their test items. Therefore, the fall test will show where they are weak and, with proper *encouragement* by you, should serve as a good motivator for getting their scores back up and beyond where they were before.

The spring fitness test is the big one for both the students and you. It answers the questions as to whether the children have been encouraged and motivated to work hard enough to bring up their scores. Also, if the scores are disappointing for most of the children, then you need to take another close look at your physical education curriculum. Are you giving them enough time for running? Do they spend enough time on the bars, the climbing ropes, and the climbing poles to build up arm and shoulder strength?

The *AAHPERD Presidential Physical Fitness Test* or the *President's Challenge Test* are highly recommended.

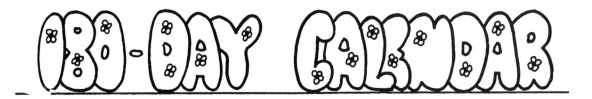

Day	GRADES 4-6	
1. ORIENTATION Student's first day (usually a short day)	16. Running The bars "Four Square"	31. Running The bars Soccer
2. Class format (Chapter 2) Running (Chapter 2) The bars (Chapter 3)	17. Running The bars "Four Square"	32. Running The bars Soccer
3. Running The bars; Practice fitness test items	18. Running The bars "Four Square"	33. ACTIVITY OF CHOICE
4. Running The bars; Practice fitness test items	19. Running The bars "Four Square"	34. Running The bars Soccer
5. Running The bars; Practice fitness test items	20. Running The bars "Four Square"	35. Running The bars Soccer
6. Running The bars; Practice fitness test items	21. Running The bars Soccer (Chapter 17)	36. Running The bars Basketball (Chapter 19)
7. Running The bars; Practice fitness test items	22. Running The bars Soccer	37. Running The bars Basketball
8. Running Fitness testing	23. Running The bars Soccer	38. ACTIVITY OF CHOICE (tire routines)
9. Running Fitness testing	24. Running The bars Soccer	39. Running The bars Basketball
10. Running Fitness testing	25. Running The bars Soccer	40. Running The bars Basketball
11. Running Fitness testing	26. Running The bars Soccer	41. Running The bars Basketball
12. Running The bars; "Four Square" (Chapter 13)	27. Running The bars Soccer	42. Running The bars Basketball
13. Running The bars "Four Square"	28. ACTIVITY OF CHOICE (teacher's or children's choice)	43. ACTIVITY OF CHOICE (tug of war)
14. Running The bars "Four Square"	29. Running The bars Soccer	44. Running The bars Basketball
15. Running The bars "Four Square"	30. Running The bars Soccer	45. Running The bars Basketball

Day	GRADES 4-6	
46. Running The bars Basketball	61. Running Circuits	76. Running Rhythms
47. Running The bars Basketball	62. Running Circuits	77. Running Rhythms
48. ACTIVITY OF CHOICE (game)	63. ACTIVITY OF CHOICE (game)	78. ACTIVITY OF CHOICE (relays)
49. Running The bars Basketball	64. Running Rope jumping (Chapter 22)	79. Running Rhythms
50. Running The bars Basketball	65. Running Rope jumping	80. Running Rhythms
51. Running The bars Relays (Chapter 15)	66. Running Rope jumping	81. Running Rhythms
52. Running The bars Relays	67. Running Rope jumping	82. Running Rhythms
53. ACTIVITY OF CHOICE (tire routines)	68. ACTIVITY OF CHOICE (circuits)	83. ACTIVITY OF CHOICE (circuits)
54. Running The bars Relays	69. Running Rope jumping	84. Running Rhythms
55. Running The bars Relays	70. Running Rope jumping	85. Running Rhythms
56. Running The bars Relays	71. Running Rope jumping	86. Running Rhythms
57. Running The bars Relays	72. Running Rope jumping	87. Running Rhythms
58. ACTIVITY OF CHOICE (tug of war, Chapter 14)	73. ACTIVITY OF CHOICE (circuits)	88. ACTIVITY OF CHOICE (circuits)
59. Running The bars Relays	74. Running Rope jumping	89. Running Rhythms
60. Running (due to cold weather, may have to move inside); Circuits (Chapter 16)	75. Running Rhythms (Chapter 23)	90. Running Rhythms

Day		GRADES 4-6	
91. Running Rhythms	106. Running Gymnastics	121. Running The bars Volleyball
92. Running Gymnastics	107. Running Gymnastics	122. Running The bars Volleyball
93. Running Gymnastics	108. Running Gymnastics	123. ACTIVITY OF CHOICE (tug of war)
94. ACTIVITY OF CHOICE (four square)	109. ACTIVITY OF CHOICE (relays)	124. Running The bars Volleyball
95. Running Gymnastics	110. Running Gymnastics	125. Running The bars Volleyball
96. Running Gymnastics	111. Running Gymnastics	126. Running The bars Volleyball
97. Running Gymnastics	112. Running Gymnastics	127. Running The bars Volleyball
98. Running Gymnastics	113. ACTIVITY OF CHOICE (game)	128. ACTIVITY OF CHOICE ("Four Square")
99. ACTIVITY OF CHOICE (relays)	114. Running Gymnastics	129. Running The bars Volleyball
100. Running Gymnastics	115. Running Gymnastics	130. Running The bars Volleyball
101. Running Gymnastics	116. Running Gymnastics	131. Running The bars Volleyball
102. Running Gymnastics	117. Running; Volleyball (Chapter 18), outside weather permiting	132. Running The bars Volleyball
103. Running Gymnastics	118. ACTIVITY OF CHOICE (tire routines, Chapter 9)	133. ACTIVITY OF CHOICE (tire routines)
104. ACTIVITY OF CHOICE (rope jumping)	119. Running The bars Volleyball	134. Running The bars Volleyball
105. Running Gymnastics	120. Running The bars Volleyball	135. Running The bars Volleyball

136. Running
   The bars
   Volleyball
	151. Running
	   The bars
	   Softball
		166. Running
		   The bars
		   Practice fitness items

137. Running
   The bars
   Softball (Chapter 20)
	152. ACTIVITY OF CHOICE
	   (tug of war)
		167. ACTIVITY OF CHOICE
		   (rope jumping)

138. ACTIVITY OF CHOICE
   (tug of war)
	153. Running
	   The bars
	   Track (Chapter 25)
		168. Running
		   The bars
		   Practice fitness items

139. Running
   The bars
   Softball
	154. Running
	   The bars
	   Track
		169. Running
		   The bars
		   Practice fitness items

140. Running
   The bars
   Softball
	155. Running
	   The bars
	   Track
		170. Running
		   The bars
		   Practice fitness items

141. Running
   The bars
   Softball
	156. Running
	   The bars
	   Track
		171. FITNESS TESTING

142. Running
   The bars
   Softball
	157. ACTIVITY OF CHOICE
	   (relays)
		172. FITNESS TESTING

143. ACTIVITY OF CHOICE
   (game)
	158. Running
	   The bars
	   Track
		173. FITNESS TESTING

144. Running
   The bars
   Softball
	159. Running
	   The bars
	   Track
		174. FITNESS TESTING

145. Running
   The bars
   Softball
	160. Running
	   The bars
	   Track
		175. ACTIVITY OF CHOICE

146. Running
   The bars
   Softball
	161. Running
	   The bars
	   Track
		176. FIELD DAY
		   Preparation

147. Running
   The bars
   Softball
	162. ACTIVITY OF CHOICE
	   ("Four Square")
		177. FIELD DAY
		   Preparation

148. ACTIVITY OF CHOICE
   (tire routines)
	163. Running
	   The bars
	   Track
		178. FIELD DAY

149. Running
   The bars
   Softball
	164. Running
	   The bars
	   Track
		179. FIELD DAY

150. Running
   The bars
   Softball
	165. Running
	   The bars
	   Track
		180. ACTIVITY OF CHOICE

Organizing the P.E. Class⸺2

It is very important that you get your physical education classes off to a good start at the beginning, so the first part of this chapter offers step-by-step suggestions for developing very important objectives during the early class meetings in the fall.

The second part of this chapter deals with a basic daily format. There are many important activities, such as running, developmental activities, skill activities, games, and so on, that should be covered during the class. Therefore, so that you don't spend all of the class time on just one activity, you need to set time allotments on the activities you intend to use during that period so that you can get them all in. Suggestions for breakdown of time allotments and the appropriate activities for particular grade levels are also presented in this chapter.

KINDERGARTEN

Here you are, we hope, in a multipurpose room or gym, with your kindergarten class at the beginning of the school year. You know how very important it is that you get your class organized and started off correctly. This beginning experience can set the tone for your physical education for the rest of the year. So what do you do first with the students? What do you want to establish with this class at the beginning?

Awareness Drill

This drill will help you get started. The "Awareness Drill" is just one of many methods that can be used to get classes organized and ready to go. With this drill, you want to establish the following:

♦ Listening skills and control
♦ Terminology that will be used in the activities
♦ Knowing the locomotor and nonlocomotor skills

First. Have your class sit quietly at one end of the multipurpose room, listening carefully to what you are saying. As a starter with this group, you may want to point out the empty area of the multipurpose room and get the class into a discussion of space. Begin with such questions as "Children, what is space?" "Who can tell me what it is?" and so on.

After a discussion of space and establishing some meaning of it, ask them to walk out quietly into all that space (general space) and find their very own little space (personal space) and sit down in it when they hear you say "Off you go." Their space should not be close to anyone else's space or to the walls or to any equipment that may be around. Say to the students, "Can you do this? Then off you go, walk quietly, and find your own space and sit down."

Second. After they are seated in their own spaces, you may have to move those who are sitting too close to someone else, the walls, or any equipment to a better position. Be sure to explain to the students why you are doing this. Next, teach the children the magic words "And stop." Explain to the students that when they hear you say "And stop," they must stop, look, and listen to your next directions. They must not talk or move about when you are talking.

Third. Once the children know what to do when they hear "Off you go" and "And stop," they are ready to learn how to move in space in many different ways. Have the students stand in their own (personal) spaces. Ask them to look around and see all the empty spaces around and in between their classmates (general space). Tell them that when you say "Off you go," they are to walk carefully in these empty spaces without touching anyone else and without talking, while constantly changing directions and using all the space so that they will not bunch up. Now give the "Off you go" signal. Let the children walk for about 15 seconds and then give the signal "And stop." Go over what you saw. It may be that some were bumping into others, some ran, a few were bunched up and not using all the space, and some were laughing and talking and paying little attention to what they were supposed to be doing. Go over these mistakes with the children and continue this same routine until the class is following your directions (listening) and responding to your commands (control).

Without these listening skills and control, you and your class will have a difficult time doing the many different, challenging, and sometimes complicated activities to come.

Safety is also a big factor. Many of these activities will be exciting and vigorous—but potentially dangerous—if you have little control over your class.

Just as soon as the children show a positive response to this drill, introduce locomotor skills. Have them run under control, skip, jump, hop, leap, slide, and gallop. Each one is explained briefly:

♦ Walk—Transferring weight from one foot to another while moving at a moderate rate of speed.
♦ Run—Similar to walking but at a faster pace, remaining in the air longer between steps.
♦ Skip—Hop step right/hop step left/continue.
♦ Leap—Shifting weight from one foot to another with long stretching strides each time.
♦ Hop—Going into the air on one foot and landing on the same foot.
♦ Jump—Taking off into the air with two feet at the same time and landing on two feet at the same time.
♦ Gallop—Leaping on the right foot/stepping with the left, and bring it beside the right/continue.
♦ Slide—Stepping to the side with the left leg, then sliding the right foot to the left foot; it's a step left/close right rhythm (when done faster, a small hop is done with the step-slide).

Spend the time needed in this early drill to establish the listening skills and control so that you will be able to lead your class successfully and safely through many exciting and challenging physical education activities. It will be a happy and rewarding experience for both you and your class in many ways.

GRADES K-3

The following ideas are to help you set up your 30-minute K–3 physical education classes. These suggestions should be used after you have introduced the "Awareness Drill" to your class. It is hoped, at this point, that most of the class has established listening skills and control.

Bring your class into the multipurpose room quietly. This will help set the tone for the rest of the period. Have them check their shoes to see if they are properly tied. A good safe knot is the double bow, which will stay tied. Have them remove any unnecessary coats, sweaters, and jewelry that could be dangerous to themselves or others.

The following is a breakdown of the class period with time allotments. (See the sample chart.)

1. First part of class (5–10 minutes): This consists of warmups, such as "Awareness Drill," "Run Break," and "Running." (See the "Warm-ups" description that follows.)
2. Second part of class (10–20 minutes): This time slot is for the regularly scheduled physical education activity, such as rope jumping, ball activities, hula hoop activities, and so on.

SAMPLE CLASS PERIOD (K-3)

	MINUTES			
FIRST PART of Period — Running or Awareness Drill	10	5	10	10
SECOND PART of Period — Regular Scheduled Physical Education Activity	20	20	15	10
THIRD PART of Period — Game	0	5	5	10
MINUTES	30	30	30	30

3. Third part of class (5–10 minutes): When possible, end the class with a game or activity that reinforces or complements the activities they had in class that day. Or use a passive activity to let the students cool down after a vigorous physical education session.

Warm-ups

Change the warm-ups frequently so that the children will not get bored or tired of them. For instance, after the kindergarten class has mastered the "Awareness Drill" and seems to be tiring of the regular routine, modify it slightly. Place a cone or marker in each corner (leave room to run around the outside of it) of the room. Then teach them to follow a leader around these four corners while running in a single file. During the run, signal by calling "Break!" On this signal, the children immediately go into the "Awareness Drill," running in and out of empty spaces without bumping, and so on. After about 5 seconds, signal "Freeze!" The children should stop in their tracks and wait for the next directions. At this time, slip the locomotor skills back in between each "Break" and "Freeze." For example, you might announce "Skip," then call out "Break." The children immediately begin to skip into the empty spaces for about 5 seconds until you say "Freeze." Continue this routine by putting a different locomotor skill in each time.

Some days, you may want to let the children run quietly and follow a leader in a single file around the outside of the cones, which are located in the four corners of the room, to music. If so, the following directions will save a lot of chaos and confusion:

♦ Play appropriate music.
♦ Follow directly behind the person in front.
♦ Never push or touch the person in front.
♦ Do not pass. (This is dangerous, especially indoors.)
♦ Do not talk.
♦ Do not speed up or slow down. Keep a steady pace.
♦ Do not run side by side.
♦ Run quietly so that you can hear the music.

When a group is running single file with no passing allowed, this group is geared to its slowest runners. You may want to put a smaller area inside the larger area for the slower children to run in.

A Final Thought

Thus, to get the most out of your 30-minute physical education periods for grades K–3, you will need to go over each day's lesson plan and decide how much time you are going to allot to the three parts of your period. For instance, if you think your class is in good running condition, you may want to spend only 5 minutes in the warm-up (or first part) of the period running (remember that these 5 minutes include not only running but getting students ready to run and a brief cool-down walk afterward) in order to maintain their condition. This will give you 20 minutes in the second part to work on the regularly scheduled physical education activity for that day and 5 minutes in the third part with an activity for unwinding.

Or you may think your class is in poor shape in their running. You may then want to give 10 minutes of the first part of the period to running, 15 minutes of the second part to the scheduled physical education activity, and 5 minutes to the third part for an activity for fun. You will have to make these decisions for yourself.

When you are doing your outside activities, you may want a full 10 minutes for the first part, especially if you have outside apparatus (such as the bars described in Chapter 3) because this will involve a run and a short workout on the outside apparatus. Then schedule the last two parts of the class as discussed earlier.

GRADES 4-6

The tone of your physical education class could very well be set by the way the class is allowed to enter the multipurpose room or the teaching area. If the children are allowed to come into the room in a loud and disorderly manner, you may have to spend half the class period trying to settle them down so that you can teach. The class should walk into the teaching area in a quiet and orderly manner. Remember, your physical education class is an *instruction* period, *not* a time for the children to "let off steam." If your physical education class is well planned and organized, the children will be able to let off steam in a productive, orderly, and controlled manner.

The physical education periods are divided into three sections:

1. Running (see "Running" later in this chapter)
2. Fitness and developmental activities (see Chapters 3 and 4)
3. Regular scheduled physical education for the day, such as soccer, volleyball, "Four Square," and so on.

Because many elementary physical education classes are scheduled for 30 minutes, it is imperative that all classes begin and end on time. To incorporate these three important sections successfully into a productive class period takes good planning, organization, and discipline. For instance, the daily run should seldom be over 3 (or at the most 5) minutes in duration. Next, if outside, the work on the bars (*when organized*) should not take over 10 minutes. This will leave approximately 15 minutes for the regular scheduled physical activity. All three of these sections are very important, so try to give each section enough time for positive results. Remember, it is consistency that counts. Running and developmental activities (the bars or the circuits) must be done every day when possible if measurable results are expected.

Daily Format

The following is a possible daily format for a beginning 4–6 physical education program with limited equipment and facilities. Again, the class period (whether indoors or outdoors) can be divided into three sections as follows:

1. Running (3 to 5 minutes)
2. Fitness circuit (10 minutes)
3. Regular scheduled physical education activity for the day (15 minutes)

First. The running area can be established around the circuit stations. (See the illustration.) Use old bicycle tires to set up your circuit area where it will include the pull up (chin-ning) bars. If possible, have approximately 35' to 50' between stations so that the students can travel around the outside of the tires when doing the running portion of the class period.

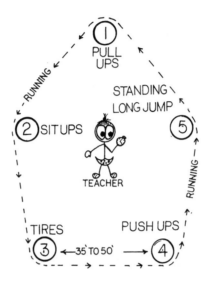

The running (time it for 3 to 5 minutes) around the outside of the bicycle tires in the circuit should pose no problem as long as it is done in an orderly manner.

Second. On the first day you introduce the class to the circuit, take the students around the circuit, and show them how the assigned tasks at each station are properly and safely done. Next, divide the class into five squads and assign each squad to a station. Practice performing the tasks and rotating until every squad has been to each station. It will be time well spent if one class period is used for practicing just the circuit to make certain the class thoroughly understands how the circuit operates. In order to finish the five-station circuit in approximate-ly 10 minutes, stand in the center of the circuit and time the activity. Allow 1½ minutes at each station and then give the squads 30 seconds to rotate. A brief description of the five activi-ties used in the circuit follows:

1. Pull-ups—See Chapter 3.
2. Sit-ups—With the knees flexed and the arms crossed in front of the chest, curl up and touch the thighs with the elbows. Return to the starting position and repeat.
3. Tires—Set up a single row of at least six truck tires. See Chapter 9 for routines that can be used.
4. Push-ups—*Regular* push-ups are for those with enough arm and shoulder strength to do them correctly. Put weight on the hands and toes as shown. Keep the body straight at all times. Lower the body and touch the chest to the ground or floor and return to the starting position. Repeat as many times as possible in the time limit.

   Modified push-ups are for those who lack the arm and shoulder strength to do a regular push-up correctly. The procedure is the same as it is in the regular push-up except that the weight is placed on the knees rather than on the toes. Move on to regular push-ups as soon as the children are ready.
5. Standing broad jump—Stand behind the take-off line with the feet several inches apart. As the arms are swung backward, bend the knees. Then with an explosive movement, extend the knees and swing the arms forward vigorously as you jump forward.

Feel free to replace any of these tasks with activities you think may be more appropriate. The items just listed are merely suggestions.

Third. This longest portion of the class period is used for the regular scheduled physical education activity for the day.

The Bars ————————————————————3

The bars should be added to the K–3 curriculum to fill a gap that seems to exist in many physical education programs. Physical fitness testing shows that many boys and girls are weak in both flexor and extensor arm strength. Even children who are heavily involved in after-school athletic programs such as soccer, football, basketball, baseball, and softball are also weak in this area.

Therefore, to try to remedy this situation, set up areas on your school grounds that include four simple pieces of gymnastic apparatus: chinning bars, vault bars, monkey bars (horizontal ladder), and parallel bars. A fifth piece of equipment could be climbing poles (see Chapter 12).

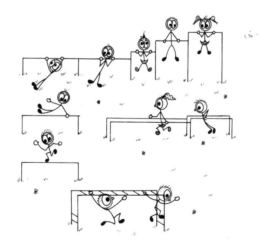

After instructing the children in the proper use of each piece of equipment and the safety factors involved, have the students run and perform a series of short gymnastic-type activities that take approximately 10 to 15 minutes of the 30-minute period. This time is well spent since the children are being exposed to organized arm flexor-extensor activities that they so vitally need.

You will get good participation and cooperation from most of the children, but there are always a few who will be very challenging to motivate, especially the obese. Regretfully, there is no pat solution for these problems except to continue to explain patiently and quietly what this equipment is designed to do for them and to encourage them to do the very best they can. Do not lose your patience and embarrass these children, either in front of the class or behind their backs. *Always* praise *any* effort the children make, no matter how slight.

CONSTRUCTION AND APPROXIMATE COST

The drawings and dimensions of each piece of equipment used in this chapter are found in Chapter 26. All the equipment is made from 1½ " black pipe and can be put together and set up by the school maintenance people. In most cases, the cost of this equipment can be taken on by the PTA as a project. After the equipment is put together and set up, give the bars a good primer coat of paint and then give each of the four sections a different color of paint. This serves two purposes: (1) the paint makes them more attractive, and (2) color coding is a big help when assigning stations and when referring to a specific piece of equipment. To keep the bars attractive, they should be sanded and painted every two or three years depending on the part of the country in which you live.

The cost of putting up a set of bars is approximately $400, which includes buying the pipe, welding, and setting up. Of course, this figure can vary due to inflation and other factors.

CLASS ORGANIZATION

For an average class size of 28 children, you will need four squads of 7 children each. (If you include climbing poles, you need five squads of 5 or 6 children each.)

Some teachers form permanent squads while others have the class line up, count off, and form new squads each day. This, of course, takes a little longer. If you have permanent squads, you may have to shift children around for a better balance of squads when students are absent.

Look at the accompanying illustration.

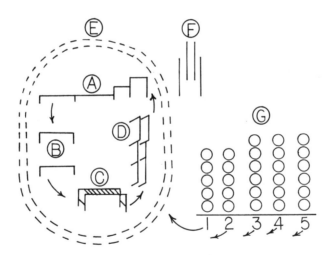

If squads are already formed, have the children line up at (G) by squads. If not already divided, have the students line up in a straight line and count off by either four's or five's and then quickly line up in their squads. This gives you time to make any announcements that may be needed. This explanation describes a class that has already been trained and has been in action for a few weeks.

After you have made your announcements, say "Squad 1, go!" Squad 1 peels off and follows the running path around the bars (E). Squad 2 follows right behind squad 1. Squads 3, 4, and 5 follow the same routine. They should run two times around the bars (the running path) and then go immediately to their assigned station: Squad 1 to the pull up bars (A, red); squad 2 to the vault bars (B, white); squad 3 to the monkey bars (C, blue); squad 4 to the parallel bars (D, yellow); and, if you have climbing poles, squad 5 to that station (F, multicolored).

As soon as the squads get to their stations, they go to work on the activity. The length of time at each station is 1½ minutes. At the end of this time, call out "Rotate!" All squads immediately hit the running path (E) and run another full lap around the bars before going to their next station—A to B, B to C, C to D, D to F, F to A.

Continue this routine until all squads have performed at each station. Remember, they will run two laps around the bars in the beginning and one lap after each rotation. At the end, if they have been motivated, they will have had a good workout from running and gymnastic-type activities.

NOTE: If the bars are to be effective, they must be used regularly in grades K–6. They will not be effective when used only now and then. So, weather permitting and when possible, begin your outdoor activities with the bars. When two classes are outside at the same time, they can take turns using the bars the first part of the period and the last part of the period.

ANOTHER IMPORTANT POINT TO KEEP IN MIND: At the beginning of each new school year, review the activities and safety procedures at each station before turning the class loose on the bars.

THE CHINNING BARS

If your students in grades K–2 have never been on the bars before, start them on the lower end of the chinning bars and teach them how to do a forward hip circle.

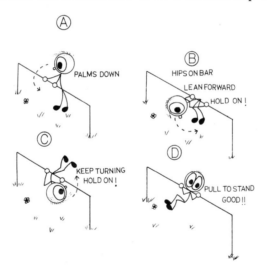

After a demonstration by a child, the majority of the children will be able to do a decent hip circle. There will be a few who will need help, however, so spot each child who needs help by putting your hand behind his or her head and following it all the way under. Some children will have a tendency to let go before they finish the move, so watch out for this.

Once the children have the circle down pat, have them do five or six in a row. You can encourage those who have mastered this skill to work on the reverse hip circle, which is a much more challenging skill. (See the illustration.)

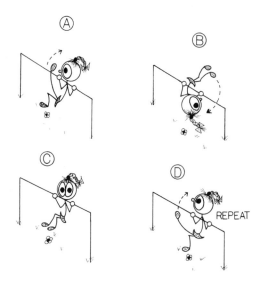

This skill is similar to the "Rear Circle Mount" (explained later in this chapter) except that it is done from the squat position: (A) From the squat position (palms up), vigorously raise one leg forward and upward, and at the same time push off from the ground with the other foot. (B) Pull hard with the arms and make both legs go up and over the bar. (C) After passing over the bar, come back to the squat position. (D) Repeat.

If grades 2 and 3 have been exposed to the bars since kindergarten, some of the children should be ready for modified or regular pull-ups in the medium area. Some of the taller students, including girls, can work on pull-ups on the lower high bar if needed. After mastering the hip circles, encourage the girls to work on modified and regular pull-ups even though they may be doing "bar hangs" on their physical fitness test later. Many girls in this age group are capable of doing regular pull-ups if they are encouraged and motivated to do so.

Pull-ups will probably be the most challenging item on this circuit for both you as a teacher and for the children as performers. Pull-ups and bar hangs are difficult for most children.

Also be aware that, even if children have been working on the bars since kindergarten, there are still going to be those who will have a difficult time doing pull-ups and bar hangs. Number one in this group will be the obese children; others are the recent transfer students from other school systems with poor or no physical education programs, and still others are the few who are lazy and just don't care. This group will always be around and be a constant challenge to all teachers.

Remember that even your best "pull uppers" and "bar hangers" are going to be in for a shock during fall fitness testing if they do not continue to work on these items during the summer vacations. As a result of easy summer living and growth spurts, many of them will find that their pull-ups or time on bar hangs have dropped considerably. You will now have to confront their discouragement and disappointment with sincere encouragement and enthusiastic motivation. Explain what has happened and why it has happened. Explain what they must do to overcome it. Most of the children in this group have what it takes to continue to work hard and snap back.

Progressions for Pull-ups

Hang Downs. These may be of some help to those children who are obese or who just do not have the arm strength to do one pull-up.

Place these children at the medium area. Have them grasp the bar with the palms forward, bend their knees, and pull their feet up behind them. Lower themselves slowly until their knees touch the ground or until their arms are straight. Have them stand up immediately and repeat this procedure four or five times. Stress lowering themselves as slowly as they can each time.

Modified Pull-ups. These are a good progression from the hang downs. This time, use the low or medium section of the pull-up bars.

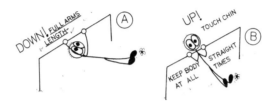

Have the children position themselves under the bar as shown in A in the illustration. Reach up and grasp the bar. While keeping the body straight, the children should pull up and touch the chin to the bar. (See B in the illustration.) Slowly lower the body (keeping it straight) to the starting position. Repeat. When they can do this in good form for five or six times, have them occasionally try a regular pull-up. The body *must* be kept straight if the children are going to get any benefit from this exercise.

Bar Hangs. Bar hangs can also be used as a progression to regular pull-ups and are still a requirement for girls on some of the physical fitness tests.

Using the medium height area of the chinning bars, have the children stand facing the bar, grasping it with the palms forward. Keep the elbows at the sides, chin over the bar without touching it. Tighten the stomach muscles; then bend the knees and lift the feet off the ground. Hold the chin over the bar, *without touching it,* as long as possible.

If you can, motivate girls to do regular pull-ups at an early age. Keep them at it because any girl who can do regular pull-ups will usually find bar hangs easy to do.

Regular Pull-ups. Jump up and grasp the bar with the palms forward. Pull the body upward until the chin is over the bar. Lower the body to a full arm's length and continue. Try to set good habit patterns early by not kicking the feet and wiggling the body while doing pull-ups because, when testing pull-ups on the fitness tests, only those done in good form will be counted.

Muscle-ups. This is strictly an advanced exercise for those children who can easily do seven or eight regular pull-ups in good form. The muscle-up is an excellent activity because it exercises both the arm *flexors* and the arm *extensors* plus most of the muscles in the upper body. Begin this exercise as you do the regular pull-ups—from a dead hang (arms straight).

(1) Swing the hips forward slightly; then arch the back as the body is pulled upward, curling the body slightly as the knees are lifted a bit. (2) As the head passes over the bar, roll up the elbows and move the head forward over the bar. (3) At the same time, push the body up to a straight-arm leaning rest position. (4) Lower the body to the hips-forward position (see 1 in the illustration) and repeat as many times as possible.

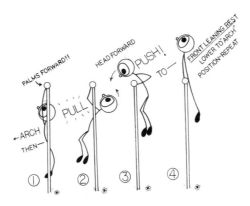

Rear Circle Mount. This can be a change of pace *only* for those who are doing well with their regular pull-ups. A series of rear circle mounts is an excellent exercise for the arm flexors and the abdominals when done repeatedly one after another.

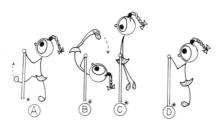

Have the person face the bar at the medium height area (chest high): (A) Grasp the bar with both hands and vigorously raise one leg forward and upward. (B) At almost the same time, push off the ground with the other leg and make both legs go over and backward over the bar. (C) As you pass over, rest your hips on the bar and stop your body as it reaches a straight-arm support position. (D) Dismount and repeat.

THE VAULT BARS

These are vault bars, *not hurdles*. Keep the hands on the bar when vaulting!
The vault bars are designed for agility along with a little stamina if the children continue to run between the vault bars (after each vault) for approximately 1 minute and 30 seconds. This is tougher to do than it sounds, so children have to learn how to pace themselves.

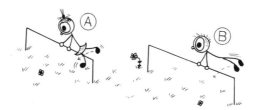

Start the kindergarten children by having them place both hands on the vault bar, step over it with one foot, and then bring the other foot over after it. (See A in the illustration.)

Repeat the same procedure from one side to the other. After practice with this step, encourage students to bring the lead foot up high, keep their body weight over their hands, and push off with their back foot and try to clear the bar without their legs touching it. (See B in the illustration.) *Keep hands on the bar when doing this!* Some of the kindergarten children will be too small to do this in the beginning, so let each one progress at his or her own rate.

For those who are ready to go into regular vaults, place both hands on the bar. Then, while keeping the body weight on both hands, kick both legs to the side and then up and over the bar. (See the illustration.)

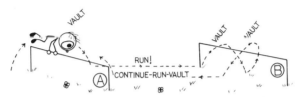

As the feet touch the ground, release the bar and run to the next bar (B) where they vault, turn, and vault again before running to the other bar (A) again. Continue this routine for approximately 1½ minutes as soon as the children can work up to it. They will probably enjoy the vaulting more than the running, so you will have to encourage them to run in between the bars.

Now and then some of the children are going to bump a knee when vaulting a bar, and it will obviously hurt for a few minutes, but it seldom happens twice to the same person.

MONKEY BARS

Children fondly refer to the horizontal ladder as the monkey bars; therefore, that's what it'll be called here.

The monkey bars are usually the most popular piece of apparatus for grades K–3. The monkey bars can also be used with grades 4–6 if the children are challenged enough.

Safety. No horseplay is ever allowed on the monkey bars. No one is ever allowed to stand or sit on top of the bars. Always let the person in front of you get halfway across the monkey bar before you start. If the other person is slow, give him or her more time. The monkey bars can be a "blister maker," so at the beginning of each outdoor session, have the children go easy until they have gotten used to the apparatus.

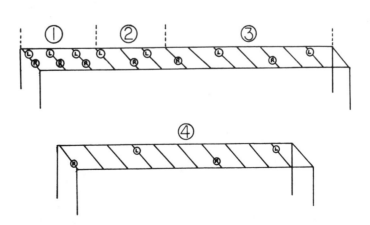

In the beginning, most of the kindergarten children will need some support and encouragement to build up their self-confidence and strength. But let them strike out on their own as soon as possible. In a matter of a few weeks, most of them will be able to handle the equipment very well. The obese child and a few others will continue to need help. You will soon know who they are, so be prepared to assist these children for a while.

The hand progressions for the small children will be from one rung (cross-bar) to the next. See the illustration: (1) one hand at a time to the same rung; (2) alternate hands to alternate rungs, which is where body rhythm begins to come in so that they can easily reach the next rung with one hand; (3) the big body swing and the big arm stretch so that students can skip one rung; and (4) the really big swing and stretch to skip two rungs.

The distance from the top of the monkey bar to the ground is approximately 6′6″, so most children in grades K–3 should have plenty of leg room. But the long-legged third and fourth graders along with most of the children in grades 5 and 6 will find that they have to keep their knees bent so that their feet will not drag.

Skipping the Bars. By the fourth grade, most of the children who have been working on the monkey bars since kindergarten have developed the rhythm and swing needed to skip every other rung as they travel along the monkey bar. There will be a few well-coordinated long-armed fourth, fifth, and sixth graders who can successfully skip two rungs as they travel along the monkey bars. Therefore, unless they are obese or a new transfer student or have physical problems, all the children should be encouraged to skip one rung or more by the sixth grade.

Hand Walking the Side Rail. As shown in the illustration, the child grasps the side rails and, by rhythmically swinging the body from side to side and alternately sliding the hands along the side rail, travels the length of the monkey bar.

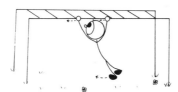

Casting Along the Side Rails. Be very careful with this one. Only your well-coordinated children should try it. It is a good idea to spot the child on his or her first few attempts. The "cast" is very similar to the one done on the horizontal bar.

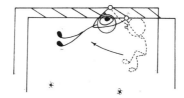

To begin, the person grasps the side rails, leans back, pulls knees up and shoots the feet straight forward and out. (Be careful so that the feet don't hit the rungs.) As the legs are forcefully extended, let both hands slide forward, regrasp, let the body swing back, and then repeat the same process.

THE PARALLEL BARS

The parallel bars are included to develop *arm extensor* strength by using progressive activities. The children in an average squad will range in arm extensor strength from weak to strong. Therefore, use the following progressions so that the weak will be challenged by activities that most of them will eventually be able to perform successfully and other activities that will challenge the stronger.

The progressions listed in order of difficulty are cross riding seats, hand walking a side rail, hand walking along both rails, and dips. When a squad is on the parallel bars, each individual should be doing the activity that challenges his or her ability.

Most of the kindergarten children will not be able to do many of these activities because of their size and strength. Usually we introduce the kindergarten children to the parallel bars by having them hang on one of the side rails and see how far they can work their way along the rail by sliding their hands in the direction of the high end. Most of the children will have to bend their knees to keep their feet from dragging. *This is not an arm extensor activity.*

Another method of travel for the younger students on the parallel bars is called the *submarine.* Hanging under the bars and bending the knees so the feet will not drag, see how far the children can go by swinging the body from side to side while at the same time alternately sliding the hands forward. *This is not an arm extensor activity.*

Cross Riding Seats. Begin this activity by jumping to a straight-arm support at the end of the bar facing along the bar: (A) Swing the legs up between the bar. (B) Spread the feet as soon as they swing above the bars. (C) Lean forward and regrasp the bars between the legs. (D) Then lean forward and place body weight on the hands, while at the same time swinging the legs up between the bars. (E) Then swing down and up to the cross riding seat. Repeat the steps.

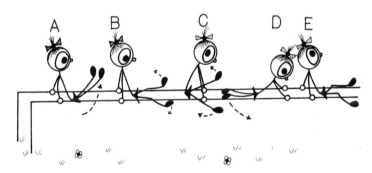

Hand Walking the Side Rail. This activity places a little more work on the arm extensors while at the same time taking part of the weight on the front of the body. (See A in the

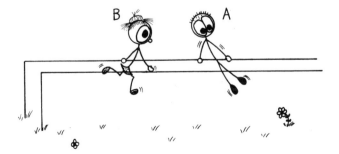

illustration.) Begin by grasping a side rail and jumping into a straight-arm support position. Travel along the bar by alternately sliding the hands along the bar as the weight shifts from one hand to another. Keep the front part of the body in contact with the bar as it moves along the bar. Encourage increasing the distance traveled each time.

If students drop to their feet, have them quickly remount and continue from the same spot.

Hand Walking Along Both Rails. In this exercise, all the body weight is taken on the hands. To begin, grasp a bar in each hand. (See B in the illustration.) Then jump to a straight-arm support position facing along the bars. To hand walk, lean the weight over one hand and slide the opposite hand forward. Then quickly shift weight to the hand that was sliding and place the other hand forward. Continue walking this way as far as possible. Again, if students drop to the ground, have them quickly remount the bars at the *same spot* and continue. CAU-TION: If there is pain in the sternum area (middle of chest), have that child cease this activity until he or she can be checked by a doctor.

Dips. Dips will be the most challenging exercise on the parallel bars if done correctly. Dips give the arm extensors almost a full range of motion. Good hand walking is a prerequisite to working on the dips.

For this exercise, children will use the high section of the parallel bars unless they are very short. To begin, have the child go to a straight-arm position (see A). Then lower the body between the bars as far as it will go (see B). While the body is being lowered, lean the upper body forward slightly at the same time. As soon as the body has been lowered as far as it will go, push back up into the starting position. SUGGESTION: As soon as a child can do one dip correctly, let him or her do *sets of ones* until he or she can do two consecutively. Then let the child do sets of twos until he or she can do three dips consecutively, and so on.

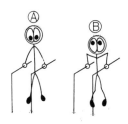

CLIMBING POLES

If climbing poles are included in your circuit, see Chapter 12 for progressions and safety instructions.

Bean Bags ══════════════════════════════ 4

Bean bags can be one of the best tools available for developing eye-hand coordination and for presenting a wide variety of exploratory activities to preschool and lower primary children.

Bean bags are also inexpensive, so make sure there is one for every child in the class. When using bean bags, it is important to follow sequences from the simple to the more difficult challenges. IMPORTANT: Remember to do bean bag activities before introducing your students to ball-handling skills.

BEAN BAG MAINTENANCE

Parents can help to make bean bags for the students. If some parents make three or four each, there should be enough bean bags for all your students.

The bean bags should be either 5″ × 5″ or 6″ × 6″. Children like bright colors, so if the parents are going to make two, three, or four bean bags, each bean bag should be a different color.

Dried beans and peas, sand, gravel, and rice are usually used as the filling. If bean bags contain edible substances such as beans, peas, or rice, they are going to attract mice. One solution is to store them in large plastic jars, such as those that contain mayonnaise. Your cafeteria staff may be willing to donate the large containers that have been emptied.

Be sure to keep a needle and thread handy so that you can patch a split bean bag promptly.

POINTS TO KEEP IN MIND

Keep the following points in mind when doing the following bean bag activities:

1. Give each challenge in a loud and enthusiastic voice.
2. Begin with easy challenges and move slowly to the more difficult.
3. Walk around your students while they are solving these challenges. Give a lot of eye contact and encouragement.
4. Let your students know you are interested in each and every one of them.
5. Be aware that some of the best bean bag challenges will come from the children themselves. Always encourage them to come up with new ideas and congratulate them for their efforts.

BEAN BAG SEQUENCES TO GET
INDIVIDUAL STUDENTS STARTED

- Can you toss your bean bag straight up in the air and catch it? (Analyze the proper way to toss the bean bag into the air. Stress the follow-through and "looking" the bean bag back into their hands.)
- Can you toss the bean bag up and catch it without moving your feet? (Discuss the importance of tossing the bean bag straight up in front of themselves.)
- Can you softly and quietly catch your bean bag? (To catch quietly, the hands and knees must give a little with the bean bag.)
- Can you toss the bean bag into the air and clap your hands before catching it? Can you clap two times?
- Can you toss your bean bag into the air and catch it with the same hand? Can you do the same thing with the other hand?
- Can you toss your bean bag into the air and catch it on the back of your hand? (Talk about having to "give" with the hand when the bean bag lands to make it "stick" on the hand.)
- Can you do the same thing with the other hand?
- Can you throw your bean bag in front of your chest with one hand and catch it with the other hand? Can you throw it the same way to the other hand? (Remind students to keep their eyes on the bean bag as it goes from one hand to the other.)
- Can you toss the bean bag into the air, then reach down and touch the floor before catching the bean bag?
- Can you toss your bean bag into the air and catch it right in front of your nose? Can you catch it in front of your chest? Your belt? Your knees? Your feet?
- Can you toss your bean bag into the air—don't wait for it to come down to you—and jump up and catch it? If this is done correctly, your arms will be straight and your feet off the floor when it is caught.
- Can you place the bean bag on two hands with your palms up and flip the bean bag over a half turn and catch it? Can you flip the bean bag a full turn and catch it?
- Can you place the bean bag on one hand with the palm up and flip the bean bag a half turn and catch it in the same hand? Can you flip the bean bag a full turn and catch it?
- Can you do this same routine with the other hand?
- Can you balance the bean bag on top of your head and slowly sit down without the bean bag falling off your head?
- Can you stand up without the bean bag falling off your head?
- Can you balance the bean bag on your knee and hop on the other foot without dropping the bean bag from your knee?
- Can you put the bean bag on the other knee and do the same thing?
- Can you toss the bean bag into the air and sit down and catch it? Can you toss the bean bag while still sitting and catch it after you stand up? Can you alternate up and down (be sitting before you catch it and be standing before you catch it)?
- Can you throw your bean bag up and catch it without moving from your sitting position?
- While sitting cross-legged, can you toss the bean bag into the air and then stand up and catch it?
- Can you hold the bean bag in one hand at arm's length in front of the body, and then

drop the bean bag and catch it before it falls to the ground? Can you do this using your other hand?

- ◆ Can you hold your bean bag over your head with one hand, drop it, and reach across your body with the other hand and catch it before it hits the floor? Can you do the same thing with the other hand?
- ◆ While lying on the floor on your back, can you toss your bean bag in the air and catch it in the same hand without moving your body? Can you do the same thing with the other hand? How many times can you do this without missing?
- ◆ Can you put your bean bag on your head and skip around the room without bumping into anyone else or letting your bean bag fall off your head?

ADVANCED CHALLENGES FOR INDIVIDUAL STUDENTS

- ◆ Can you place the bean bag on your instep and walk carefully around the room without the bean bag falling off? Can you do the same thing with the other foot?
- ◆ Can you place your bean bag on one instep and hold this same foot in the air while you hop on the other foot? Can you do this without the bean bag falling off? Can you do this using the other foot?
- ◆ Can you put the bean bag on one foot and kick the bean bag up into your hands? Can you do the same thing with the other foot? Can you do the same routine with the bean bag between the knees?
- ◆ Can you put the bean bag on one heel, kick it up behind, turn, and catch it before it falls to the floor?
- ◆ Can you place a bean bag between your feet and then jump your knees up in front of you so that you can catch the bean bag in your hands?
- ◆ Can you lie on your back with a bean bag on the toes of one foot and then kick the bean bag into your hands? Can you try it with the other foot? Can you try it with both feet?
- ◆ Can you place the bean bag between both feet, lie flat on the floor on your back, bring your feet over your head, and touch the floor without dropping the bean bag? Can you do it again?
- ◆ Place your bean bag on the floor right in front of your feet. Can you carefully move your bean bag around the room by tapping the bean bag forward with the inside of one foot and then with the inside of the other foot? Do not kick the bean bag way out in front of you—it should be kept close enough so that you can quickly put a foot on top of it when the teacher signals "Stop." Can you move your bean bag around the room without bumping into anyone else? Can you change directions as you move around the room?
- ◆ Hold your bean bag over your head with two hands. The bean bag should be held on your fingertips, and you should be looking at it. Can you tap your bean bag into the air above your head using your fingertips? Keep your eyes on the bean bag and your hands in position. Move your feet, when needed, to keep your body under the bean bag. As skills improve, tap the bean bag a little higher.

CHALLENGES FOR PARTNERS

Have the students pair off. Each pair of students needs one bean bag.

- Stand about 4' to 6' away from your partner. Can you toss the bean bag back and forth underhand to each other? Try to catch it softly.
- Can you throw the bean bag back and forth overhand? Again, try to catch it softly and make your tosses good.
- Stand about 6' to 8' away from your partner. Can you and your partner remain 6' to 8' apart and move into empty places, changing directions (as partners), and continually passing the bean bag underhand back and forth to each other? Use the empty places, make the throws good and catches soft, and do not bump into other partners. (Have the partners move slowly at first; as they become more skilled, let them speed up.)
- Can you do the same challenge except throw the bean bag overhand?
- Can you pass the bean bag back and forth to your partner while using the same hand for both throwing and catching?
- Can you do the same thing using the other hand?
- Can you do the same thing, except clap your hands before catching the bean bag?
- Face your partner about 5' away and—on signal—both of you slide in a circular direction to your right. As you slide to the right, can you toss the bean bag back and forth to each other? (Students will find it necessary to lead each other with each throw.) Can you do the same thing by circling to the left?

STUDENT-MADE CHALLENGES

After the students have had a chance to work on the challenges just suggested, let them work on their own sequences of challenges. Be sure to stress that each challenge should follow the one before it as smoothly as possible. For example,

1. Throw the bean bag into the air and catch it softly with both hands.
2. Immediately and smoothly take it down to the feet, place the bean bag between the feet, and jump the bean bag back into the hands.
3. Immediately throw the bean bag back into the air and clap three times before catching it.
4. Then throw the bean bag back into the air and turn around completely before catching it.

Now, from all the challenges that have been covered by the class, ask each student to work up his or her own routine. Stress again to flow smoothly from one challenge to another and to see how many of these items can be worked into his or her very own routine.

Hula Hoops ——————————————— 5

Hula hoops are used not only for twirling around the hips, waist, and arms; they also present the opportunity for a large variety of exploratory experiences in grades K–3.

Although commercial hula hoops are available, you might want to make your own. (See Chapter 26.)

HULA HOOP CHALLENGES

The following are hula hoop activities designed to get you and your students started.

♦ Place your hoop flat on the floor with your toes up against the hoop. Can you *jump* in and out of your hoop until you hear the signal "And stop"? (Repeat the same procedure, but substitute *hop* and *leap* periodically.)

♦ Can you jump into your hoop and turn halfway around before you land? Can you jump out of your hoop and do the same thing? Continue.
♦ Can you jump in and out of your hoop and turn *all the way around* before you land?
♦ Can you jump into your hoop and land in a low position (a crouch)? Staying in your low position, can you jump out and land in a high position?
♦ While standing in the middle of your hoop, how high can you jump? (Discuss how you jump high by swinging the arms, bending the knees, springing upward and pushing off with the toes, reaching up, etc.). Practice jumping for a while.
♦ While you are still standing in the middle of your hoop, can you jump high in the air and click your heels together before you land? Can you jump in and out of your hoop doing the same thing?
♦ While standing in the middle of your hoop, can you jump high in the air, hug your knees to your chest, and then let go before you land? Can you do this as you jump in and out of your hoop?

39

♦ Still standing in the center of your hoop, can you jump high in the air and slap both heels at the same time before landing? Can you jump in and out of your hoop while doing the same thing?

♦ Pick up your hoop. Can you balance your hoop on your head with the hoop hanging in front of you and with your hands out to your side? Do not touch the hoop with your hands! Can you slowly step through the hoop one leg at a time? Can you go back through?

♦ Place your hoop on the floor again. Can you place both hands in your hoop, and, while you are looking at your hands, can you kick your feet up in the air so that all your weight is on your hands? How long can you keep your feet in the air?

♦ Put the hoop on the floor. While standing inside your hoop, look around to see where all the other hoops are. On the signal "Off you go," run carefully from one hoop to another (without bumping into anyone else) and *leap* over each hoop as you come to it. On the signal "Stop," stand in the nearest hoop. (A variation to this is to ask students to place a body part, such as a foot, knee, or elbow, inside the hoop when they hear the signal "Stop.")

♦ Can you roll your own hoop about the room into empty spaces? Try changing directions frequently, but do not let the hoop get away from you or bump into anyone else. (Explain how the children will have to stay right beside the hoop as it rolls so that they can guide it and keep it under control.)

♦ Can you spin your hoop like a top? As it begins to slow down, how many times can you step in and out of the hoop with one foot before it completely stops?

♦ While standing in one spot with your hoop in one hand, can you roll your hoop out in front of you so that it will come back to you? (You will have to explain how to put "back swing" on the hoop as it is released. This will take practice.)

♦ (This challenge comes after the children have learned how to make the hoop roll back to themselves.) Can you make your hoop roll back to yourself? As it rolls back to you, can you run by the side of the hoop and step or run through the hoop without knocking the hoop down? (Again, this will take a lot of practice.)

♦ This time when you make the hoop roll back to yourself, can you pick up a leg high and let the hoop run under it? Can you jump in the air with spread legs and let the hoop roll between your legs? (Be sure the students can jump high enough to do this.)

♦ Can you "jump rope" with your hula hoop? How many times can you jump without missing?

♦ You will need a partner for this challenge. Keep your own hoop and turn to face your partner, who is standing 5' or 6' away. Can both of you roll your hoops to each other at the same time and catch them before they fall? (Explain that the children will have to try to keep the hoops from bumping as they pass each other.)

♦ Partners will use only one hoop this time. The partner with the hoop (1) stands 5' or 6' away from his or her partner without the hoop (2). Partner 1 then rolls the hoop with backspin so that partner 2 can practice running through the hoop. Next, partner 2 rolls for 1, and the activity continues.

♦ This time, partner 1 holds the hoop horizontal to the floor at knee or midthigh height. Partner 2 jumps into the hoop and immediately rolls out, stands up, takes the hoop from 1, and holds it for 1 who does the same routine. Have partners repeat this routine until the teacher says "Stop."

♦ Whether done individually or with a partner, *sequences* are very important because they give the children a chance to use the challenges they have already done as well as to use routines they make up themselves. For example,

With the hoop on the floor and with both hands and feet touching the edge of the hoop, make a bridge shape with the tummy upwards. Now, turn over so that the tummy is downward and balance yourself on two hands and one foot. Next, turn sideways so that one hand and one foot are on the hoop. Finally, stand up and balance the hoop on top of the head and climb through. Make the flow from one move to the next as smoothly as possible. (Next, give students a chance to work up sequences with a partner. Give them 10 to 15 minutes to work up their own routines, stressing a smooth flow of sequences just as in the individual routines.)

♦ Play ***musical hoops.*** Each child finds an empty space, puts his or her hoop down, and stands in the middle of it. On the signal "Off you go," they are to run about the room stepping into hoops that are at that moment empty. On the signal "And stop" or when the music stops, they are to locate quickly and stand in the middle of the first empty hoop they see. Stress no talking or noise when running so that they can concentrate and hear the signals. Explain that you are taking away one hoop and that one person will end up with no hoop to get into. This is similar to the old favorite "Musical Chairs."

SUGGESTION: Instead of making the child who is left without a hoop sit the game out, leave him or her in and continue to take out two hoops next time, then three, four, and so on. You can repeat this activity five or six times, but don't keep them running too long before stopping each time. Stress moving quietly and quickly, having fun, and being a good sport.

VARIATION: Ask the children to decide upon three different positions. For example, position 1 is standing in the hoop on one leg, position 2 is placing hands inside the hoop and feet outside the hoop, and position 3 is curled up in the middle of the hoop with weight on both feet. In this game, call out one of the three numbers instead of saying "Change." The children have to think how they must arrive in the hoop, as well as being quick to find a new hoop. As in musical hoops, let the child who was "left out" in the game remain and take out an extra hoop each time.

♦ Play ***shipwreck.*** This begins with the same routine as in *musical hoops*. On the signal "And stop" or when the music stops, everyone finds a hoop to stand in. Remove two hoops after each "And stop." Now, if a child does not have a hoop of his or her own to stand in, that child quickly gets into a hoop with someone else. Continue the routine until the hoops are filled with as many children as they can safely hold.

♦ Circle the Cones- Roll hoop if it goes over a cone- score a point.

♦ Numbers Change — Ball if ball hits runner they become in the middle

♦ Hoop Tag- Tagger puts him over himself. stays on center line. Tag someone, they grab a hoop, join the tagger. Taggers must hold onto each others hoop as they try and tag other players.

Ball Activities ———————————— 6

It is fortunate that most children enjoy playing with balls because ball activities can present present a wide range of varied and exciting experiences that are fun and challenging. The early development of ball-handling skills is to serve as a foundation for the many ball activities that will follow in the next chapters, such as "Two Square, Four Square"; "Newcomb"; volleyball; soccer; basketball; softball; baseball; football; and so on. Beginning with kindergarten, it is very important for children to be exposed to a well-planned program of ball activities.

WHAT KIND OF BALL?

Use an 8½" playground ball for these activities. Cheaper plastic balls are not completely round, which can lead to considerable frustration when trying to learn how to bounce the balls. Remember, every child in the class will need a ball.

BALL CHALLENGES FOR INDIVIDUAL STUDENTS

- ◆ Can you raise the ball a full arm's length overhead, drop the ball, and count how many times you can run around the ball before it stops bouncing?
- ◆ Can you use both hands to toss the ball gently into the air just above your head? Now, with your palms up and using the fingertips, how many times can you push the ball into the air without missing it? (Stress keeping eyes on the ball at all times and using the fingertips—not the palms of their hands.)
- ◆ Can you throw the ball into the air and catch it before it hits the ground? Did you have to move to catch it? Why? (Discuss the importance of throwing the ball straight up. What happens when you throw it up forward? backward? sideways?)
- ◆ Can you throw the ball straight up into the air and catch it without moving your feet?
- ◆ Now that you are getting better at throwing the ball straight into the air, how many times can you clap your hands before catching the ball?
- ◆ This time, can you throw the ball into the air and let it bounce one time before you catch it? Did you have to move your feet to catch it? Why?
- ◆ Listen very carefully to this next challenge. Can you throw the ball into the air, and then when it lands and bounces in front of you, spin all the way around and catch it? (Stress watching the ball hit the floor *before* the child spins around.)
- ◆ Again, listen very carefully. Can you throw your ball straight up and, when it hits the

floor and bounces up, quickly run under it, turn and catch it after the next bounce? (Again, stress running under the ball *after* the first bounce, turning quickly, and catching the ball after the *second* bounce.)

♦ Sit on the floor. Now, how large an area can you cover when you roll the ball around your body without moving from your sitting position?

♦ After you have rolled the ball in front of your body and are getting ready to roll it behind your back, lie on your back and roll the ball as far behind your head as you can reach. Then, as you come back down your side with the ball, sit up and roll it in front of you again. Can you do this several times without stopping?

♦ From a standing position with the feet spread, how large an area can you cover while rolling the ball around the outside of your feet? (Stress transferring weight from one leg to another in order to make a wider circle.)

♦ From your standing position with feet spread, can you make a "figure 8" while rolling the ball around and between your spread feet?

♦ Be very careful with this next challenge so that you don't bump into anyone. Can you carefully roll your ball into an empty place, then run after it, leap over your ball, turn, and field it? (Stress rolling the ball slowly and carefully.)

♦ Can you bounce the ball against the wall and catch it on the first bounce? (Stress starting off close to the wall and moving back as the students become more skilled.)

♦ Can you bounce the ball off the wall and catch it before it hits the floor? (This is called "volleying" the ball. Begin close to the wall as you did in the previous challenge.)

♦ How many times can you volley the ball off the wall in 15 seconds? (Wait until students have developed some skill before you try this one.)

♦ Can you keep the ball bouncing while using two hands?

♦ Now, can you keep the ball bouncing while using one hand? (Discuss the mechanics of dribbling—using fingertips, pushing the ball rather than hitting it, using the wrist, etc.)

♦ Can you bounce the ball with the other hand?

♦ Can you keep the ball bouncing while alternating your hands?

♦ Can you go through all the preceding bouncing routines while keeping your eyes on the teacher and not on the ball? (This will take some practice.)

♦ Can you walk forward four steps, then backward four steps, while dribbling the ball with the right hand? Can you keep the ball on your right side and bounce it with each step?

♦ Can you follow the same routine using the left hand?

♦ Can you change from right- to left-hand dribbling while walking forward and backward when I say "Change"?

♦ Can you walk around the ball while dribbling with your right hand? How about the left hand?

♦ How can you bounce the ball with one hand while moving into empty spaces, changing directions, and not bumping into anyone else? (Have students start slowly in the beginning and then speed up as their skill increases.)

♦ While bouncing the ball, can you lift one leg over the ball and then lift the other leg over the ball? Can you do this five times without stopping?

♦ Can you bounce the ball with one hand and slowly go to a full squat and back to a standing position again while still bouncing the ball?

♦ While standing and not moving your feet, can you bounce the ball continuously in a circle around your body, starting with the right hand and letting the left hand take over behind your back? Can you go in the opposite direction this time?

♦ Now, place the ball on the floor. Can you slowly move the ball around the room by kicking it with the inside of one foot and then with the inside of the other foot while moving into empty spaces? (Stress the importance of keeping up with the ball as the student moves it with each foot for control and guidance. Let the children speed up as they gain control.)

♦ Can you throw the ball straight in the air and then sit down and catch it? Did you have to move your position to catch it? If so, you are not throwing the ball straight up. Try again.

♦ From a sitting position with legs crossed, can you throw the ball up and then stand and catch it?

♦ Standing in your own spot, can you throw the ball straight up and then jump up and get it? You are doing it correctly if, when you catch the ball, your feet are off the floor and both arms are in full extension.

♦ Place the ball between your feet and squeeze. Can you jump and bring your feet up high enough to get the ball in your hands?

♦ Can you keep the ball rolling around your body (the stomach and back area) continuously without stopping?

♦ Can you dribble the ball when doing some of the basic locomotor skills, such as walking, running, hopping, jumping, leaping, sliding, and galloping?

♦ While standing and dribbling the ball, can you continue to dribble the ball as you go into a kneeling position, then into a sitting position, then back into the kneeling position, and then back to the standing position?

♦ This game is called "Dribble Tag." Every child has a ball and must dribble when moving. "It" must dribble the ball when chasing others. The person tagged by "It" becomes the new "It."

CHALLENGES FOR PARTNERS

Each pair of students needs one ball.

♦ Sit and face your partner, who is 8' away. Spread your legs. Can you roll the ball back and forth to each other?

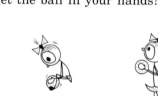

♦ Stand and face your partner, who is about 5' away. Holding the ball in two hands, can you gently toss the ball to your partner using the underhand toss?

♦ Still facing your partner, can you bounce the ball to your partner? (Stress bouncing the ball about midway between each child.)

♦ Face your partner, who is about 6' away. Both partners circle to the right using the sliding motion. While circling, can you pass the ball back and forth to each other using the underhand pass?

♦ Can you hold the ball with both hands in front of your chest and then step off with one foot toward your partner and push the ball to him or her? (Stress the stepping as they push the ball to their partner—this is called the "chest pass.")

♦ Can you chest pass the ball to each other as you are circling?

♦ Face your partner, who is 8′ to 10′ away. Can you bounce the ball to your partner using the chest pass?

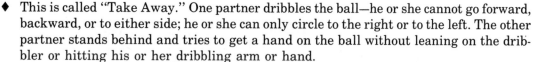

♦ Can you use the circle drill again and bounce pass the ball to your partner while circling each other?

♦ This time, one partner gets down over the ball like the center on a football team. The other partner stands about 5′ behind. On the signal "Hup," have the center pass the ball between his or her legs to the partner, then take two running steps forward, stop, turn around and face the partner who will throw the ball using a one-hand overhand pass. When the center catches the ball, he or she immediately gets down over the ball and centers it again to the partner. Continue the routine four or five times; then change positions and continue.

♦ This is called "Take Away." One partner dribbles the ball—he or she cannot go forward, backward, or to either side; he or she can only circle to the right or to the left. The other partner stands behind and tries to get a hand on the ball without leaning on the dribbler or hitting his or her dribbling arm or hand.

♦ Set up a row of hula hoops using the hula hoops holders (see Chapter 26 for making these) to hold each hoop in an upright position. With a partner on each side of the hoop, run down the row of hoops and bounce pass the ball through each hoop to each other as they go.

♦ Can you and your partner bounce the ball into the center of the hoop as you circle to the right? To the left?

♦ One of the partners puts a backward spin on the hoop and the other partner has a ball. Can you both run forward with the hoop, then follow it back on the back spin passing the ball through it while it is rolling? (This is a tricky challenge and takes some practice to master.)

BALL-AND-HOOP ACTIVITIES
FOR INDIVIDUAL STUDENTS

♦ Can you stand inside the hoop and bounce the ball inside the hoop at the same time? Can you circle around in the hoop while bouncing the ball? Can you do the same thing while changing height levels—high, medium, and low?

♦ Can you stand inside the hoop and bounce the ball on the outside of the hoop while circling with sliding steps to the right? Can you do the same thing to your left?

♦ Can you stand on the outside of your hoop and bounce the ball inside the hoop as you circle around the hoop still using a sliding motion with your feet? Change directions and hands frequently.

♦ Begin with your hoop lying flat on the floor about 2′ from a wall and stand in it. Can you toss the ball against the wall with two hands and catch it without letting it hit the ground? Can you do this without stepping out of your hoop? Continue to move the hoop away from the wall after each successful catch. What is your best distance?

♦ Can you stand behind the hoop, throw the ball against the wall so that it will bounce inside the hoop, and then catch it? Can you move the hoop back from the wall a bit and do the same thing? What is your best distance?

♦ Can you bounce the ball into the hoop so that it will bounce off the wall and back to you? Can you catch it after it bounces off the wall? (This will be difficult, so have the students begin with the hoop close to the wall.)

Carpets and Tumbling⸺7

Most of your carpet pieces can be donated by local furniture and carpet stores. The carpet samples should be large enough for the student to do a forward roll, so try to get pieces that are at least 36″ × 18″. Many furniture and carpet stores will cut the pieces to your specifications; although there may be a charge for this, carpets are a valuable piece of equipment and well worth the expense. Many parent organizations will also take on the paying for this equipment as a project.

Be sure that each student has his or her own carpet piece for the following challenges.

CARPET AND TUMBLING CHALLENGES

Remember to encourage the students to come up with their own challenges, too.

♦ Find an empty spot and place your carpet on the floor. Make sure no one else is close beside you. Can you stand on the edge of the narrow end of your carpet?
♦ Can you stand on the edge of the long side of your carpet?
♦ Can you put your toes on the edge of the long side of your carpet and jump across it? Can you turn around and jump back across?
♦ Can you put your toes on the long side of your carpet, hop over it, and land on the same foot you took off on? Can you try the same thing with the other foot?
♦ Can you leap over the narrow part of your carpet?
♦ Can you jump over the narrow part of your carpet, turning halfway around while you are in the air so that you will land facing across your carpet?
♦ Can you do the same thing when you leap across your carpet?
♦ Can you put your toes on the edge of the narrow end of the carpet and jump all the way across the long part? Are you able to do this without your feet touching the carpet?
♦ Can you leap across the long part of your carpet without letting the foot you land on touch the other end of the carpet?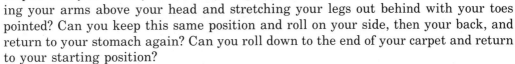
♦ This challenge is called the log roll. (Before starting this instruction, each child will need space to roll without bumping into anyone else, so make sure the class uses all available safe space.) First, lie on your stomach across the short end of your carpet. Can you make yourself very long and skinny by stretching your arms above your head and stretching your legs out behind with your toes pointed? Can you keep this same position and roll on your side, then your back, and return to your stomach again? Can you roll down to the end of your carpet and return to your starting position?

♦ This challenge is called the tucked roll. Lie on your side on the carpet in a tight curled position. Put your knees up against your chest. Put your head forward with your nose on your knees, elbows tucked in close to the body, and hands under your chin. Can you slowly rock from side to side? Can you rock a little harder and roll over? Can you roll over two or three times while holding this position?

♦ The log roll and the tucked roll are not only fun to do, they can also help keep you from hurting yourself if you trip and fall while running. You already know how to run into empty spaces and change directions without bumping into anyone else, so listen carefully to the directions for the next drill. When I say "Off you go," run into empty spaces and touch the empty carpets with your feet as you pass by. Change directions constantly, use all the space, but do not bump into anyone else. When I say "And stop," quickly find an empty carpet, put both feet on the carpet first, and then carefully go down on the carpet and do either a log roll or tucked roll. "Off you go."

♦ Standing in the center of your carpet, can you jump high?

♦ Can you jump and click your heels? Can you jump and slap your heels? Can you jump and turn halfway around before you land?

♦ Can you keep your hands in the middle of your carpet while moving your feet in a sliding motion around the outside of the carpet? Can you do the same thing in the other direction?

♦ Can you make a bridge over the narrow part of your carpet with your stomach facing the carpet? Can you make another bridge over the narrow part of your carpet with your stomach facing upward?

 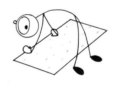

♦ Can you straddle the carpet with your feet on opposite edges of the long sides?

♦ While using short steps, can you walk down the length of your carpet and, when you get to the end, jump into the air, turn halfway around, and land with your feet on the edges as before? You should be facing the opposite direction. Can you do the same thing again?

♦ Straddle the carpet as you just did. Lean over and place your hands on the edges of the carpet and bear walk down to the end. When you reach the end, can you push hard with your hands and feet so you can get high enough in the air to do a half turn before landing? If done correctly, you will be facing the carpet in the opposite direction. Can you continue until I say "And stop"?

♦ While keeping two hands in the center of your carpet, can you jump your feet from one side of your carpet to the other? Keep your head up, your eyes on the carpet, and see how high you can kick your feet.

♦ This time, stand with your feet pointing toward the long side of your carpet. Can you put the hand nearest your front foot on the carpet and quickly follow with the other hand? Keep your head up and your eyes on the carpet. At the same time, can you kick your legs high and wide like the spokes in a wheel? Your side should be toward the mat when you land on your feet.

♦ Can you support your body weight on two hands and one foot? How straight can you make the leg that is in the air? Point your toes.

♦ Can you do the same thing while using your chin to hold a bean bag against your chest? Can you touch the bean bag with the knee of your supporting leg?

♦ Slowly straighten the leg that is in the air, and at the same time, using your arms, can you lower the back of your head and neck to the carpet and roll into a sitting position? (Holding the bean bag against the chest with the chin keeps the top of the head off the carpet and keeps the back round. The supporting knee against the chin also keeps a round back. Do not rush these sequences; some of the children will need more time than others to develop the confidence and the feeling they need to complete this routine.)

♦ Place your toes on the narrow end of your carpet so that you are facing down the carpet. Sit down on your heels and place your hands on the carpet in front of you. Tuck your chin on your chest, then slowly begin to straighten your legs and raise your hips in the air. Keep your chin tucked on your chest. Use your arms and slowly let the back of your head touch the carpet. Roll on over into a sitting position with your knees still close to your chest. This time as you complete your roll, can you reach forward with both hands, and, keeping your knees close to your chest and feet close to seat, roll on up to your feet and stand up? (Stress taking the weight on their arms and slowly lowering the back of their necks to the carpet and rolling out.)

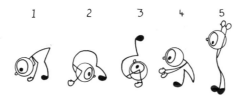

♦ This time, stand with your heels at the narrow edge of the carpet with your back to the carpet. Can you sit on your heels, lean forward with your chin on your chest, grasp your shins, pull them in tight, and rock backward as far as you can? Can you hang on to your shins and try to rock forward to your feet after rocking backward?

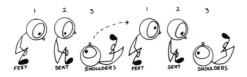

♦ From this same position, can you rock back with your chin and knees tucked close to your chest without holding them? Can you rock back and place both knees on the carpet beside one of your ears? Can you do the same routine and touch both knees by the other ear?

♦ This time, try rocking backward a little harder. Place your hands by your head—thumbs near your ears—and push hard with your hands as you rock back. Can you rock over and take your weight on your feet? (Stress keeping the chin tucked, pushing hard with the hands, and keeping the knees close to the chest all through this move.)

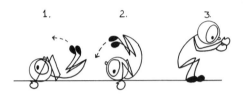

♦ Put your toes on the narrow end of your carpet so that you will be looking down the long section of your carpet. Stoop down and sit on your heels, and lean forward and place your hands on the carpet. Raise your hips, keep one foot on the floor, and lift the other ("up leg") in the air behind you. Kick up high and hard with your "up leg." How high can you get both feet in the air when you do this? Practice this a few times. Now, can you kick your legs straight up in the air—keeping the body and arms straight and covering your ears? This time, try to find your balance and hold it as long as you can. If your legs come down in front of you, can you quietly put your feet down? If your legs go over backward, can you gently lower yourself to the back of your neck and roll out just like you did in the forward roll? Don't get discouraged; this one takes a lot of practice. (It is important that the students learn how to roll out safely if their feet go over.)

Wands———————————————8

Wands can be fun and challenging, but they can also be very dangerous if not used correctly and with good discipline.

The playground is the ideal place to hold wand activities. This gives the children plenty of room to spread out and to keep a safe distance from each other while doing this particular activity. Most gyms and multipurpose rooms are also large enough for wand activities. Most classrooms, however, are just too small for these activities to be done safely.

Wands can be made from ⅝" plastic tubing, ½" dowels or old broom sticks, or tomato stakes cut between 25" to 30" in length. Hollow plastic tubing might be the best to use because it is light and quiet, and usually comes in bright colors.

You will need a wand for each child.

IMPORTANT SAFETY NOTE: Allow no horseplay with the wands! To avoid temptation, have the students put the wands on the floor or ground whenever you are giving instructions. Keep the children spread out a safe distance from each other. There must be no sword fighting with the wands; this is how children can be poked in the eye. Discipline must be maintained at all times when using wands.

WAND ACTIVITIES FOR INDIVIDUAL STUDENTS

♦ Can you balance your wand? How long can you make it stand without touching it?
♦ Can you balance your wand long enough to swing a leg over it?
♦ After balancing your wand, how many times can you run around it before it falls?
♦ Can you hold your wand between your legs and jump halfway around? Can you jump all the way around without dropping your wand?
♦ Can you jump a half turn while holding your wand between your feet? How about a full turn?
♦ Can you balance your wand across your toes? How high can you bring your leg before the stick falls off?
♦ Can you put your heel on top of your wand and hold it there? Can you keep your heel up and hop around the wand?
♦ Can you balance the wand in the palm of your hand? Be sure you are far enough away from your neighbors so that you won't hit anyone with the wand if it falls.

♦ Can you balance the wand on the back of your hand? Can you make yourself as short as you can and then as tall as you can without dropping the wand?

♦ Stand tall with your arm straight in front of you. Balance the wand on the back of your hand. How high and how low can you move your hand without dropping the wand?

♦ Can you hold your wand by the end and carefully flip it and catch it by the other end? (You may have to demonstrate this.) If successful, can you do it with the other hand? (Make sure students are far enough apart.)

♦ Can you balance the wand on the back of your hands? Now, can you quickly pull your hands from underneath the wand and catch it before it hits the floor?

♦ Hold the wand in your hands, palms up and open. Can you toss the wand high enough to turn your hands over and catch it on the back of both hands?

♦ Can you hold the wand across your back with the help of the elbows? Now, cross your legs and sit. Can you stand up?

♦ Hold the wand on the back of your hands in front of you and raise your arms and let the wand slowly roll down to your chin. Slowly lower your arms and let the wand roll off your fingertips. Can you catch your wand before it hits the floor?

♦ Hold the wand in front of you with one end up and the other end down. Flip the wand a half turn and catch it. Can you do the same thing in the other direction? How many times can you do this without missing?

♦ Can you hold your wand in front of you with two hands and step through one foot at a time? Can you go back through?

♦ Hold your wand in front of your body. Can you jump through with both feet without letting go with your hands?

♦ Can you use your wand as a jump rope by turning it under your feet?

♦ Grasp your wand near one end with one hand. Hold the wand, with the end pointing down. Can you release the wand and reach across your body and try to catch it before it hits the ground? Can you try this with the other hand?

♦ This time, grasp your wand near the bottom. Holding it straight, can you release your grasp just enough to let the wand slide through your hand? Then, can you try to regrasp it again as close to the end of the wand as possible? Now try it with your other hand.

♦ Balance your wand. Can you let it go, spin all the way around, and try to catch it before it hits the ground?

EXERCISES

For the Neck

♦ Hold your wand behind your head. Push hard with your hands and resist with your neck. Hold for a count of five.

♦ Hold the wand under your chin. Push up with your hands and resist with your chin. Hold for a count of five.

For the Arms

♦ Hold the wand under your hips. Pull up with your hands and push down with your hips. Hold for a count of five.

For the Arms and Chest

♦ Place your hands about 6″ apart on your wand. Push your hands *in* hard. Hold for a count of five.

For the Arms and Shoulders

♦ Place your hands about 6″ apart on your wand. Pull your hands *away* from each other hard. Hold for a count of five.

WAND ACTIVITIES FOR PARTNERS

♦ Can you and your partner each balance your own wand? On the signal "Go," can you and your partner swap positions and get to your partner's wand before it falls? Can you try this with three people? Four people?

♦ Face your partner across a line or jump rope. Both of you grasp the wand firmly. On the signal "Go," can you both try to pull the other across the line? (Be sure to match the partners as evenly as possible.)

♦ Sit and face your partner across a line or jump rope, feet braced against each other. Both of you grasp the wand firmly. On the signal "Go," can you both try to pull the other *up* and *over* the line?

♦ Face your partner. Both of you hold one end of the wand with one hand, and your leg with the other hand. Can you both try to pull the other person off balance or make that person let go of the leg or wand?

Tire Routines ———————————— 9

Old school bus or truck tires can make a positive contribution to your efforts of developing agility, balance, and stamina in your students. Many tire shops will give you all the old tires you need free of charge. Also, many of them will haul the tires to your school if you tell them they are to be used in your physical education program. It never hurts to ask!

Tires present an opportunity for a wide variety of activities for grades K–6. In grades K–3, many different challenges can be presented: (1) single tire routines, (2) squad drills, (3) flea jumps, and (4) circuits. (These will all be discussed later in the chapter.)

In grades 4–6, tires continue to play a big part in the development of the children. These classes will no longer be doing the individual challenges as done in grades K–3 on single tires, but they will continue the following activities: (1) squad drills, (2) partner activities, (3) circuits, and (4) relays.

If you are just starting your physical education program, the following suggestions for using tires will be helpful:

EQUIPMENT NEEDED: Old school bus tires or old truck tires that still have firm casings. Car tires are not large enough or firm enough for these activities.

NUMBER OF TIRES NEEDED: For the activities described here, you will need a total of 32 tires for the outside activities. This represents 24 tires for grades K–3 and 32 tires for grades 4–6.

SAFETY:Wet tires are a hazard because they can be slick; make sure tires are dry before you use them. Don't let children play inside stacked tires. When tires have been chained up outside during the summer months, watch out for yellow jacket and wasp nests inside the tires when you begin using them in the fall.

STORAGE: Let's be realistic. Storage—both outside on the playground and inside in the multipurpose room or gym—can be a problem in many schools. Some schools are able to leave their outside tires unchained and on the ground with very little vandalism during the after-school hours. Unfortunately, other schools find it impossible to leave their tires unchained or locked up after school hours. If you think you will need to lock up your tires after school hours, the following suggestions may be of help.

To chain up and lock your tires, you will need a tree or a stout pole against which the tires lean. You also need a chain to run through the tires to secure them to the tree. The chain that most schools use is size 2–0. It is sometimes called *cow chain* or *weld chain.*

All of this may sound like a lot of work, but two capable upper elementary children can handle this chore very well.

To figure how much chain you will need for your outside tires, measure the length of the tires after they are stacked against the tree, multiply this number by 2 and add 2′ to the total. This should give you all the chain you will need.

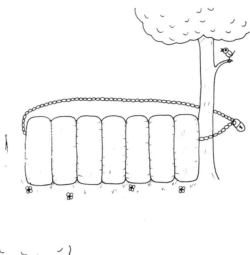

Sixteen tires are usually adequate for indoor activities. If space permits, it is very handy and convenient if you can put a stack of four tires in the four corners of the multipurpose room or gym. REMEMBER: Do not let the children play inside the tires when they are stacked!

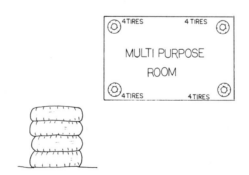

WHO PUTS THE TIRES OUT WHEN NEEDED: This is no problem for children in grades 4–6. Most third grades and some second grades, too, may be able to handle this chore successfully. When using the tires indoors, assign two children to each stack of four tires.

It will be their responsibility to take the tires from the stack and set them up for whatever activity is planned. It is very important when taking tires off the stack, and when stacking them back up, that both children work together and carefully move the same tire together. These truck tires are too heavy and awkward for most children to move by themselves.

The kindergarten, first grade, and most second-grade teachers can have some of the older children come in and set up the tires for their classes *under their supervision.*

The unlocking and putting the outside tires out for use can be handled very easily by two or three children from grades 4–6. They should be put out before classes begin in the morning and locked up again after the last class at the end of the school day.

SAFETY TIP: Now is an excellent time to teach children how to lift heavy objects. They should keep their back straight and lift with the legs. Demonstrate this yourself and have the children practice.

SINGLE TIRE ROUTINES
FOR GRADES K–3

Every child should have his or her own tire that is located at least 3' away from the nearest tires. This gives each child room to experiment with the following challenges without bumping into classmates who are engaged in the same activity. It also gives you room to circulate constantly among the tires while giving directions, encouragement, and praise when needed.

- ◆ Can you walk around the rim of your tire? Run? Skip? Hop? Slide?
- ◆ Straddle your tire. Can you jump up and turn half way around before you land with your feet spread on the rim? Can you turn all the way around?
- ◆ Can you stand in the middle of your tire and jump out, turn, and jump back in? How quietly can you do this? As you jump out of and into your tire, can you do a half turn before landing?
- ◆ Get into a push up position with your hands on the rim of the tire and your feet on the ground outside the tire. How many times can you walk around your tire while you are in this position? Keep your back straight while doing this.
- ◆ Straddle your tire again. Can you jump into the middle of your tire and then jump back on your tire in the straddle position again? Can you continue to do this until I say "And stop"? Can you do a half turn each time before landing?

- ◆ Stand in the middle of your tire. Can you jump high enough in the air to spread your legs and bring them together again before you land with both feet in the center of your tire? Now it gets tougher! Can you do a one quarter turn as you jump and spread your legs before landing?
- ◆ Straddle your tire again with your feet on the edge of the tire. Can you jump into the air and click your heels once before landing in the straddle position again? Can you click your heels more than one time? Can you do a turn and click your heels before landing?
- ◆ Get down into the push-up position. This time, your feet should be on the rim of the tire and your hands on the ground outside the tire. Can you "hand walk" around your tire? Don't sag in the middle, and keep your back straight. Can you go all the way around

to your starting place, and then reverse and go all the way around again? This is a tough challenge!

♦ Get into the frog jump position on your tire. From this position, can you push off with your hands and feet high enough in the air to do a one quarter turn? Both hands and feet should be off the tire while you are turning. Can you do a half turn? A three quarter turn?

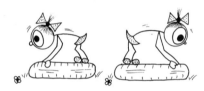

♦ Stand straddling your tire. Can you jump high enough to bring your knees up to your chest? Can you pull your shins in tight with your hands and then quickly let go and land straddling the tire again? (This is the *tuck* position. It will take a lot of practice for some children to do it correctly.)

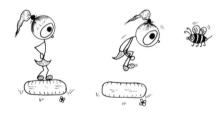

♦ Straddle your tire. Can you jump high enough in the air to slap both your heels at the same time before landing back into the straddle position on your tire? Can you turn in the air while doing this?

♦ Straddle your tire. How far can you spread your feet apart when you jump in the air? Don't forget to straddle your tire when you land.

♦ Straddle your tire with a jump rope in your hands. Can you jump rope in the straddle position? How many times can you jump without a miss? Can you make the rope go under your feet two times before landing?

♦ This time, straddle your tire with one foot forward in front of you and the other foot on the tire rim behind you. Hold your jump rope in your hands. As you jump, can you change the forward foot to the back position and the back foot to the forward position each time the rope goes over your head?

♦ Straddle your tire with your jump rope in your hands. Can you turn in the air on each jump? How many jumps does it take you to turn all the way around to your starting position?

♦ Straddle your tire with a jump rope in your hand. Can you click your heels as the jump rope passes under your feet?

LANE FORMATIONS FOR GRADES K-6

The formation shown here is called the "lane or squad formation." It shows four lanes of six tires in each lane. If you have 28 children in your class, there will be four squads of 7 children in front of each row of tires. Six tires in each lane is plenty for the K-3 classes. The 4-6 classes should have eight tires in each row when possible. Do not use these drills as relays in grades K-3; rather, let the children learn these moves without pressure. If the 4-6 classes have been doing these routines since kindergarten, they can use them as relays occasionally if they do them correctly and safely.

In the following illustrations showing the foot and hand positions, there will be only three tires shown. REMEMBER: There will be six tires for grades K-3 and eight tires for grades 4-6 when outside; there will be four tires in front of each squad in grades 4-6 when inside.

The following illustration shows the two positions used in these activities: (A) the frog jump and (B) standing positions.

- ♦ *Run Through:* Step in the middle of each tire as you run through them.

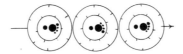

- ♦ *Jump Through:* Jump with both feet entering the center of each tire.

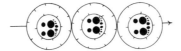

- ♦ *In and Straddle:* Jump in the center of the tire; then jump to a straddle position on the next tire.

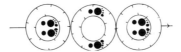

- ♦ *Straddle-Straddle:* Straddle jump each tire.

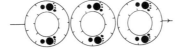

- ♦ *Alternate:* Jump (both feet together) with one foot landing on the ground inside the tire while the other foot lands on the rim. Jump to the other side of the next tire with opposite foot reaction.

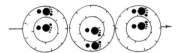

♦ ***Straddle Half Turn:*** Jump from tire to tire in the straddle position with a half turn in the air.

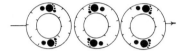

♦ ***Hop:*** Hop along the row of tires on the same foot and hop back along the tires using the other foot.

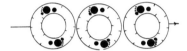

♦ ***Jump Over:*** Straddle jump over every other tire.

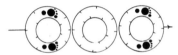

♦ ***Frog Jumps:*** Push off with the feet but land on the feet and hands on the next tire at the same time.

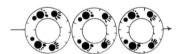

♦ ***In-and-Out Frog Jumps:*** Same as the frog jumps except that the feet go inside the tires one time and on the rim of the tire the next time.

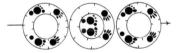

♦ ***Frog Jump Half Turns:*** Follow the same directions as in frog jumps except try to make quarter turns while in the air. Can you make half turns?

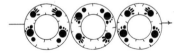

This is just a beginning! Encourage your students to create new moves and to name them.

PARTNER ACTIVITIES FOR GRADES 4–6

Use the same tire arrangement as is used in the single tire routines. (Each tire is located at least 3′ away from the next tire.) When selecting partners, be sure to select children who are near the same height, weight, and ability. *Be very careful with these activities.* Most classes will handle them very well and have a great experience, but some classes will not be able to handle them safely. If there is a negative response, don't do them.

♦ ***Power Push:*** Both children straddle their tire facing each other with hands held up to shoulder height, palms facing partner's palms. The action is palms against palms; you cannot push against any other part of the partner's body. The object is to make your partner step off the tire with either foot.

♦ ***Power Push Pull:*** Both partners straddle the tire and face each other. Grip each other's hands with the fingers interlocked. The object is to make your partner step off the tire either by pushing or pulling. The hands must stay locked together.

♦ *"Chicken Fight":* Partners straddle the tire and face each other. Each partner crosses his or her own arms across the chest while holding the elbows in tight with his or her hands. With knees slightly bent and feet shoulder width apart, move around the top of the tire in a sliding motion and try to bump your partner off the tire using the shoulder only. Do not use elbows.

♦ *"Lame Dog Fight":* Almost the same routine as the "Chicken Fight" except that each partner is holding one leg with one hand and has the other hand held close to the chest. The object is to bump the partner off the tire or make the partner let go of his or her leg. Only use the shoulder for bumping.

"FLEA JUMPS"

Flea jumps involve putting large truck tires or school bus tires halfway in the ground in a planned sequence and challenging the children to see if they can jump from tire to tire without stepping off a tire in the sequence.

To set up the flea jumps, you will need 15 large truck or school bus tires. Select the ones that still have firm casings with wide openings. Wide openings are important so that the half that goes into the ground can be filled and packed tightly with rocks and dirt.

There should be some sort of purpose or pattern in the arrangement and sequence of the tires when they are put into the ground. They should present a challenge for all concerned. They should be easy enough for the primary grades to experience success and hard enough to challenge the upper elementary group. To accomplish this, notice the arrangement of the tires in the following illustration.

Notice that the tires numbered "1" through "5" are set up where the long jumps are located so that the primary children can take these "short cuts" instead of trying to make the long jumps themselves. Even with the short cuts, some of the younger children will be challenged to complete the sequence eventually.

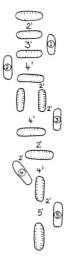

Since only a few children can be on the flea jumps at one time, this activity should be part of an outdoor circuit so that there will not be a long line of children waiting and wasting valuable time.

SAFETY: Make sure that the tires are dry and that the bottoms of the children's sneakers are dry and free of mud before doing this routine.

SUGGESTED LAYOUTS
FOR OTHER TIRE ROUTINES

♦ *V-Jumps (for grades 3–6):* This vigorous fitness routine is usually done inside, but can easily be done outside also. In the beginning, do not make the gaps of the "V" too wide. Let the students experience success; then gradually widen the gaps as the students get stronger and more skilled. IMPORTANT: Do not use this drill as a relay.

You will need 16 big tires and 16 cones or old gallon milk jugs for turning points.

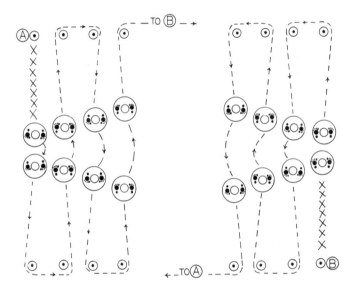

Divide the class in half: squad 1 and squad 2. Line up squad 1 to start at A and line up squad 2 to start at B. On the signal "Go," each person follows the squad mate in front at a safe distance in case of a fall. The squads follow the pattern shown in the illustration. When each squad finishes the "V" in its area, that squad follows the squad leader to the opposite area as shown. Squad 1 will follow on the outside of the formation to B while squad 2 follows its squad leader to A, where the students continue the routine.

SAFETY: Do not have the children do more repeats than they can handle. When they get tired, they get careless and have more falls. Squad members need to keep a safe distance from the person in front at all times. If a runner falls, the person directly behind should stop and raise both hands until the person who fell has a chance to get up and continue.

♦ *Box Formation (for grades K–6):* This routine is usually done indoors because of the mats involved. Again, this is not a relay; you want to encourage the children to do the skills correctly—not to see who can do them the fastest. This drill involves running and using some of the tire challenges (run through, straddle-straddle, alternates, etc.) used earlier and an appropriate roll on the mat when the students finish the tasks on the tires. The type of roll students will use depends on their grade level and how proficient they are in the rolls. For instance, the younger children will probably use the log roll or the tucked roll. Older children might use forward and backward rolls.

You will need 4 tumbling mats, 16 truck tires, and 4 cones or gallon milk jugs.

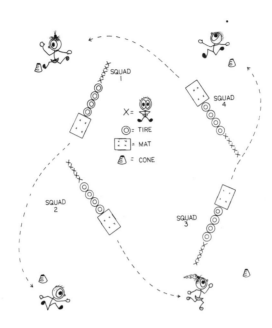

Divide the class into four squads and assign each squad to one of the four stations. (See the illustration.) The squads will line up behind the tires in a straight line. On the signal "Go," the first person in each squad, who will be followed by his or her squad mates at a safe distance, will follow the planned routine. For instance, the first person in squad 1 will run through the tires and land on his or her feet first on the mat and then do a log roll or forward roll (whichever he or she is qualified to do). Then that student will jump up and run around the formation on the outside of the cones until he or she and the squad come to squad 2. The student gets into line and does the same routine from this station and then from stations 3 and 4 until the student and the squad get back to their home base at station 1.

To add variety, you can assign different ways to travel along the tires at each station. A complete circuit for the four stations is called a *lap*.

SAFETY: Squad members must follow at a safe distance from the person in front. Always land on your mat with your feet first, and then go into your roll. *Never dive from the last tire into a roll.*

The Parachute —————— 10

How did we ever get along without parachutes! The children love them, and there is something magical about them. Not only are parachutes graceful and beautiful, they also have so many uses in physical education. In minutes you can give your students a tough arm-and-shoulder workout, and you won't hear one complaint. That's because the students were having so much fun that they didn't realize they were doing all that work!

Parachutes usually used in schools are the standard "personnel" parachutes—approximately 25' across. If possible, try to get parachutes from a war surplus unit if you have one in your area. Usually, you have to put your name on a waiting list. Most catalogs advertising elementary physical education equipment also carry parachutes; however, these are more expensive, so perhaps the PTA might become involved to obtain them for the school.

There are excellent parachute records commercially available that include the activities described in this chapter. The records also include many other activities done to music with good instruction. You might want to first go over the basics with the children orally, then let them put the routines to music. Two good records to look for are *Parachute Play* and *Pop Rock Parachute.*

"RIPPLES AND WAVES"

To make "ripples," put the class into a circle around the parachute. Have the children grasp the edges firmly with both hands, palms down, and at waist level. Now, shake the parachute vigorously! (This is a good warm-up.) To make "waves," have half the class raise its end of the parachute while the other half of the class lowers its end of the parachute. Repeat with each half of the class doing just the opposite of what they did before.

"MERRY-GO-ROUND"

Have the children grasp the parachute with one hand and all face the same direction. On your signal, the class will go around in a circle using whatever form of locomotion you call out. On your next signal, the class will pivot in the opposite direction, regrasp with the other hand, and continue.

"THE TENT"

Begin with the parachute flat on the floor. The class is in the stoop position grasping the edges of the parachute. On the signal, everyone—without moving his or her feet—stands up pulling the parachute off the floor and raising their arms to full extension overhead. The parachute will billow overhead like a big tent. Keep the arms extended and do not let go or walk toward the center.

"POP-UPS"

Follow the same procedure as in "Ripples and Waves," except that any number of balls are thrown on top of the parachute. The bouncing balls will sound like popping popcorn as they pop up in the air. (This gives the arms and shoulders a good workout.)

"COMBAT"

Use the same formation as in "Ripples and Waves." Divide the class into two teams such as the Greens and the Blues. Place one ball in the center of the parachute. On the signal "Go," both teams try to shake and bounce the ball off the parachute on the other team's side.

CHANGE PARTNERS

Number the class off into fours (1-2-3-4) and follow the instructions given for making the "tent." When the parachute is in the full tent position, call any number from 1 to 4. The numbers called will change places with each other by running under the tent to their new positions. When the numbers just called are in their new positions, repeat the same process again and call different numbers to change this time. Repeat until all the numbers have been called. Later, you can have the children do different locomotor skills (skipping, jumping, hopping, etc.) as they change positions.

"THE MAGIC CARPET"

Follow the same procedure as in making the tent. When the students' arms are in full extension and the parachute is in the full tent position, on your signal the class will turn loose at the same time and let the parachute glide to the floor.

"THE IGLOO"

Have the students follow the same procedure for making the tent. When the parachute is in the full tent position, have the children pull the edges of the parachute to the floor and place their knees on the edge of the chute and hold their arms in the air.

"INSIDE THE IGLOO"

Follow the same procedure for making the "igloo." When the chute is in full tent position, have the class pivot in place (turn halfway around), kneel down, and pull the parachute down on top of them. Keep the knees on the edge of the parachute to keep the air inside.

NUMBERS CHANGE

Use the same procedure for making the "igloo." When the children pull the parachute over them, have them sit on the edges and lean back against the parachute. The children are numbered off 1-2-3-4. When a number is called, these children will change places by crawling under the parachute.

"THE SUNFLOWER"

Use the same procedure for making the "igloo," except the children will lie on their stomachs with their heads inside the parachute and their forearms on the edges. On the signal "Out," everyone at the same time will poke their heads outside the parachute. On the signal "In," they pull their heads back in. On the signal "Turn," the children turn over *in place* onto their backs. Then, using the same procedure, they will poke their heads in and out on the signals.

"THE WAVE"

To make the wave go smoothly all around the circle is a real team effort in timing and staying alert. Begin with everyone holding on to the parachute and in a stoop position. On the signal "Begin," an appointed student (A) stands with his or her arms straight overhead. The person (B) next to the appointed student begins his or her stand when (A) is halfway up. When (B) is standing tall, (A) should be halfway down and (C) should be halfway up. Continue this motion, person to person, all the way around the circle. This takes practice, but is a lot of fun.

"THE BALLOON"

Use the same procedure as in the tent. As the students stand and raise their arms to full extension, they should all walk toward the center of the circle. The parachute will billow up toward the ceiling like a big balloon.

Rope Climbing ——————————— 11

Most children in grades K–3 will be challenged with the lead-up activities to rope climbing, and if they continue to work hard on these drills and follow the progressions, they should become good rope climbers in their upper elementary years. But, there will be a few precocious youngsters in the lower elementary group who will be ready to climb a rope long before the majority of their classmates. Don't penalize this small group and keep the students on lead-ups just because some people say that only fourth-graders are ready to climb. If they have the strength and skill to climb, let them go for it—but *restrict* the height gradually to 8' to 10' and make certain they *understand and practice* all safety rules listed later before turning them loose.

In some cases, the installation of indoor climbing ropes can present problems. If you are fortunate enough to be using a gym, putting up ropes presents no big problem, but many multipurpose rooms are not designed with climbing ropes in mind. However, most school maintenance personnel are good at figuring out how to get things done, so if you want climbing ropes in your program, call on the expertise of these people to help get the job done.

Climbing ropes and all the hardware needed for safe installation can be purchased from most sports equipment companies. IMPORTANT: Use only ropes and the proper fittings made for climbing ropes.

Ideally, there should be four ropes. In most seven-station fitness circuits, there will be four children in each squad, so this will give each child a rope to work with at that station.

The length of the ropes should almost touch the floor, so you will have to order your ropes according to the height of the ceiling in your gym or multipurpose room.

SAFETY: Here are important safety rules to follow:

1. Tie climbing ropes together and pull them up and out of the area when not in use. Tell the students that they are not to be used unless you (or another supervising adult) gives permission and is present to supervise their use.

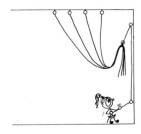

2. Do *not* tie big knots at the end of the ropes. The children like to sit on them and swing, which is very dangerous because
   a. The ropes are too close together to do this.
   b. Once the knots are put in, they become very tight and are difficult to get out.
   c. These ropes are for the activities that lead up to climbing and for actual rope climbing; they are not for sitting on and swinging.
3. Do not encourage a child to climb higher than he or she is capable of because the climber must always remember to save enough strength to come back down safely.
4. Place a mat under each climbing rope.
5. Do *not* have a spotter holding the rope under a climber.
6. Stress to the students that they are never to make remarks to a climber that may make him or her laugh and lose concentration.
7. Work hard on the progressions to rope climbing. This will develop the grip and arm flexor strength needed to safely climb the rope.
8. When climbing, the hands go hand over hand with leg and foot pressure. When coming down, go hand under hand with leg and foot pressure. *Never slide down the rope.* Serious and painful burns to the hands and legs will result from sliding.

Now for the rope climbing progressions. Have each child master the easier progressions before moving to the next, more challenging progressions.

STRAIGHT-ARM HANG

Begin by standing in front of the rope. Stand on tiptoes and reach up the rope as high as you can with both hands. Grab hold of the rope and hang on as you lift both feet off the floor. How long can you hold on? Ten seconds? Good. The next progression is to stand in front of the rope again, but this time *jump* as high as you can, grab the rope, and hang on as long as you can.

BENT-ARM HANG

Begin by standing in front of the rope, grab the rope in front of you so that your hands are in front of your chest. Hold on tight, put your chin on top of your top hand, and bring both knees up in front of you. Squeeze the rope between the legs and feet. How long can you hold this position? Good. Now, do the same thing except this time lift your legs up behind you and see how long you can hold this *bent-arm* position without using the legs and feet. Next, see how high you can *jump* up on the rope and hold the bent-arm position without using the legs and feet.

JUMP, BENT-ARM HANG, BICYCLE

Jump up as high as you can and grab the rope in the bent-arm position. While hanging on, make your legs go around as if you are riding a bicycle. How long can you do this and hold the bent-arm position? Ten seconds?

JUMP, BENT-ARM HANG, LEGS OUT FRONT

Jump again to the bent-arm position. While keeping your legs straight, can you bring them up and stick them out in front of you (90°)? How many times can you do this while keeping the arms bent and without letting go? Ten times?

JUMP, BENT-ARM HANG, TOUCH ROPE WITH TOES

Jump again to the bent arm position. While keeping your legs as straight as you can, can you bring your feet up and touch the rope above your head?

UPSIDE-DOWN HANG

Stand in front of the rope. Reach up as high as you can and hold on with both hands. Can you swing your feet forward and upward so that you are hanging upside down? Lower yourself slowly and carefully. Can you do it again? (In the beginning, you should spot this one.)

PULL TO STANDING POSITION

Lie flat on your back where you can reach up and grab the rope with both hands. Can you keep your body rigid and straight and pull yourself up to a standing position? Good. Now, carefully lower yourself and do it again.

SITTING TOE TOUCH

Sit with the rope between your legs and grab the rope in the bent-arm position. Can you pull your seat and legs off the floor and touch the rope with your toes? How many times can you do this?

CLIMBING ROPE "PULL-UPS"

Stand in front of your rope. Can you jump up and grab the rope in a straight-arm hang position? From this position (do not use your feet), can you pull yourself up so that your chin touches your top hand? How many times can you do this?

USING HANDS, LEGS, AND FEET TO CLIMB ROPE

If you have done all the progressions up to this point successfully, you should be ready to climb the rope. Reach up and grab the rope in a straight-arm position with the rope between your legs. Pull with your arms and bring your knees up at the same time. Now squeeze the rope between your legs and at the same time pinch the rope between the feet by pushing the rope against the ankle of one foot with the bottom of the other foot. (Many of the children will come up with other ways of pinching the rope with the legs and feet. If their way works, let them use it.) REMEMBER: *Hand over hand* when going up; *hand under hand* when coming down with leg pressure on the rope.

USING ARMS ONLY TO CLIMB ROPE

There will be very few primary and upper elementary children who can climb a rope in this manner because of the arm flexor strength required. But in case that rare young individual comes along, this is the way it is done. As the title indicates, the child will use the arms only—no legs and feet allowed. Have the rope between the body and legs. Extend the legs in front of the body, almost at right angles to the trunk. While climbing, shift your weight from side to side and kick your legs in a scissors or walking motion with each arm pull. REMEMBER: Hand under hand when coming down, with leg pressure on the rope.

TEMPORARY HOLD POSITION

It would be a good safety procedure to have those children who can climb (using feet and legs or otherwise) to learn and practice this hold position. Have them make a *stirrup* by putting the rope on the outside of one foot: then reach down and pull the rope up against the inside ankle. This makes a temporary rest position if needed.

Pole Climbing————————12

Climbing poles are an excellent addition to the physical education program. The activity is fun to do and can be a good supplement—along with rope climbing and pull-ups—for developing arm flexor and leg adductor strength.

This equipment presents a real challenge and obviously has a great appeal to children. Climbing poles are relatively inexpensive and with good care will last a long time.

But with all these exciting contributions to the physical education program, do not become complacent to the possibility of injuries. Never turn the children loose on the climbing poles *until they have completed the progressions and are thoroughly familiar with the safety procedures.*

As in rope climbing, there will always be a few youngsters who will be able to climb the pole the first time they touch it. They should be allowed to skip the progressions and work on climbing *only* if they have had a thorough period of instruction in the safety factors and practice them.

Limit the height that the primary children can climb to 10'. If they are capable of doing more, let them climb the pole several times in a row but go no higher than 10' each time.

How Many Poles Are Needed? As in rope climbing, four poles are ideal. For class instruction, you can have four squads with seven children in each squad working on one pole. Climbing poles are also excellent stations for your outdoor fitness circuits. In a seven-station fitness circuit, there will be approximately four children rotating at each station, so this would give each child a pole to work on.

Length of Pole. Most black pipe lengths come in 21' lengths.

Diameter of Pole. For safety, a pole that will be 16' above the ground should have a diameter of 2½".

How Deep in the Ground Should the Poles Go? The pole should be sunk 5', with the sunken end encased in cement.

Cost of Poles. The cost, of course, will vary. At the time of this writing, the cost of black pipe is approximately $2.50 per foot.

Painting the Poles. Painting keeps the poles from rusting and makes them attractive. Use a good primer before you paint the other colors. The illustration shows a color scheme used in "Color Climbing," a class activity that is explained later in this chapter. The illustration also shows the pole with different colors every 2' except for the bottom brown section which is 6'. The top two colors—blue and red—are for grades 4–6 only.

SAFETY: Here are important safety rules to follow:

1. No one climbs the pole until he or she has mastered the progressions and is thoroughly familiar with all the safety rules. (Make sure those students who are able to climb the pole without doing the progressions know and practice all safety rules.)
2. Assign only one person on a pole at a time.
3. No one stands directly under a pole when someone else is climbing.
4. Never try to make a climber laugh when he or she is climbing. The climber could lose his or her grip and fall.
5. When coming down the pole after a climb, come down with a hand under hand motion. Never slide down—a pole can burn your hands and legs.
6. Do not encourage a child to go higher if it looks as if he or she is tiring. The child must keep in mind that he or she has to save enough energy and strength to come down safely.

Now, on to the progressions. The progressions in pole climbing for children in grades K–3 are limited because of the diameter of the pole (2½″) and the small hands of the children in this group. Ideally, if the children can work on the climbing ropes indoors during the cold and wet months, they will be able to strengthen their grip and develop some arm flexor strength that will be a big help during the warm days in the spring when they can work outside on the climbing poles.

JUMP TO BENT-ARM POSITION—LEG SQUEEZE

Stand facing the climbing pole and grab the pole in a reaching straight-arm position. Jump to a bent-arm position and, at the same time, bring your knees and feet up. The climbing pole will be between your legs. Squeeze the pole between your legs and feet. Hang on tight in this bent-arm position. Can you hold it for 10 seconds? When you come down, *do not drop;* rather, keep your knees in the up position, and lower yourself the rest of the way down with a hand-under-hand motion. Ease off the leg and foot squeeze as you come down. To build strength, repeat this progression several times.

JUMP TO BENT-ARM POSITION—NO LEGS

Stand facing the pole. Jump as high as you can and grab the pole in the bent-arm position. Squeeze the pole in close to your body. Now, without using your legs and feet, how long can you hold yourself off the ground in this position? Can you lower yourself to the ground with the hand-under-hand motion? Repeat.

ADDRESSING THE POLE

After successfully working on the two previous progressions, some of the children should be ready to work on climbing the pole. Stand close to the pole with the straight-arm grip. This is called "addressing" the pole.

JUMP TO BENT-ARM POSITION—LEG SQUEEZE

This is the same position the children worked on in the first progression.

LEG SQUEEZE—HANDS SLIDE UP

Squeeze the pole with your legs and feet and, at the same time, *slide* your hands upward 4″ or 5″. (Four or five inches in the beginning may be high enough. Later, when the students are more confident and have developed more strength, they will probably reach higher.)

ARM PULL—KNEES UP

Pull hard with the hands and arms and, at the same time, ease the squeeze on the pole enough with the legs and feet to bring the knees and feet upward. As soon as the knees and feet are up again, repeat the procedures described in the previous slide progression. (Remember to limit the climb to 10′ for these youngsters.)

COLOR CLIMBING

This activity should be used only after the children's initial introduction to the climbing poles, where they are given a chance to practice the progressions and a thorough explanation of the safety rules.

Remind the children that their own personal desire along with peer pressure to climb higher may cause them to forget to save enough strength to climb down safely. But after children have climbed for a while, they adapt to this situation very well. Being able to make this decision for themselves is a definite part of pole climbing.

The purpose of "Color Climbing" is not only to offer the children a definite challenge to improve their climbing skills, but more important to ensure a safe climbing sequence.

Situation. There are four climbing poles and approximately 28 children, so there will be four squads with 7 children in each squad. Assign each squad to a pole and have each squad line up in a straight line behind its pole.

Have each child in each squad climb one time on the pole. Next, have the squads rotate clockwise to the next pole, where everyone will make one climb again. Continue to rotate and climb until every child has had a chance to climb all four poles. (The reason for rotating poles is to make it fair for all so that no squad has a "better" pole.)

Scoring. To score in the white area, the child must climb or jump to the white area and hang there in the bent-arm position for 5 seconds. To score in the green or orange, the student must climb and touch that particular color. If a child can climb and touch orange on all four poles, that student becomes a "pole cat" (or whatever else your students may want to designate for this honor).

	WHITE				GREEN				ORANGE				POLE CAT
TAD									1	2	3	4	★
CINDY	1	2	3	4									
SALLY									1	2	3	4	★
JO	1	2											
KATHY					1	2	3	4					
BO									1	2	3		
ANNE	1												
ETC.													

If, in the beginning, a child is skilled enough to climb up past white to green or orange, that is fine. White is a challenge for those less skilled.

Let's check a hypothetical class that has just finished "Color Climbing" and see how the students were scored.

Tad and Sally were able to climb and touch the orange area on each pole so they are both "pole cats" and get a big star in that column. Bo missed touching orange on his fourth pole, but he will get another chance on another day. Cindy was able to jump up to the white area and hold the bent-arm position for 5 seconds so she is looking forward to getting into the green next time. Jo was able to do the same thing on her first two poles but missed on her last two. Anne is very excited—she was able to hang in the white on her first pole for the first time.

"Two Square" and "Four Square"———13

"Two Square" and "Four Square" are excellent activities to reinforce the ball skills introduced in Chapter 6. Two Square will give the children one of their first "ball" games involving very simple rules they must follow.

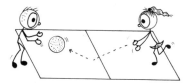

"Four Square" will follow "Two Square" with more skills and rules to be mastered.

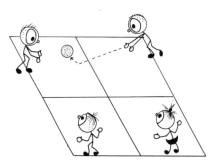

If done correctly, these activities will contribute to the development of eye-hand coordination, agility, quickness, sportsmanship, and other positive factors.

"Four Square" can become one of the most popular activities in your physical education program if it is presented correctly, and if you insist that the children play by the rules at all times consistently. When the rules are not enforced, chaos prevails and results in the loss of an excellent teaching and learning opportunity for all concerned.

Most "Four Square" courts are either 10′ × 10′ (four 5′ squares) or 16′ × 16′ (four 8′ squares).

They can be painted on hardtop surfaces by laying them out first with a chalk line, then putting down masking tape and painting between the masking tape with a paintbrush and "traffic" (parking lot) paint. Or you can lay out your court with a chalk line and use a rented line painter (sometimes called a striping machine). It is then a simple job to follow your chalk lines and put the paint down with this machine. (See Chapter 26 for more details.)

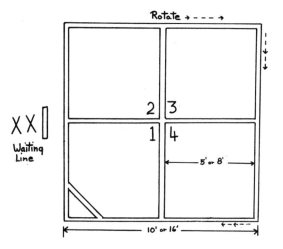

How many courts do you need? Four courts will be perfect for one class of 28 children. This allows 7 children for each court—4 in the squares and 3 in the waiting line.

"TWO SQUARE"

Most first-graders can do a good job with "Two Square" if they have had a good unit on ball activities in kindergarten and first grade. Put your good, fair, and poorly skilled students together in homogeneous groupings. If you have four "Four Square" courts, you will have more than enough two-squad courts. As shown in the illustration, have four students at each "Two Square" court, whereby there is one player in the square and one behind each player.

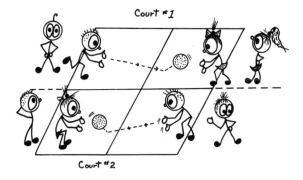

The *first progression* in the "Two Square" court is for the players to toss the ball (two-hand toss and catch) into the other player's square. The ball must bounce *one* time before it is caught. The player who catches the ball then tosses it right back into the other court again. This continues until someone misses or drops the ball or hits a line with the ball. When this happens, that player drops out and the person behind comes in.

The *second progression* is only for those who are ready for it. Leave the slower students on the toss-and-catch progression as long as they need it. The second progression is called "catch, drop, hit." It is just what it is called—first you catch the ball, then drop it (do not bounce it), and then hit it with both hands (underhand) to the person in the other square, who will follow the same procedure. Continue until someone misses or hits a line.

The *third progression* is usually for second-graders and third-graders (although there may be some first-graders who can handle it). In this progression, you skip the catch and the drop. Let the ball bounce one time in your square, then hit the ball underhand with both hands to the person in the other court, who will do the same to you. Continue until someone misses or hits a line.

"FOUR SQUARE"

There are many different directions for playing "Four Square." The following directions and rules are by no means the official ones. However, they have worked very well. Some changes were made through trial and error; others were selected by the children as a good solution to some problem areas we ran into. If your own rules work, then use them.

A simple way to go over the game of "Four Square" is to have the entire class line up around the outside of one of the "Four Square" courts with their toes on the outside line. Then ask the class to take one big giant step backward. Select four children and place one in each square. Now you are ready to demonstrate.

Notice that each square in the illustration is numbered. Number 1 is the server. (AUTHORS' NOTE: Some directions make our number 2 actually number 1 because the "extras" always enter this box first when someone misses. But our students wanted the server's box to be number 1 because that is the box they work so hard to get into—to be number 1!)

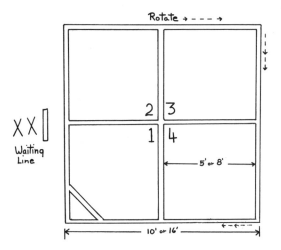

The server puts the ball into play by dropping (not bouncing) the ball with both hands and hitting it into any of the other three boxes with an underhand motion. Whoever receives the ball lets it bounce once and then, in turn, hits the ball with two hands (if possible) to any of the other three boxes with an underhand motion.

This exchange continues until someone makes one of the following mistakes:

- Allowing the ball to touch any other part of the body except the hands.
- A player hits the ball before it bounces one time.
- A player lets the ball bounce more than one time before he or she hits it.
- A player hits down on the ball and causes it to bounce higher than the receiver's shoulders.
- A player carries the ball when he or she hits it.
- A player stops the ball before it bounces (stops it with the hands) and lets it bounce before hitting it.
- A player taps the ball, and it hits any line, either inside or outside.
- A player hits the ball into his or her own square.
- If a player argues with the referee (this will be explained later), he or she may have to sit out 5 minutes of the game to "cool off."

If you are eliminated, go to the end of the waiting line and wait for your next chance to play, which is usually not a long wait. When a player is eliminated, the first player in the waiting line moves into square 2 while the other players, depending on which player was eliminated, move one square toward 1. For instance, if the player in 2 is eliminated, there will be no rotation; the first player in the waiting line just moves into square 2. If the player in 3 is eliminated, the player in 2 moves into square 3 and the new player moves into 2. If the player in 4 is eliminated, the player in square 3 moves into 4, and the player in 2 moves into 3 while the new person moves into 2. If the server is eliminated, then there is a complete rotation—2 moves to 3, 3 moves to 4, 4 moves to 1, and the new player moves to 2.

Positions

For a better game, teach the children how to position themselves in their square in relation to which square the ball is in. The illustration shows where the students should be located so that they will not be caught out of position. Play in the back and middle of your square when facing the ball.

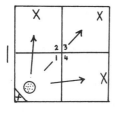 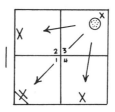

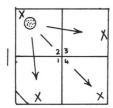 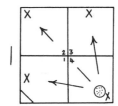

Arguing

Let's be realistic—there is a lot of arguing and fussing in most games of "Four Square"! Unless it is nipped in the bud, it will soon spoil the game for everyone. By making the first person in the waiting line the referee each time, you can cut down on the griping tremendously. This way, each child has his or her own turn to be referee, which helps develop some empathy toward others' "calls." If a child argues about a call given, have that child cool down a few minutes by sitting away from the court to watch the game. When the player can come back into the game without fussing, he or she is allowed to play again. Eventually, if you enforce this consistently, a major part of the griping is stopped. It also gives the children an opportunity to have the responsibility of being a referee.

Variation for Grade 1

After mastering the toss and catch on the "Two Square" courts, you may want to give your first-graders the opportunity to play "Four Square Toss and Catch." This means they will also have to learn how to rotate and become familiar with the additional rules for "Four Square."

Variations for Grades 5-6

After the basic game of "Four Square" is learned, add new variations to further challenge the students. Encourage the children to come up with ideas of their own, too. (NOTE: When playing the variations involving a server, the server must call out the new activity loud enough for everyone concerned to hear before beginning.)

"Doubles." Play the same game of "Four Square" as described earlier—the only difference is that there are two players (partners) at each square, one in the square and the other waiting outside the square. As soon as one partner hits the ball, he or she quickly gets out of the square and the partner steps in the square prepared to hit the next ball. Then he or she quickly gets out while the partner returns to the court again. Regular "Four Square" rules are used, so if one partner fouls, both partners go to the end of the waiting line. This is a great activity for quickness and concentration.

"Around the World." The server loudly calls out "Ready" and then "Around the World." If the server serves to the right, the ball will continue going around the court to the right until the server yells "Left" as the ball lands in the server's court. Then the server hits the ball to the left and begins a new rotation. Continue until someone fouls.

"War." The server loudly calls out "Ready" and then "War." The server serves to one of the squares. Then the person in that square hits the ball back to the server. These two players continue hitting the ball back and forth to each other until one of them fouls or until the server yells "Cease Fire." Then the regular "Four Square" game continues while the game is still in play.

"Battle." The server loudly calls out "Ready" and then "Battle." The server serves to any of the squares. Whoever receives the ball must always return the ball to the server. This continues until someone misses or until the server yells "Cease Fire" as the ball is returned to the server's court. Then the regular "Four Square" is continued without stopping the game.

"Numbers." The server loudly calls out "Ready" and then a number from 1 through 4. For example, if the server calls out "3," the server would then hit the ball to square 3. The student in square 3 can then return the ball to any other court thereafter but the ball must always be returned to 3. Continue until someone fouls.

Tug-of-War Routines━━━━14

You won't have to do a selling job with this activity! Children and adults all over the world have participated in many forms of tug of war for hundreds of years, and it will probably continue to be a favorite activity for many more years to come.

When dividing your class into two teams, it is extremely important that you match them up as close as possible to size and ability. You will probably have to make several trial runs to finally balance out your teams. It is not a good idea to let the children pick their own teams—all the "stars" want to be on the same team. Tug of war is fun and challenging if you have two well-balanced teams.

Don't try to make a full 30-minute session of tug-of-war activities alone. If you do, you will have lots of children with very sore hands, they will be very tired, and their enthusiasm for tug of war may be at a low ebb for awhile.

Instead, follow the regular daily format of running first, then tug of war for 10 or 15 minutes, followed by a brief session with a passive game to let them cool down before going back to their classrooms. A short, vigorous, and enthusiastic session of tug of war will leave them looking forward to the next time they have tug of war scheduled.

Safety. Have two teams paired off as evenly as possible. When you signal "Stop" after a win, everyone (winners and losers) should ease off the rope—*never* let go of the rope until told to do so. Caution the children to get back on their feet as quickly as possible when they fall during a pull. *Never* wrap the rope around the hand or arm! The last person in line should *never* wrap the rope around his or her waist. You should always check the tug-of-war rope before using it for signs of wear and tear.

Rope Size and Length. A 1″ diameter hemp rope is satisfactory for grades K–3. Grades 4–6 should have 2″ ropes. Remember, a new hemp rope will be hard on the hands for a while. The sticky fibers seem to smooth out after the rope has been used for a time, so plan shorter sessions when you have a new rope.

The length of the rope can be 50 or 60 feet. At the time of this writing, the cost is approximately 60 cents a foot for 1″ rope. Two-inch rope, of course, is more expensive.

ORGANIZATION

The following three steps in organizing a safe and orderly tug-of-war session have been successful in many physical education classes, field days, and special programs:

1. The class has already been selectively divided into two teams. Assign each team to its half of the rope. *Do not pick up the rope.* Ask students to stand on their right-hand

side of the rope. Next, have each team "stagger" its teammates—one person on the right and one on the left; do this all the way down the line. All team members are now standing in a staggered position beside the rope, and no one has touched the rope except you. At this point, hold the rope with a hand on each side of the flag.

2. When everyone is in position, give the command "Pick up your ropes"; team members pick up the rope *without pulling.* Your next command is "Take up the slack." The team members gently pull just enough to straighten the rope. Have a slight pause to make sure that neither team has more pressure than the other. Your next command is "Set," whereby everyone should now be poised and ready for the signal to pull.

3. The third command is "Pull!" As you say "Pull," immediately let go of the rope and step back into a safe position so that you can see all the markers. From this position, you can also stop the pull if anyone gets into trouble .

FIVE SUGGESTED TUG-OF-WAR ACTIVITIES

Pull for Distance

Securely attach the flag to the center of the rope. Then place the flag in the center of the markers. The markers can be two jump ropes that are placed 6' apart (or any other distance you feel is appropriate for your students).

Another method is to place two cones 6' apart. On your signal "Pull," carefully watch the flag—the team that pulls the flag across the cones (or jump ropes) wins.

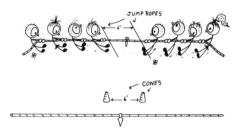

Pull for Time

For this pull, you need only one jump rope or one cone. Place the flag directly on the rope or in line with the cone. After the teams have lined up properly, tell the students that the pull will be timed for 30 seconds. The team that has the flag on its side of the rope or beyond the cone on its side wins.

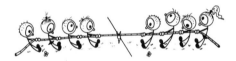

Pull for the Flag

Stretch the tug-of-war rope on the ground and place a cone or gallon milk jug (half full of sand) at 4' or 5' from both ends of the rope. Place a flag, a ball (Nerf™ ball or playground ball), or some other object on the cones that the last person on each team can either grab or knock off. The last person on each team should hold on with one hand and face the cone at the end of his or her rope. On the signal "Pull," both teams try to pull hard enough so that the end person can grab the flag or knock the ball off the cone. The team that does this first wins.

Marine Corps Tug of War

This pull can be set up for pull for distance, pull for the flag, or pull for time. The only difference is that after the teams have staggered themselves correctly, they either lie on their stomachs or on their backs with their feet touching the rope. On the signal "Pull," everyone jumps up, grabs the rope and starts pulling. Usually the team that gets more hands on the rope faster wins this pull, which is a good quickness drill.

Sprint Tug of War

Stretch the rope out as shown in the illustration and set up for pull for distance, pull for the flag, or pull for time. Measure 10' or 15' away from the rope at opposite sides and draw a line or put down jump ropes behind which the teams line up. On the signal "Pull," both teams sprint for the rope, pick it up, and start pulling. Again, the team that gets more hands on the rope first usually wins.

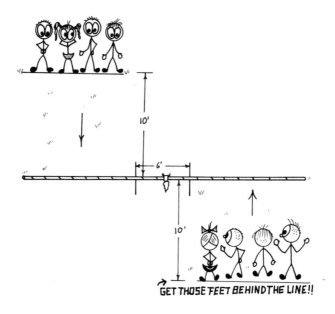

GET THOSE FEET BEHIND THE LINE!!

Relays———————————————15

Most children find relays fun and exciting, especially when the leadership is skilled and enthusiastic and the relays are conducted and organized properly. Relays are also one of the teacher's best tools for

♦ Fostering teamwork.
♦ Teaching how to win or lose graciously.
♦ Teaching how to follow rules and directions.
♦ Developing and reinforcing skills (locomotor skills such as running, skipping, galloping, etc.).
♦ Developing fitness in a way that is fun.

Nothing spoils relays faster than

♦ Having only two relay teams.
♦ Having a teacher who is obviously bored and not enthusiastic.
♦ Having a teacher who is unprepared and unorganized.
♦ Using poor rules and enforcement.
♦ Having all the best performers on the same team.
♦ Giving vague directions.

So be enthusiastic and have good organization so that the children will thoroughly enjoy, benefit greatly, and look forward to relay days.

GENERAL SUGGESTIONS

It is very helpful in determining winners if each runner sits in his or her regular place behind the team after he or she has run.

Keep the lines straight and close. During the excitement of a relay, children have a tendency to pull out of line to watch and cheer for their runners. That is fine, but they can still see and cheer while keeping their lines tight and straight and not block their teammates' progress.

Occasionally, you still see a well-meaning teacher who has the class doing relays in two long lines. The children soon get bored and end up scrapping and losing all their enthusiasm. So always have at least four teams to a relay unless you have a very small class. There should be about six to eight people on each team.

Simple scoring for four-team relays can be

5   points—first place
3   points—second place
2   points—third place
1   point—fourth place

As you will see, there are many different types of relays, so use a variety to keep the children enthusiastic. This makes relays much more fun for all concerned. And it can't be said enough—your enthusiasm for relays is reflected by the students, so be very enthusiastic and supportive of your relay program.

ORGANIZATION

Relays are more fun and exciting when the competition is close. Be aware that many times most of the best performers will want to be on the same team. As stated before, this can spoil your relays. It is no fun when the same team wins all the time. To give an example of how to set up your four teams, let's use the most common formation called the lane method.

Divide the class into four teams by having the whole class line up on a straight line and then have them count off by fours (1–2–3–4, 1–2–3–4, etc.). Next, have all the 1's line up in a straight line on the starting line, then the 2's, the 3's, and the 4's. Then have the children do a few simple relays. Now juggle the teams around (moving some of your faster and slower children to other teams) until you have all four teams as close to being equal as possible. Very seldom will your relay teams have an even number on each team. So, if you have seven children on three teams and six on another, most of the time you can find one child on the short team who will be glad to run two times (first and last positions).

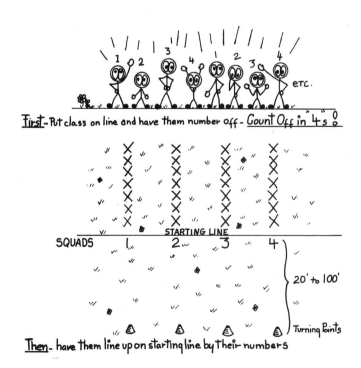

Starting

Children in this age group usually use a standing start for lead-off runners on each squad. Be consistent in your starting commands, and make certain all four teams get an equal start.

Have the lead-off runners "Take your marks" (place the toe of their front foot against the starting line). Then "Get set," a short hold while you make sure all four runners are ready to go, and then "Go!" *"Yell loud enough for everyone to hear.* If someone starts before you say "Go!" bring everyone back and start all over again. It is really disheartening if one team is allowed to get away with a head start and is not called back—especially if that team wins!

Passing the Baton or Tagging Off

Look at the illustration. After the lead runner (1) has circled the turning point (A) and is on the way back, have him circle around the back of his team as shown, then run up to the front of his team and pass the baton or tag off the next runner (2). The lead runner (1) then goes to the back of the squad's line and sits directly behind and in close to the next runner (6) in line. As each runner goes, all the sitters scoot up one place. This method takes a bit of practice, but it is worth the effort for more orderly and controlled exchanges.

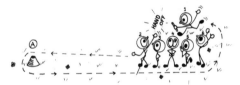

Using Safe Batons Whenever Possible

A baton will eliminate a lot of fussing about a runner leaving before he or she was actually tagged. The illustration shows how to make a safe baton out of newspaper and masking tape.

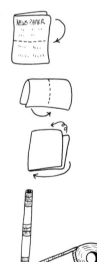

1. Fold one section of newspaper in half.
2. Then fold this section once more in the middle.
3. Roll tight toward the fold.
4. Then tape both ends and middle with masking tape.

Turning Points

Always use an object such as a pylon, milk jug (one quarter full with sand), and so on, for the turning points. *Never* use a wall for students to tag and turn because children may stumble and fall into the wall at full speed.

MODIFIED AND TRUE RELAYS

Modified relays are used for grades K–12. They are especially handy for grades K–1 when introducing relays to this particular age group for the first time. *True relays* would prove a bit complicated for grades K–1. It is easier to introduce the modified relay with the lane method.

Modified relays are run in heats, and each heat is started separately. The first child to win in each heat wins a point for his or her team. For instance, if there are seven children on a team, it would be possible to win seven points. (If this happens, check to see that the "stars" are not on the same team; in that case, the teams need to be reorganized.) Keep in mind that modified relays are run in many varieties for the upper age groups, too.

True relays are a continuous team effort. For instance, on the signal "Go!" all team members run consecutively until the last person has finished. The first team to get everyone back to their original position wins. True relays are run from a variety of relay formations (which are explained later).

EQUIPMENT NEEDED FOR RELAYS

The list of equipment that follows is used in most of the relays, at one time or another, in this chapter. The cones, jump ropes, and playground balls will be the only store-bought items; the rest is either free for the getting in your community or can be hand made.

32 Used Bicycle Tires

Many local bicycle shops will be glad to save used bicycle tires for you. Bicycle tires are used in most of the relays in this chapter to mark (1) team positions and (2) individual positions. This eliminates having to put down lines of all shapes and sizes both indoors and outdoors.

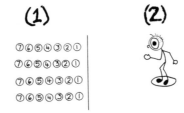

8 Cones or Plastic Gallon Milk Jugs

The cones can be purchased and will last a long time with good care. Or the children can bring gallon milk jugs from home; fill them one quarter full with sand. Be sure to tape the tops on securely.

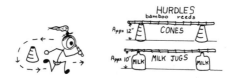

8 Carpet Squares

Carpet squares, usually old samples used in local furniture stores, are often donated to the school's physical education program. Small carpet squares can be used for sit-ups in some of the relays.

4 Bamboo Reeds

These reeds should be approximately 1″ to 1½″ in diameter and 5′ or 6′ in length. Furniture stores may assist if they have rugs with bamboo in the center. Or farmers with farms that have bamboo patches as wind breaks are usually glad to donate as much as you need. Bamboo reeds are used to make hurdles. (See the illustration accompanying "Cones or Plastic Gallon Milk Jugs.")

8 8½" Playground Balls

These can be purchased, but, if you are giving your students a unit on ball activities, you will already have a supply on hand.

8 No. 10 Tin Cans

These are used to hold the playground balls. The cans are available from your school lunch room. Be sure to hammer flat any sharp edges around the openings.

8 Short Jump Ropes

These can be purchased, but again, if you are giving your students a rope-jumping unit, you will already have a supply on hand. The jump ropes will be shown in the following relay diagrams as in the illustration here. The jump ropes are always placed on a bicycle tire to keep them in a certain location in relation to the other equipment.

← JUMP ROPE
← BICYCLE TIRE

1 School Bus or Truck Tire

This item is optional. It comes in handy in setting up the spoke relay, which is described later.

RELAY FORMATIONS

The following seven relay formations will be explained, along with examples of each:

Lane method	Spoke
Box	Hexagon
Circle	Octagon
Shuttle	

Lane Method

The lane method involves placing the teams in parallel columns behind a starting line. A turning point (pylons, gallon milk jugs, balls, etc.) should be placed directly in front of each team at a distance determined by the physical condition of the class and the type of relay to be run. The race involves having each runner, in turn, run from the starting line around the turning point and back to her team where she tags off the next runner (see "Passing the Baton or Tagging off.") The first team to get everyone back into his or her original position wins.

Remember, from the lane method as well as most of the other formations, you can use some of the basic locomotor skills (skipping, galloping, sliding, jumping, hopping, etc.) in your relays.

Also from the lane method you can use some of the self-testing skills and stunts shown in the following illustration. Some of these are quite vigorous, so make the distance to travel shorter than you would for running, and so on. See illustration on next page.

Potato Race. You need 16 bean bags, 4 no. 10 tin cans, and 16 bicycle tires. (NOTE: The illustration shows only one team. Remember, there are three more teams.) On the signal "Go!" the first runner (1's) takes off and picks up bean bag A, returns, and puts it in her team's no.

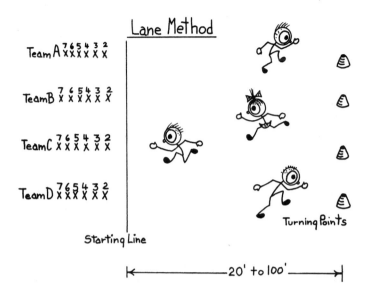

10 tin can (X). She then does the same thing with B and C. When she picks up bean bag D, she circles her team and puts the bean bag into the can. As soon as 1 places the last bean bag in the can, runner 2 pulls one bean bag out of the can and places it in the first tire A, returns and pulls another bean bag out of the can and places it in the second tire B, continuing until all the bean bags are in the tires. The team continues alternately to put the beans bags out and to bring them back in. The first team to get everyone back into their original position wins. An old and popular relay, the children love this one.

Jump Rope Relay. You need 4 cones or milk jugs and 4 short jump ropes. (NOTE: The illustration shows only one team. Remember, there are three more teams.) On the signal "Go!" the first person (1) on each team takes off, jumping rope as he circles the turning point and returns to his team. He circles around behind his team (still jumping) and gives the rope to 2, who continues with the same routine. The first team to get everyone back into position wins.

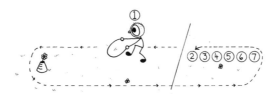

Hurdle Relay. You need 8 cones or gallon milk jugs and 4 bamboo reeds or broomsticks for hurdles, 4 cones or gallon milk jugs for turning points, and 4 paper batons. (NOTE: The illustration shows only one team. Remember, there are three more teams.) On the signal "Go!" the first runner (1) on each team leaps one hurdle on the way to the turning point and then leaps the same one on the way back. If a bamboo reed is knocked off the cones, the runner has to stop and put it back up. (Tell the children not to get discouraged because other runners will knock them off, too.) Each runner circles his or her team and passes the baton to 2. The first team to get everyone back into position wins. Later, try adding another hurdle about 12' from the first one.

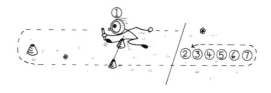

Jump Stick Relay. You need 4 wands or broomsticks with rounded edges and 4 cones or milk jugs. (NOTE: The illustration shows only one team. Remember, there are three more teams.) On the signal "Go!" 1 takes off with her wand or broomstick and runs around the turning point and heads back toward her team. Child 2 has turned sideways and is ready to take one end of the wand. Children 1 and 2 hold the wand low and, as they move back through their team, each person jumps the wand. When they get to the end of the line, 2 takes off for the turning point while 1 takes her place at the end of the line. While 2 is running, 3 has positioned himself sideways as 2 had done and is prepared to carry out the same procedure. The first team to get everyone in his or her original position wins.

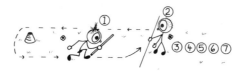

Throw and Duck Relay. You need 4 8½" playground balls or Nerf™ balls and 24 bicycle tires. (NOTE: The illustration shows only one team. Remember, there are three more teams.) Have all four teams line up as shown in the illustration, with 1 behind the starting line. On the signal "Go!" 1 throws the ball to 2, who throws it back to 1 and stoops down. Child 1 then throws to 3, who throws it back to 1 and stoops. Continue this procedure until 6 catches the ball. Child 6 holds the ball and yells "Change!" Everyone then drops back one position (1 goes to 2, 2 goes to 3, etc.). Child 6 is now in 1's old place, so he continues the same routine as explained. Continue until everyone is back in his or her original position. The first team to do this wins. (For kindergarteners and some first-graders, use Nerf™ balls instead of playground balls.)

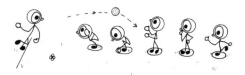

Change Relay. You need 28 bicycle tires, 4 cones or milk jugs, and 4 8½″ playground balls. (NOTE: The illustration shows only one team. Remember, there are three more teams.) On the signal "Go!" all 1's run to the turning point, holding the ball behind their backs. As they round the turning point, they place the ball between their knees and jump back to their teams where they circle behind their teams and hand the ball off to the 2's, who continue the same routine. Continue until everyone is back to their original position. The first team to do this wins.

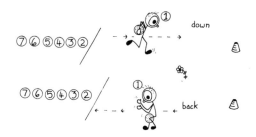

Box Relay

Here are two variations of the box formation.

The Box No. 1. You need 28 bicycle tires, 4 cones or milk jugs, and 4 paper batons. The task involved is running. This is a simple running relay to introduce the children to the box formation. On the signal "Go!" all 1's pull out and circle the box formation in a clockwise direction. As soon as each runner gets back to his or her own tire, the baton is passed to 2 who repeats the same procedure. The first team to get everyone back into their original position wins. You might want to have each runner sit in his or her own tire when finished running. This can also be run as a modified relay.

The Box No. 2. This can be a modified or a true relay. You need 32 bicycle tires, 4 carpets, 4 jump ropes, 8 cones or milk jugs, and 4 bamboo reeds. The tasks involved are running, hurdling, rope jumping, and sit-ups.

In *progression 1,* notice that in front of each team is a jump rope (inside a bicycle tire) and a carpet. Each team will use its own equipment. On the signal "Go!" all 1's pick up the jump rope in front of their team, do 20 speed jumps, put the rope back into the tire, and then do 10 correct sit-ups, if possible. Then they run out through their tires and run around the formation leaping four hurdles. As soon as they get back into their own tires, they touch off the next runner, and the relay continues.

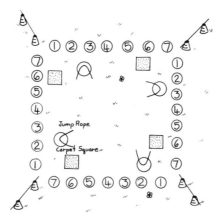

In *progression 2,* follow the same procedure except that on the signal "Go!" the runners will do 20 speed jumps with the rope, circle the formation, do 10 sit-ups, then circle the formation, and tag off the next runner.

Progression 3 is a tough one! Follow the same procedure except that on the signal "Go!" the runners will circle the formation, do 20 speed jumps with the rope, circle the formation, do 10 sit-ups, then circle the formation, and tag off the next runner. This is a very demanding routine, so make sure the class is in good physical shape before trying it.

Circle Relay

Here are two variations of the circle formation.

The Circle No. 1. You need 28 bicycle tires and 4 paper batons. The task involved is running. This simple relay from the circle can be either a modified or a true relay. Arrange your teams in the quarter sections as shown in the illustration. If this is to be a modified relay, no batons are needed. If it is a true relay, each 1 should have a homemade paper baton. In both the modified and true relays, *the runners all run around the circle in the same direction.* Make this absolutely clear! This relay is usually run clockwise. Explain and demonstrate before the students run. If you are running a modified relay, the first runner back inside his or her tire wins a point for the team. If it is a true relay, the baton is passed to the next runner when the present runner steps into his or her tire. The first team back into its tires wins.

The Circle No. 2. You need 28 bicycle tires, 8 cones or milk jugs, 4 bamboo reeds, 8 hula hoops or bicycle tires, 4 jump ropes, and 4 8½" playground balls. The tasks involved are hurdling, rope jumping, bouncing balls, and running. Lead the class into this one gradually. It is a good fitness relay, and you can make this one almost as physically demanding as the class can handle safely. Keep in mind that the more tasks you give the runners, the longer the rest of the children have to stand and wait even though they are usually jumping up and down and calling encouragement to their teammates.

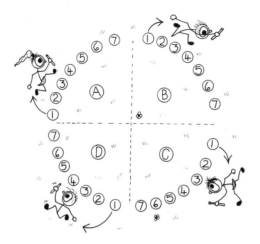

Progression 1 is a true relay. On the signal "Go!" the 1's run into their own section where they each pick up the ball and bounce it 10 times with each hand inside the tire. Then they go directly to the jump ropes and speed jump 20 times. *They must place the ropes back into the tires.* As soon as they have done this, they will run out through their own tire and run completely around the circle, leaping each hurdle (four of them) before entering their own tire and tagging off runner 2. Notice that they are not using a baton because they have to use their hands to perform the tasks. The first team to complete this routine wins.

In *progression 2* on the signal "Go!" the first runners will run around the circle, leap four hurdles, enter through their own tires, complete both tasks, run out through their own tires again, and run around the circle and back to their own tires where they tag off 2. The relay continues in the same manner.

Make sure students are physically ready for *progression 3* before starting. On the signal "Go!" all 1's run around the circle, leaping the four hurdles. Each runner runs into her section through her own tire and bounces the ball inside the tire 10 times with each hand. Then she goes out through her own tire, runs around the circle, enters through her tire, and does 20 speed jumps. She runs around the circle again and touches off the next runner. Continue until every team member has completed this routine.

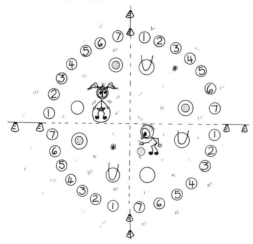

Shuttle Relay

You need 4 paper batons. In the shuttle relay, each team is divided into two sections. As shown in the illustration, team A is divided into A-1 and A-2, and they face each other as shown. The same is true for teams B, C, and D. On the signal "Go!" the first runners (1's), who have the batons, run to the other half of their teams, circle around behind their teams, and pass the batons to 2's. The first runners immediately go to the end of their teams and sit. The 2's follow the same procedure. Continue this routine until everyone has run and there is a complete change of positions at the end. The first team to do this wins. When the children learn this relay, you might include basic locomotors and hurdles for variety.

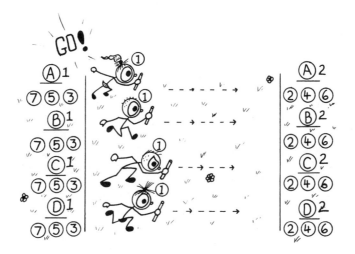

Spoke Relay

The spoke relay gets its name from the shape of the formation. There are many exciting possibilities from this formation. Explained here are three examples for grades K–3.

Spoke No. 1. You need 28 bicycle tires, 1 truck tire (optional), and 4 paper batons. The task involved is running. This relay can be either a modified or a true relay. It is an easy introduction to the spoke so that the children can get used to running in this new formation.

A simple modified relay is the same from the spoke as it is in the lane method except for the routes. There is no turning point. The runners run around each squad, including the end of their own squad. Then they go on in and get into their tire. The first runner in his or her tire wins a point for the team. Continue this same routine until all children have had a chance to run. The team with the most points wins.

When used as a true relay, follow the same directions for the other true relays except for the routes again. On the signal "Go!" all 1's pull out to their right, circle the spoke and hand off the baton to 2's. The 2's must wait in their tire until they are given the baton. Continue this routine until all seven runners on each team have run. The first team to get all seven runners back in place wins.

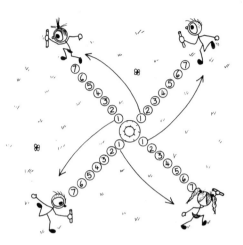

Spoke No. 2. This can be either a modified or a true relay. Follow the same routines as in spoke no. 1 except that there are four hurdles each runner must negotiate. If a runner knocks down a hurdle, she must stop and set it up again before she can resume her run. In the meantime, the other runners can run to the outside of the hurdle when someone is setting a hurdle back up. (The other runners do not have to step the hurdle that is being set up.) Remember, the runner always returns to the tire on the same side he or she came out. In other words, the runner must have stepped *four* hurdles before returning to his or her tire.

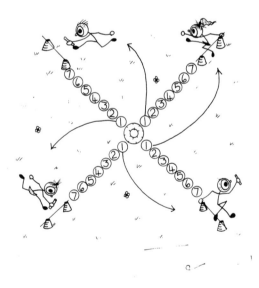

Spoke No. 3. You need 28 bicycle tires, 1 large tire (optional), 8 cones or milk jugs, 4 bamboo reeds, 2 jump ropes, 2 8½″ playground balls, 2 chairs, and 2 carpets. The tasks involved are hurdling, bouncing balls, rope jumping, sit-ups, and step-ups. This can be either a modified or a true relay. The routine is the same as in spoke no. 2 except that each runner must perform a task before stepping each hurdle.

For example, let's follow Sally (see the illustration) through this routine. On the signal "Go!" Sally comes out of her tire to her right, picks up a jump rope, and speed jumps 20 times. She puts the jump rope back into the bicycle tire, leaps the first hurdle to the next station, and does 10 sit-ups the best she can. Then she leaps the second hurdle to the next station where she does 20 step-ups correctly in the chair. (To be done correctly, the child steps up with one foot, brings the other foot up, then steps down with one foot then follows down with the other foot. As soon as she gets both feet back down she counts *one,* the same routine for *two,* etc.) After completing the 20 step-ups, Sally leaps the third hurdle to the next station where she bounces the ball inside the bicycle tire 10 times with each hand. Then she leaps the fourth hurdle and returns quickly to her tire. If this is a modified relay and Sally is the first to get back in her tire, she wins a point for her team. If it is a true relay, she tags the next person off and this child will follow the same routine.

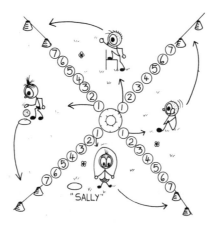

If you think your class is in good shape physically, you can make this relay more challenging by having the runner take a full lap around the formation before each new task. For instance, on the signal "Go!" all 1's do the task that is in their area; then they run all the way around the formation. After leaping the fifth hurdle, they are in the next station where they complete the next task. Continue this routine. After finishing the last task, they leap the hurdle and go directly to their tire where they tag off the next runner. These runners have taken three laps around the formation and have performed four tasks. This is a good fitness workout!

Hexagon Relay

Here are two variations of the hexation formation.

Hexagon No. 1. This can be a modified or a true relay. You need 24 bicycle tires, 8 cones or milk jugs, 6 no. 10 tin cans, 6 8½″ playground balls, and 4 bamboo reeds. The tasks involved are running and hurdling. The hexagon formation has an advantage and a disadvantage. The advantage is that there are 6 children activated at one time instead of 4. The disadvantage is that it is set up for only 24 children rather than the average 28. But on a simple relay like this one, you could have four teams with 5 runners and two teams with 4 runners if you have two outstanding youngsters who would like to run first and last for the two short teams.

This relay is simple to introduce the children to the hexagon formation. It is very similar to some of the others we have already done. The illustration shows that the 1's, on the signal "Go!" have run into the center of the formation and have picked the playground balls off the no. 10 tin cans located in front of their teams. From here they have run out through their tires and run around the hexagon (four hurdles) and back through their tires to the center of the formation where they placed the balls on their tin cans, quickly returning to their tires and tagged off the 2's. The first team to get all four runners back into position wins.

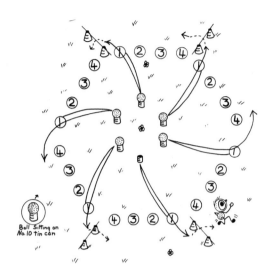

Hexagon No. 2. You need 30 bicycle tires, 6 jump ropes, 8 cones or milk jugs, 6 carpets, and 4 bamboo reeds. The tasks involved are running, hurdling, sit ups, and rope jumping. This time everyone will be doing something at the same time. There is a lot of action and thinking going on during this short but very active relay. Most third-graders can handle it with a little practice if they have worked on the progressions. There may be a few second-grade classes that can do it, so don't count them out. Grades 4–6 should have no problem.

On the signal "Go!" the 1's jump rope 20 times while the 2's pull out and run around the formation (four hurdles). When each 2 returns through his tire, he jumps rope while 1 runs through her tire and runs around the formation. At the same time on "Go!" the 4's pull out and run around the formation (four hurdles) while the 3's do 10 sit-ups. As each 3 finishes his sit-ups, he runs out of his tire and circles the formation while the 4's do their 10 sit-ups. When all have finished, the same routine is repeated except that 1 and 2 will run and do sit-ups, while 3 and 4 will run and jump rope. The first foursome to complete all the tasks and be back in their tires wins.

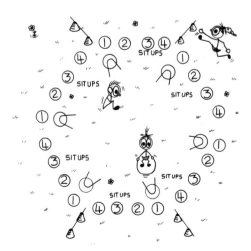

Octagon Relay

Here are two variations of the octagon formation.

Octagon No. 1. This can be a modified or a true relay. You need 24 bicycle tires, 8 no. 10 tin cans, and 8 8½″ playground balls. The tasks involved are running and hurdling. The octagon is very similar to the hexagon except you will have eight people running at one time instead of six. Hurdles are optional.

On the signal "Go!" all 1's run into the formation and pick up their playground balls that are located in front of their teams. They will then run out through their tires and circle the formation. As soon as they get back to their teams, they run back into the center of the formation—through their tires—and put the balls back on top of the tin cans. Next, they get back into their tires and touch off the 2's who follow the same routine. Continue until everyone is back into their tire. The first team to do so wins.

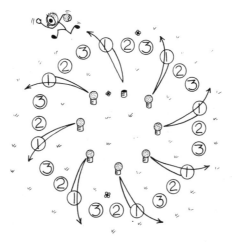

Octagon No. 2. You need 32 bicycle tires or 24 bicycle tires and 8 hula hoops, 8 carpets, and 8 jump ropes. The tasks involved are running, rope jumping, and sit-ups. If your class can handle hexagon no. 2, they can probably handle this one, too. Again, this relay involves a lot of action and a lot of thinking going on at one time.

The following directions are for runners 1, 2, and 3. *All stations will be active at the same time.* On the signal "Go!" follow along with the illustration.

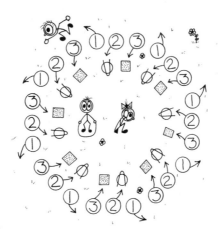

♦ The 1's will pull out and circle the formation. Entering through tire 3, they will do 10 sit-ups on the small carpets. Next, they move over to the jump ropes, where they will do 20 speed jumps. Then they will quickly move back to tire 1.

♦ The 2's will move up to the jump ropes, where they will do 20 speed jumps. Next, they will exit through tire 2 and circle the formation. Then they will enter through tire 3 and do 10 sit-ups on the small carpets. They will then quickly move back to tire 2.

♦ The 3's will move to the small carpets and do 10 sit-ups. Next, they will move over to the jump ropes and do 20 speed jumps. Then they will exit through tire 1, circle the formation, and quickly return to tire 3.

The first team to get everyone back into position wins.

Circuits————————————————16

Circuits can be one of the best teaching tools that a physical educator has if they are done properly. This activity gives the children a variety of challenging tasks on small pieces of movable equipment.

There are many types of circuits. An example of a primary circuit is shown here.

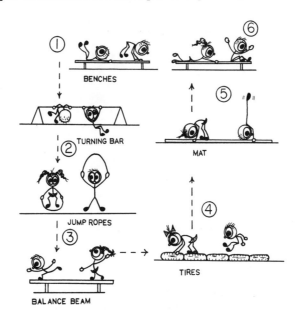

In this particular circuit, there are six stations with a different task at each station. A squad of about four children each (depending on class size) is selected and assigned to each station. Before the circuit can be used, the children should be familiar with the tasks involved and the safety precautions to be observed at each station. Walk the class around the circuit in the direction you want them to rotate when changing stations. Explain and, using one of the children, demonstrate each task and its safety factors thoroughly. Explain to the children that they will be at each station for only a few minutes. Then they will be asked to "Stop" and "Rotate" to the next station as a squad. In the primary circuits, the children are usually asked to walk to their next station for safety reasons. They will continue this routine until each squad has worked on each task at the six stations.

For an added plus, which involves a little more work on your part, the squads can be given the responsibility of setting up the equipment at their assigned stations. This also involves putting it away themselves when the session is over. This responsibility can be a valuable experience for the children along with the benefits derived from the activities involved. The "setting up, participation, and putting away" are always done under your direction and supervision.

The following pages will suggest some ideas for safely setting up different pieces of equipment for use in primary circuits. On some of the suggested items, you will be referred to the chapter in this book on that particular subject.

LIFTING

This is an excellent opportunity to teach the children the proper way to lift heavy objects. This should become a lifetime habit, so take the time to explain and demonstrate the proper way to pick up heavy objects.

BENCHES

See the "How to Make" section for directions on construction. Two benches will be needed for circuit activities, so that the children will not have to wait in line to perform. These benches are heavy and cumbersome, so it is suggested that you select some of the larger and stronger members of the class to lift and move these items. When moving the benches, have a child on each end and one on either side as shown. Everyone must lift at the same time and lower at the same time.

The following routines help the children get started on different ways of traveling down the bench. Later, encourage them to think of different ways of traveling down the bench that have not yet been used. Be sure to *stress safety!*

♦ Begin with both hands on the bench and both feet together and on the floor on one side of the bench. Slide hands forward and bring both feet on top of the bench. Slide hands forward and jump both feet to the floor on the other side of the bench. Continue this same routine by moving the hands and jumping on the bench and jumping down to the other side again. Do this routine all the way to the end of the bench.

♦ Move by going up-straddle-up-straddle-up-straddle all the way down the bench.

♦ Move by going up and all the way over—up and all the way over to the other side. Continue alternating the jump all the way down. Keep the feet together if possible.

♦ Lie on your stomach and pull all the way down.
♦ Lie on your back with the knees and feet up. Push all the way down.

♦ Put both knees on the bench with the hands forward. Pull both knees to hands, reach forward, and do the same thing again. Repeat all the way down.

♦ Sit on the bench with hands in the air, knees bent, and heels touching the bench. Reach out and pull with one heel and rotate the hip forward on the same side. Then do the same thing with the other side. Repeat this procedure all the way down.

♦ This backward roll is an advanced move. *Do not attempt this until the backward roll has been mastered on the mat.* Carefully spot the child in the beginning.

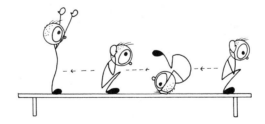

♦ This forward roll is also an advanced move. Again, *do not attempt this until the forward roll has been mastered on the mat.* Be sure to spot the child.

♦ Do not put hands on the bench; this is all leg work. Jump up onto the bench and jump down on the other side; then repeat to the other side. Continue all the way down.

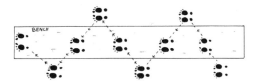

♦ Straddle the bench and then jump up. Straddle up and straddle down all the way along the bench.

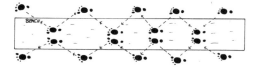

♦ Be careful—this one takes good leg strength. *Keeping feet together,* jump over to the other side, then jump back again. Move forward as you do these jumps.

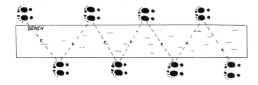

Placement of Benches

There are four different ways to set up and use the benches:

♦ Side by side, at least 3' to 4' apart

♦ Side by side with mats for jumping and rolling; *no diving*

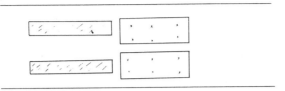

♦ End to end to make a long bench

♦ Side by side with mats; this time put a stretch rope in front of each mat for the children to jump (*not dive*) over

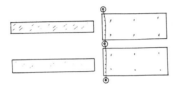

TURNING BAR

See the "How to Make" section for directions on construction. This piece of equipment comes in three sections: two "A" frames and one section of pipe (which includes two bolts, one for each end). Assign one person to each of the "A" frames. These can be easily moved by dragging. Have two children carry the pipe, with one child on each end so that no one will be poked by the ends of the pipe.

Set up the turning bar by placing the pipe on the two "A" frames and then putting the two bolts through the pipe where the holes have been drilled. This will keep the pipe from turning.

When moving the mat to place under the turning bar, use four children as shown. You may have to give this group a little help.

To keep the turning bar from tipping over, there must be two children "riding horse" on each end of the bar when the bar is in use. Be sure that this group takes turns at "*riding horse*" and performing.

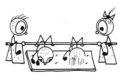

♦ **Front Hip Circle:** This is the easy one. Have the child lean over and place his stomach on the bar. While holding on with both hands, have him duck his head under the bar and bring his hips and legs on over after him. Keeping his hands on the bar at all times, he comes back to his feet and repeats the same procedure.

♦ **Back Hip Circle:** This move is definitely more challenging, involving much more arm flexor and abdominal strength. While the child holds on to the bar with both hands, have him scoot both feet under the bar as shown. He should keep one foot on the mat and the other in a raised position. Teach him to scissor the raised leg and vigorously push off with the foot on the mat at the same time so that the feet will go up, back and over the bar. At the same time, he must pull hard with the arms so that the body will follow the legs and the hips over the bar. With his hands still on the bar, he should land on his feet, then scoot the feet under the bar again, and repeat. (This move will take a lot of practice for most children.)

ROPE JUMPING

This squad has an easy job, so you may want to put your smallest children in this group. Their job will be to put out four short jump ropes.

The object at this station is to see how many times each child can jump his or her rope in the allotted time. If they miss, have them begin again immediately and keep the same count.

BALANCE BEAMS

See the "How to Make" section for directions on construction. These items are not heavy, but they are awkward to handle. The job for this squad is to set up three balance beams in any shape you direct. Shown here is the "U" shape.

Have the children carry the beams at the ends so that no one will be poked.

The object is to see how many times the child can walk on the beams in the allotted time without falling off. If they do fall off, have them get back on immediately and try again. If they are successful at walking *forward*, have them try walking the beam *sideways* or *backward*.

TIRES

(See Chapter 9 for routines.) Tires are heavy and awkward so put some of your larger children in this squad. The indoor tires should be stacked four high—no more. Always use two children to *slide*, not lift, the tires off the stack when setting up the circuit.

To stack the tires safely after use (two children again), always lean the upper tire on the lower tires and pull the tire on top of the others. *Never try to lift them.*

Information and directions on different ways to travel along the tires can be found in Chapter 9.

TUMBLING

If you have a 5′ × 10′ or 6′ × 12′ folding tumbling mat, you will need four children to carry it safely. First, teach them how to fold it correctly; then put one child on each corner as shown.

The object of this station is to let the children practice the rolls they have learned to date or to experiment and see how many different ways they can safely cross the mat. Have the children cross the *width* of the mat, not the *length*. This gives plenty of space for each child to move back and forth without bumping into anyone else.

BOUNDING BOARDS

See the "How to Make" section for directions on construction. Bounding boards are often called the "poor man's trampoline." They are inexpensive to make and add a variety of exciting activities to the circuit.

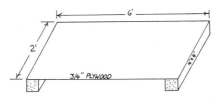

IMPORTANT: Bounding boards will break if not taken care of. It is strongly recommended that this equipment be used only with primary-age children. The equipment just can't take the weight of the larger children.

- ◆ Jump for height. Reach up with those arms.
- ◆ Jump two times, then pull your knees up as high as you can. Repeat.
- ◆ *Scissors:* As you go up, spread your front leg forward and the rear leg backward. Then quickly bring them back together again before you land. On the next bounce, do the same thing with the opposite legs. Continue.
- ◆ *Tuck:* As you go up, hug your knees close into your body. Quickly let go and bounce into the same position. Continue.
- ◆ Jump two times, then "spread eagle." Can you touch your toes when you do this?

- ◆ Jump two times and turn halfway around. Can you turn all the way around?

♦ Place several bounding boards in a row. Can you jump from one bounding board to another and land on the mat feet first, then do a roll?

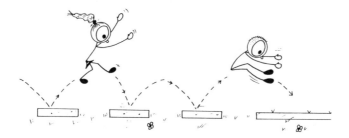

♦ There are many more activities that can be done on bounding boards, such as jumping up and clicking heels, slapping both heels, bicycling legs as you go up. Rope jumping is also great fun on bounding boards. Always encourage the children to think up new activities on this equipment.

INNER TUBES

It used to be easy to find old, used but repairable, truck inner tubes from either your local school bus garage or at most local trucking lines in your area. Most of these outfits now use tubeless tires, so if you are interested, you may have to buy new tubes. (Make sure you buy the large truck inner tubes.) This is still a very cheap price for a piece of equipment that has many uses in physical education. However, like any rebounding equipment, it is fun to use but can be very dangerous if not used correctly. The children should not use this equipment unless they have had thorough instruction in the activities involved and the safety procedures that go along with the activity.

The following illustration shows how to set up an inner tube rebound station. All you need for a rebound station in a circuit is one large inner tube, a mat, and three or four children. To keep the tube stable, two children take turns sitting on the outside edges as shown. The rebounder begins by stepping up on the back section of the tube. From here, he jumps to the front section of the tube and rebounds by letting the tube bounce him up. *Go for height, not distance.* If children go for distance, there is a chance of hyperextending the back when landing.

Once they have practiced enough to have developed control and get good height, they are ready to try a few of the more challenging moves listed next.

- ◆ *Tuck:* Go for height. Quickly bring the knees up and squeeze the legs into the body with the arms. Let go and land on the feet.
- ◆ *Spread Eagle:* Go for height. Spread the legs and try to touch the toes if possible. Bring the feet back together quickly and land.
- ◆ Go for height. Make a half turn before landing. Later, if you have mastered the half turn, carefully go for a full turn, a little bit at a time.
- ◆ Bounce and go! This is a vigorous activity and fun for the lower grades. For this activity, it is best to have two children on a tube at one time, or three very small children. The action is bouncing and moving forward. Try to catch the person in front.

CIRCUIT PROGRESSIONS

The following three circuit progressions go from very simple to more interesting and challenging each time. Except for adding inner tubes and bounding boards, most of the same equipment is used in each circuit.

The following three illustrations (see circuits 1, 2, and 3) show good basic circuit layouts with which to begin.

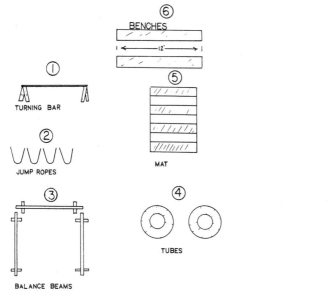

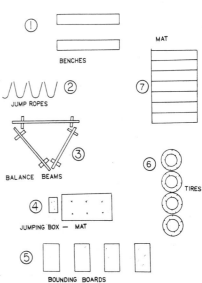

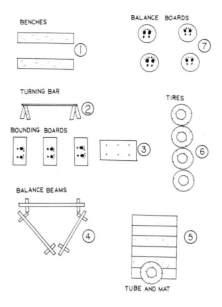

In the next illustration (see circuit 4), bounding boards have been added along with the jump ropes at station 3. The children love to jump rope on the bounding boards. The other new addition are the inner tubes—two children to a tube and the action is bounce and go. Stations 1 and 4 have no new equipment, just a mixture of the original pieces. At station 1, the task is to travel in a square pattern alternating on a bench and balance beam. Station 6 also has a mixture of the original equipment. Here, students travel down the tires and up the balance beam.

In the next illustration (see circuit 5), the benches at station 1 have been put end to end for a longer challenge. Station 2 is set up for inner tube rebounding. Station 3 is the same. Station 4 is set up for jumping from one bounding board to another down to the mat where they will land on their feet and roll. Station 5 is set up for bounce and go. Station 6 is set up for jumping rope on the tires.

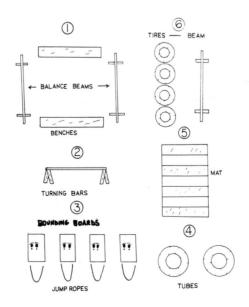

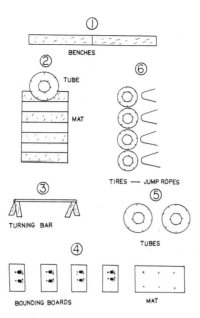

There are many different variations you can make in your circuits to keep them challenging and fun. Again, encourage, the children to come up with ideas of their own for new combinations.

The next circuit is called a "fitness circuit" (see circuit 6) and is usually used by the upper primary grades. We have found that a good motivating device for performance is to have the class divided into pairs. One partner will be a *counter* while the other partner is the *performer*. At the end of the allotted time, they reverse rolls, and the counter becomes the performer and the performer becomes the counter. There are four stations with 3 couples at each station. This is set up for a class of 24 children.

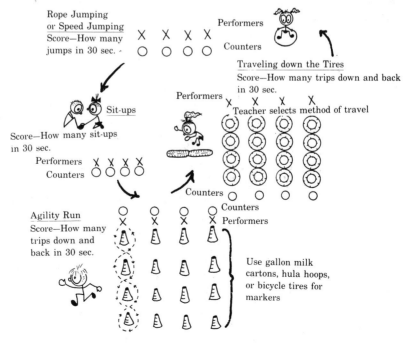

After going over each station carefully, divide the class into four squads of six members. There will be three couples at each station. One partner will be the performer and the other partner will be the counter. On the signal "Go," the performer performs for 30 seconds (or whatever time limit you want) when "Stop" is called. The couples switch rolls for the next 30 seconds and then rotate. To keep the enthusiasm high, have the class run all the way around the formation before going to their next station. Continue this routine until everyone has performed at each station. Change the tasks at each station frequently to keep this circuit from becoming boring.

The next circuit (see circuit 7) is called a "sports circuit" because of the different sports skills that are involved. The routine with the performers and counters are the same as explained in the fitness circuit. Also, change the skills at the four stations frequently so that this circuit will always be fun and challenging.

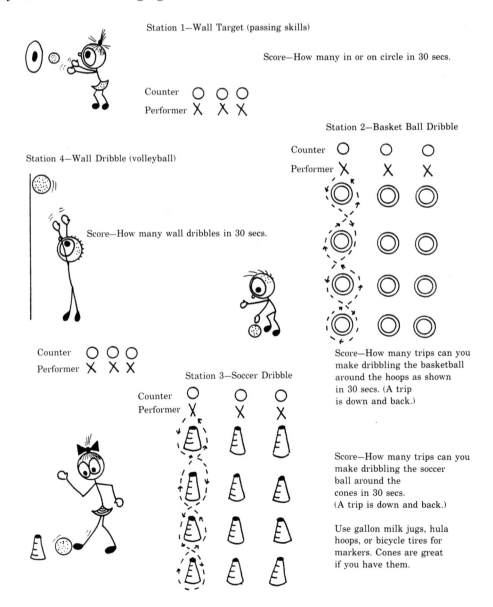

Station 1—Wall Target (passing skills)

Score—How many in or on circle in 30 secs.

Counter

Performer

Station 4—Wall Dribble (volleyball)

Score—How many wall dribbles in 30 secs.

Counter

Performer

Station 2—Basket Ball Dribble

Counter

Performer

Score—How many trips can you make dribbling the basketball around the hoops as shown in 30 secs. (A trip is down and back.)

Station 3—Soccer Dribble

Counter

Performer

Score—How many trips can you make dribbling the soccer ball around the cones in 30 secs. (A trip is down and back.)

Use gallon milk jugs, hula hoops, or bicycle tires for markers. Cones are great if you have them.

FOUR-ITEM CLASSROOM FITNESS CIRCUIT

Circuit 8 can also be done in the multipurpose room, the gym, or outside. When done in a classroom, space is always a problem. Let's be realistic, some classrooms may be too small to accommodate this activity, but the majority of the classrooms can handle this one if the desks are pushed into the positions as shown in the illustration. Make sure that all pencils, books, and so on, are picked up off the floor before you begin the circuit.

Even though most of your students already know how to perform these four items, have some of your top children demonstrate each activity in the areas designated for them before you begin.

Divide the classroom into four areas and place three or more couples in each area. One of each of the couples will be the counter and the other partner will be the performer. The events will be timed for 30 seconds. At the beginning of each time period, the couples swap jobs—the performer becomes the counter and the counter becomes the performer. When both couples have performed in their area, there will be a rotation. The 1 group will go to 2, 2 to 3, 3 to 4, and 4 to 1. This procedure is followed until everyone has been a counter and a performer in each of the four areas.

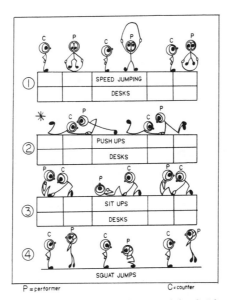

*The performer must touch the counter's hand with his chest for it to count. How many can you do in 30 seconds? (There will be three partners doing push-ups in this area.)

- ♦ *Station 1—Speed Jumping:* How many times can you jump in 30 seconds?
- ♦ *Station 2—Push-ups:* Encourage doing regular push-ups if possible. If students cannot do a regular push-up correctly, have them do modified push-ups (on their knees, keeping backs straight). Notice the counter is on his stomach with his hand under the performer's chest.
- ♦ *Station 3—Sit-ups:* Cross the arms across the chest, and curl up so that the elbows touch the legs. Do not reach out with the elbows. How many can you do in 30 seconds?
- ♦ *Station 4—Squat Jump:* Put hands on head, fingers locked. Drop to ¾ squat (*not a full squat,*) spring up and back down to a ¾ squat. Continue. How many can you do in 30 seconds? Do not go down to full squats as this could possibly harm the knees.

FITNESS CIRCUIT FOR A LARGE CLASSROOM

Circuit 9 obviously requires a large classroom to be successful. If you do not have a large classroom, use a multipurpose room or gym, or go outdoors.

This circuit is drawn up for 28 children, although it can easily handle fewer. Seven stations are shown. Each person has a partner, and each takes turns being the performer and the counter. All events go on at the same time for 30 seconds. Then the performer becomes the counter and the counter becomes the performer. After both partners have performed at their station, they rotate to the next station (1 to 2, 2 to 3, 3 to 4, etc.). This same procedure continues until each person has done all seven of the activities. Make certain all pencils, books, and so on are off the floor before you begin.

For circuit 9, you need 8 hula hoops (4 for shuttle run, 4 for bean bag toss), 6 bean bags (4 for shuttle run, 2 for bean bag toss), 6 short jump ropes (2 for speed jumping, 4 for bean bag toss), 6 chairs (4 for over and under, 2 for step-ups), and 2 reeds or broom handles (for over and under).

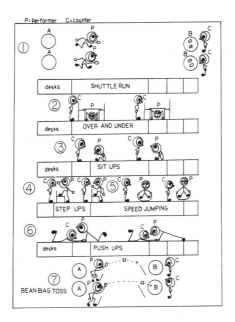

- ♦ *Station 1—Shuttle Run:* On the signal "Go," the performers start from hoop A, run to hoop B to pick up one bean bag, and run back and place it in hoop A. Then they return to hoop B, pick up the other bean bag, and also place (don't throw) it in hoop A. Then they run down and circle around hoop B and return to hoop A, pick up one bean bag and return it to B, then return to A, pick up the other bean bag, and return it to B. Then they circle A as they did B and continue. How many times did you move these bean bags in 30 seconds?
- ♦ *Station 2—Over and Under:* Two chairs face each other with a reed going from one to the other as shown. On the signal "Go," see how many times you can step over and then crawl under the reed in 30 seconds.
- ♦ *Station 3—Sit-ups:* With arms crossed on the chest and knees up as shown, how many sit-ups can you do correctly in 30 seconds?
- ♦ *Station 4—Step-ups:* The performer stands in front of his chair as shown. To do one step-up, the performer steps on the chair with one foot, brings the other foot up beside

it, and then steps down with the original foot followed by the other one. That is a complete step-up. How many complete step-ups can you do in 30 seconds?

♦ ***Station 5—Speed Rope Jumping:*** How many times can you jump the short rope in 30 seconds?

♦ ***Station 6—Push-ups:*** Encourage doing regular push-ups if possible. If students cannot do a regular push-up correctly, have them do modified push-ups (on their knees, with backs straight). Notice the counter is on his stomach with his hand under the performer's chest. The performer must touch the counter's hand with his chest for it to count. How many times can you do this in 30 seconds? (There will be two partners doing push-ups in this area.)

♦ ***Station 7—Bean Bag Toss:*** The two performers have one bean bag in their hands and are standing behind a short jump rope located in front of their hoops. On the signal "Go," the performers toss their bean bags at hoops B. If the bean bag lands in the hoop or on it, it counts one point. If the bean bag slides in and touches the hoop, it counts nothing. Immediately after tossing the bean bag, the performer runs to hoop B, picks up his bean bag, turns, and, from behind the jump rope, tosses the bean bag to hoop A. The performer continues this same routine for 30 seconds. How many points can you get in 30 seconds?

Soccer ══════════════════════════════ 17

Driving past schools and recreation areas in the fall, you see fields full of children playing soccer. Some of the youngsters are wearing blue jeans; other groups might be dressed in colorful uniforms complete with soccer shoes. Regardless of how the children are dressed, they all have the same enthusiastic joy of participation.

Many of these children got their start in soccer from their area recreation organization, the YMCA/YWCA, or school physical education programs. They enjoy not only the fitness benefits derived from this physically demanding activity, but they are also challenged by the strategy involved in good team play. In some parts of the country, children can continue to play soccer as one of their lifetime sports.

Some teachers may be reluctant to teach soccer because they have never played this activity and were probably not very active in sports activities when growing up. Fortunately, *enthusiasm* and a *sincere concern* for students are the main requirements for a teacher who is interested in getting children actively involved in soccer.

Without getting too technical or analytical, teachers can expose even the youngest children to the basic skills of soccer and then put them through a planned progression of simple activities that involve the skills they have covered. In this way, teachers will be excited at the enthusiasm and the natural progress that takes place in these children while participating in this exciting and challenging activity.

BASIC SOCCER SKILLS

In most games, the hands are used to move a ball, so even at this young age, children are going to be challenged to use only their feet while learning to play soccer. Children in the early elementary grades can tolerate very little formal drill or practice on skills; they want to jump right in and begin playing the game. Therefore, the skills involved should be introduced and demonstrated thoroughly but as briefly as possible. Then give the children the opportunity to put these new skills to work in organized drills and games that are fun to do and easy to control.

Dribbling

To move the ball and keep it under control while running requires moving the ball with a series of taps and pushes with the inside of one foot (not the toe) and then the other foot. The ball should not be advanced more than a yard or so with each tap. Don't let the ball get too far away from the body; if this happens, the dribbler has lost control of the ball and will soon lose it. A smooth and controlled run can be maintained by kicking the ball after every third step.

Instep Kick

A lot of power can be generated with this kick if it is done correctly. When approaching the ball, the weight-bearing foot is pointed straight ahead and is placed on the ground beside the ball as the kicking leg swings back. It is important that the knee and ankle of the kicking leg are flexed and remain in this position on the forward swing until the *knee is over the ball.* At this point, the knee and ankle are straightened; the toe is pointed toward the ground so that the ball will be contacted on the instep of the foot. Follow through with a shift of weight to the nonkicking foot. Watch out for the toes hitting the ground.

Passing—Inside Foot

When passing the ball diagonally or laterally ahead, swing the leg from the hip across the body. The ball is struck with the inside of the foot swinging in the direction the ball is intended to go.

Passing—Outside Foot

Because of the mechanics of this kick, it is used for short distances, for short passes to the outside, or for maneuvering the ball. The leg, with the knee bent, swings across the front of the body, then out to the side—striking the ball with the outside of the foot. Swing the leg from the hip.

Heading the Ball

This is for using the head to volley a ball that is coming in high. Keep your eyes on the ball until the moment of impact. Stiffen the neck, keep the tongue in the mouth with the mouth closed, and meet the ball at the hairline of the forehead with an upward and forward motion. The direction of the rebound may be controlled by the angle of the jump and head position. Practice with a playground ball first, as it may be a bit softer.

Trapping—Sole of the Foot

A slow rolling ball is trapped by reaching forward with one foot to meet the oncoming ball. The heel should be about 5″ off the ground, and the toe should be pointed up at a diagonal. As the ball rolls to the foot, it is stopped between the sole of the foot and the ground. Never step and put your weight on a ball.

Body Trapping

It is difficult to bring a traveling bouncing ball to a dead stop with immediate control as with the foot trap. In this situation, a blocking technique by the body can be used to stop or slow the progress of the ball. If the ball is bouncing chest or belt high, the rebound can be checked by taking the ball's progress on the stomach or chest while at the same time "giving" with the ball (as in catching a ball) so that the ball will drop at the feet where it can quickly be brought under control with a foot trap.

Attacking the Ball

This move involves a player who, from the side and *without touching the other player,* is reaching in with one foot to take over the possession of the ball. If successful, he will protect the ball by quickly turning his back to his opponent so that he is in position to dribble or pass.

To attack the ball from the front, the steal is made by placing a foot on top of the ball to stop it (do not stand on it) and quickly pulling it away from the dribbler. Remember, when attacking the ball, you cannot touch the dribbler.

SOCCER DRILLS GAMES

Dribbling

Equipment: To get as many children as possible active, you will need 24 markers. A mixture of items, such as cones, bean bags, milk jugs, hula hoops, bicycle tires, and so on, are fine—anything students can dribble around.

Formation: Divide the class into four squads. Then divide each squad into two sections (A and B) as shown in the illustration. Put the four squads into a box formation so that you can stand in the middle of the action and be available wherever needed.

This is a very simple dribbling drill. As shown in the illustration, the first person in line dribbles the ball around the markers as shown. When he returns to his group, he passes the ball to the next person who traps the ball and continues the drill. The dribblers now go to the end of their own line.

Explain carefully to your students that this is a drill and not a relay; they need to take their time and concentrate on learning how to do this skill correctly.

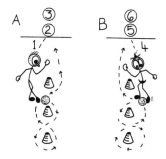

Triangles

Equipment: You need 8 playground balls and 24 bean bags or hula hoops or bicycle tires.

Formation: Again, so that more children can be more active, divide your class into four squads, then divide each squad into two groups (A and B) as shown. Again, put the squads into a box formation so that you can be in the center of the activity.

Remember, you are going to have real problems keeping the children in their triangles unless you have some sort of markers. If this drill is done on a black top, it will be a simple matter of marking the stations in chalk. If it is done in the grass, you will need hula hoops, bicycle tires, or bean bags to mark the stations.

From these triangles, the children can practice the four skills shown. For equal participation and control, let's follow group A as an example. Player 1 kicks the ball to 2 who traps the ball and kicks it back to 1. Player 1 traps the ball and then kicks the ball to 3 who traps the ball and kicks it back to 1. Then you have a simple rotation: 1 goes to 3, 3 goes to 2, and 2 goes to 1. This same rotation can be used with the other skills. The distance between the children in the triangles can be set according to the ability of the group.

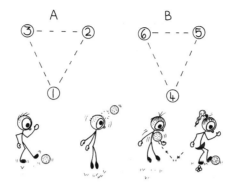

IMPORTANT: If the younger children have a problem with the rotation, simply instruct them to let (using A as an example again) 1 kick to 2 who will trap the ball and kick it to 3 who will trap the ball and kick it to 1. This can continue around the triangle as long as needed.

Dribble-Kick

Equipment: You need 20 markers, so use cones, hula hoops, bicycle tires, or milk jugs—anything to dribble around and to use for goal markers.

Formation: The distance from the end line to the goal line markers is flexible; make it whatever distance suits your class.

Divide the class into four squads and set up each one as shown in the illustration. Player 1 dribbles around the markers and beyond the end line where he tries to kick the ball by the goalie (5). Player 6's job is only to chase the kicked ball and to dribble it back to 2 who is next in line. After 1 has had his turn, he becomes the new goalie and 5 becomes the new chaser. Player 6 goes to the back of the line after dribbling the ball to 2, who has moved up one spot to the head of the line.

After the class has developed some skill, this drill can be used as a game by keeping individual scores.

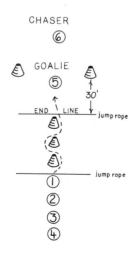

Circle-Pass-Trap

Equipment: You need 4 playground balls.

Formation: Divide the class into four squads. Give a ball to each squad and have them hold hands. (Some of the children may fuss about this!) As they hold hands, have them practice kicking the ball and trapping it. They can kick randomly to different people in the squad or they can pass the ball around the circle to the right or left.

Squad Drill

Equipment: You need 4 playground balls.

Formation: This is another formation for squad soccer drills.This one does not require markers. The only problem with this formation is that the children do not get as much participation and practice as in "Triangles."

Divide the class into four squads and set them up as shown in the illustration. Player 1 lofts a header to 2 who tries to head it back to 1. Then he lofts a header to 3 who does the same thing. Continue the same routine down the line. When 6 heads the ball back to 1, he follows the ball into 1's place and becomes the new leader. The rest of the squad moves down one place and 1 moves into 2's old place.

As you can see, this formation can be used to work on the other soccer skills, too.

Dribble-Pass-Shoot

Equipment: You need 4 playground balls, 8 cones or milk jugs (goal line markers), and 4 jump ropes (end lines).

Formation: Divide the class into four squads of partners and set up as shown in the illustration. Players 1 and 2 lead off.They must pass at least two times before they try to kick a goal.The goalie (5) does not attack the ball in this drill; he only tries to block the kick. The chaser (6) dribbles the ball back to 3 and 4, who will be the next to go, and 5 and 6 line up behind them. Players 1 and 2 are now the new goalie and chaser (who must take turns on these two jobs). Continue following this routine.

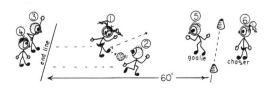

This drill can be easily turned into a game—after the students have developed their skills—by scoring the goals made by the partners.

Throw in-Trap-Dribble-Attack

Equipment: You need 4 playground balls and 8 jump ropes (end lines).

Formation: Adjust the distance between the two boundary lines (jump ropes) to suit your class. Divide the class into four squads and set up as shown in the illustration. This is a one-on-one shuttle-type activity involving throwing in, trapping, dribbling, and attacking the ball. Player 1 throws the ball in to 4, who traps it and attempts to dribble and kick the ball over A's end line. Player 1, meantime, is trying to attack the ball. If 1 can steal the ball, he tries to score over B's line. (You may want to set a time limit.) After a goal, 1 goes to the B side and stands behind 6, and 4 goes to the A side and stands behind 3. Continue this routine. To score, the ball must go over the short jump rope (end line). Feel free to make any changes to suit your needs.

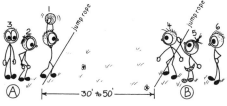

This drill can also become a game—after the class has developed their skills—by keeping individual scores.

Dribble-Pass-Shoot-Attack

Equipment: You need 4 playground balls and 20 short jump ropes (5 for each squad).

Formation: This is an advanced drill or game and should not be used unless the children are ready for it. Divide the class into four squads, and each squad into two three-person teams as shown in the illustration. This activity has team A trying to dribble and pass through three consecutive attackers to score by kicking the ball over line E. Team B (the attackers) is in a line approximately 30' apart. Each one can attack forward, but cannot go *backward* beyond his or her line. That is, 4 cannot go behind line B, 5 cannot go behind line C, and so on. This means that team A has to keep in its lanes (so that they can successfully pass to one another) if they are going to have a chance to score.

You will be wise to set a time limit. After a score, the teams change places.

SOCCER RELAYS

The next three activities are soccer relays. Relays are exciting, but they should not be used to teach skills in the beginning. During the intense excitement of a relay, there is a tendency for children and beginners to get very sloppy and careless with any skills that are used in the relay. So keep this in mind and use relays only after the children have shown improvement in their skill development. But even at this time, if they get sloppy and careless, stop the relays and go back to the drills.

"Shuttle"

Equipment: You need 8 cones or milk jugs and 4 playground balls (or soccer balls).

Formation: Divide the class into four squads (A, B, C, D) and put them into a shuttle formation as shown in the illustration. On the signal "Go," 1 dribbles the soccer ball or playground ball around the cones or other markers and passes off to 2. Player 2 traps the ball and does the same routine and passes off to 3. Continue until the teams are lined up in their original position at the opposite side of the lines. The first team in this position wins.

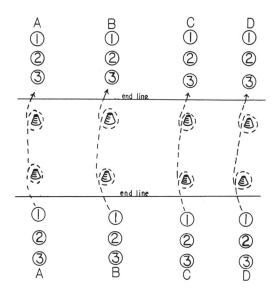

"Spoke"

Equipment: You need 24 bicycle tires or hula hoops (as position markers) and 4 soccer balls or playground balls.

Formation: Divide and set up four squads as shown in the illustration. On the signal "Go," 1 dribbles in and out of his own squad. As soon as 1 dribbles past them, the rest of the squad members move up one spot—2 to 1, 3 to 2, and so on. When 1 reaches 6's spot (which is now empty), 1 passes the ball to 5, who traps it and quickly passes the ball to 4, who traps it and passes to 3. Continue this routine until the ball reaches the new 1. The new 1 follows the same procedures listed earlier. The first team to get back into its original position wins.

"Star"

Equipment: You need 24 bicycle tires or hula hoops (position markers) and 8 soccer balls or playground balls.

Formation: Divide the class into eight squads of three people each as shown in the illustration. On the signal "Go," 1 from each squad dribbles the ball counterclockwise around the formation. In the meantime, as soon as 1 pulls out, 2 and 3 move back one tire (2 moves to 1; 3 to 2). After 1 makes the circle, he passes off to 2 from his squad who is now in the 1 tire. The old 1 now moves down and occupies the 3 tire. Continue this same routine until everyone is back in his original position.

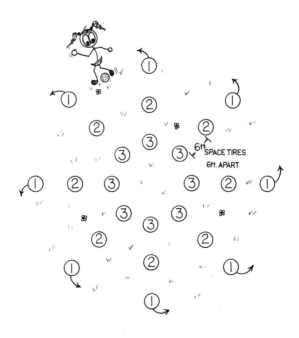

MORE SOCCER FUN

"Soccer Snatch"

Equipment: You need 4 playground balls, 8 cones or milk jugs or hula hoops or bicycle .ires, and 16 jump ropes (4 for each team, 2 for each end line).

Formation: This one-on-one activity involves quickness, attacking the ball, dribbling, and scoring. Divide the class into four teams and match them up as A and B, and C and D. Set up the playing area so that you will be adjacent to each area, as shown in the illustration.

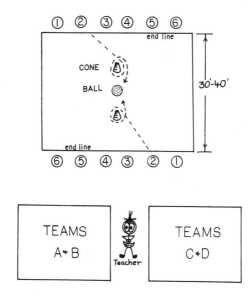

NOTE: The cones or milk jugs are included as safety features to slow down the two attacking players before they attack the ball. With no cones, the children, in their excitement, could have severe collisions when they both try to attack the ball at the same time at full speed. The cones are an excellent safety device without taking any of the excitement or challenge from the game.

The teams are numbered from 1 through 6 as shown. Then call a number. Those numbers circle the cones, try to control the ball, and score a point by kicking the ball over their opponent's end line. A 30-second time limit is recommended. Call numbers for both groups at the same time.

"Soccer Take Away"

Equipment: You need 4 playground balls, and 8 jump ropes for goal lines.

Formation: This is another one-on-one activity involving attacking, dribbling, and attempting to score. Divide the class into four squads. Then divide each squad in half (A and B) and have them face each other as shown in the illustration. The center players stand facing each other with a ball between them. When you say "Go," each player attempts to gain possession of the ball, dribble, and kick the ball over the opponent's goal line for a score. A 30-second time limit is recommended. After a score, both players go to the end of their lines and the next players move up. It is a good idea to change the players around now and then so that they will not meet each other a second time.

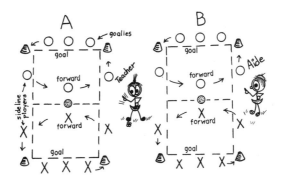

"Line Soccer"

Equipment: You need 2 playground balls and 8 cones or milk jugs for corner and midline markers.

Formation: This is another favorite. There are no standard rules, so you might want to begin with a basic set of rules and then add or delete new ones as needed to make this activity a success in your own situation.

If possible, set up as shown in the illustration, using two areas so that there is more participation by the children in the short time allowed. It would be difficult for one teacher to keep two games going on at the same time, so if you are fortunate enough to have an aide, let the aide supervise one of the games. If you do not have an aide, you may be able to use one of your students who is playing soccer in an afternoon soccer program. Some of these children can do a good job.

The object of the game is for one of the forwards to score a point by kicking the ball past the opposing goalies *below shoulder level.* If successful, both teams rotate counterclockwise and new forwards face each other.

On the signal "Go," both forwards try to get control of the ball and dribble toward their opponent's goal line for a possible score. The goalies may block the ball with their feet or bodies. They can catch the ball, but they must quickly put it on the ground and either roll it in or kick it in with the *side of the foot.* They cannot pass or punt the ball back into play. If the ball is kicked out of bounds, the sideline players who travel up and down the side lines can give the ball a push back into the playing area with the side of their feet. If the ball is kicked beyond the sideline players, they must quickly bring the ball back and roll it into the playing area. Kicking the ball out of bounds can sometimes become a real problem and slow down the game, so you may have to set a rule that when the ball is kicked out of bounds three times, the teams will rotate. Also, if there is no score in 45 or 60 seconds, the teams rotate.

"Lane Soccer"

Equipment: You need 6 cones or milk jugs for corner and midline markers .

Formation: All lines and lanes are imaginary in this game, which features three-on-three and stresses the aspect of team play and the importance of the team members playing in their lanes both on offense and defense. When you first use this particular activity, you will find yourself spending most of your time encouraging the players to stay in their lanes. Be patient. It will begin to evolve and the children will begin to see and feel the importance of position play rather than bunching up on the ball.

The object of the game is to keep possession of the ball, to dribble and pass to the opponent's goal line, and to kick the ball through the goalies (below the shoulder line) in order to score a point.

Divide the class into two teams and set up the area as shown in the illustration. There will be three forwards, four sideliners, and five goalies. In case of a score, both teams rotate counterclockwise *three* positions. Choose a team to start the game on offense. The center forward begins by passing to one of his side forwards, who attempts to control the ball and possibly dribble on down toward the goal line or pass off if he is under attack. The defense, of course, is attempting to attack the ball and go on the offense themselves.

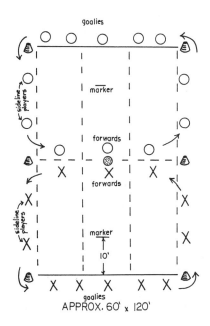

APPROX. 60' x 120'

The goalies can stop the ball with their feet or bodies, or catch the ball. In this case, they must immediately put the ball down and roll it into the field of play. Goalies may not punt or pass the ball back into action. The sideline players follow the ball up and down the field, and, if it comes their way, they kick it back into play with the side of their foot. If the ball is kicked passed them, they must quickly retrieve the ball and roll it into play. Side guards cannot score a goal when kicking the ball back into play.

After a score and rotation, the team that did not score puts the ball into play.

Set up a 2-minute time limit. If there is no score by this time, both teams rotate and the opposite team puts the ball into play.

There must be no unnecessary roughness, touching the ball with the hands, or pushing.

There is a penalty kick for violations from the penalty marker with the goalies defending: 1 point if successful; if not successful, the ball remains in play.

"Mad Dog Kickball"

Equipment: You need 1 playground ball and 2 cones or milk jugs.

Formation: Divide the class into two teams for this good fitness activity. Count off 1, 2, 3, 4, and so on. This becomes the children's kicking order. Put one team (B) in the field and one team (A) at "home." The home team gets three kicks (three people, one kick each). After 1 kicks the ball, the *whole team* (A) joins behind the kicker and follows him around the two cones (C and D). Every time the kicker (1) goes around cone C, he scores a run. (The whole team must follow the kicker in a single file to get a score.)

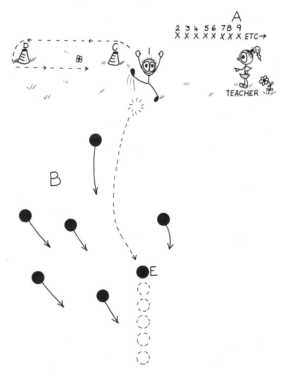

In the meantime, the team in the field (B) is converging as fast as they can on the person who caught the ball. Immediately, the team in the field lines up single file behind the person who caught the ball. The ball is then passed, from front to back, over and under to *every* person on the fielding team. When the last person in line gets the ball, he runs to the front of the line and yells "Stop." This signals the home team to stop running around the cones and to add the runs made to their score. After three kickers have had their time to kick the ball, they reverse positions—the home team goes to the field and the fielding team goes to home.

Let's follow along with the illustrations. Player E has stopped the ball, so he stands his ground while the rest of the team (black dots) line up behind him in a straight line. When everyone is lined up, player E passes the ball over and under down the line until the last person gets it. As soon as the last person gets the ball, he quickly runs *to the front of the line* and yells "Stop." Emphasize to the fielding team that they must keep their eyes on the kicked ball and quickly run in that direction so that they can line up in a hurry to stop the kicking team from scoring runs.

MODIFIED SOCCER RULES FOR GRADES 4-6

Follow this illustration as you go through the modified soccer rules.

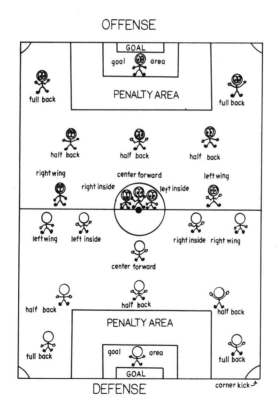

♦ *Players:* There are 11 players on a team, and each player has a definite position. The forwards (left wing or outside, left inside, center forward, right inside, and right wing or outside) play offense and attempt to advance the ball into the opponent's territory and score a goal. The halfbacks (left, center, and right) play offense in that they follow the forward line to the opponent's goal and feed the ball to the forwards. They play defense when the opponents have possession of the ball and are responsible for guarding a specific opponent. For instance, the right halfback guards (or covers) the left wing; the full backs (left and right) play defense and guard the opposite inners (left full back versus right inner). The goalie defends the goal.

♦ *Starting the Game:* The game is started with a kickoff (a place kick from the ground) in the center of the field by the center forward of the team on offense. (The opponents must be 5 yards away until the ball is kicked.) The center forward tries to kick the ball to one of his forwards.

♦ *Scoring:* A goal (two points) is scored when the ball is kicked between the goal posts and below the cross-bar.

♦ *Throw In or Kick In:* Anytime the ball goes out of bounds at the sideline, the opponents put the ball in play by throwing or kicking it in at the spot where it crossed the sideline as it went out. If it is a throw in, parts of both feet must remain on the ground. The ball is thrown overhead.

♦ *Defense Kick:* If a player kicks the ball over the opponent's goal line (not between the posts), one of the opponents is given a free kick where it went out. This may be a punt or a place kick inside the goal area.

♦ *Corner Kick:* If a player causes a ball to go out of bounds over his own goal line (outside the goal posts), a corner kick is taken by a member of the other team. The kicker may kick the ball toward his opponent's goal. If it goes between the posts, it is a score.

♦ *Fouls:* (1) Using the hands to play the ball in any way. Only the goal keeper may use his hands. Only the goal keeper may punt the ball. (2) Any unnecessary roughness. (3) Any unsportsmanlike conduct. (4) Interfering with the goal keeper when he has the ball.

♦ *Free Kick:* Any time a foul is made, the other team may take the free kick right where the foul was committed *except* in the penalty area.

Volleyball———————————18

For years, volleyball was looked upon as an activity that was played at camp or picnics; it was fun to play, but few seemed to take it seriously. Then television made it possible for us to see the teams from Japan, Russia, and other countries in action. Everyone was amazed at the skill and stamina of these superbly trained athletes. It was almost as if we had discovered a brand-new sport. Since then, volleyball has caught on in the United States and is definitely here to stay. Many junior high schools and senior high schools sponsor varsity volleyball teams for both boys and girls, colleges and universities sponsor varsity teams, and YMCAs and city and county recreation departments have league play for all ages of both sexes.

So what are we doing with volleyball in our elementary physical education programs? We actually begin laying a foundation for the children's volleyball skills in kindergarten with such activities as bean bags (see Chapter 4) and balls (see Chapter 6). These activities present many eye-hand experiences that contribute greatly to the next stage, which includes simple games that involve throwing and catching balls. To get students used to throwing over a net, we add some "low-net" activities and then go to the "high net" (6') with a game called "Newcomb," which, in the beginning, involves just throwing the ball over the net and catching it. Later, "Newcomb" becomes more sophisticated with the addition of volleyball rules, rotation, three catches and over, and so on. Even though most of the children are still in the throw-and-catch stage of development, you may find a few fifth-graders and a few more sixth-graders who may be ready to try regular volleyball, if they have had good continuity in their volleyball progressions since kindergarten. They are instructed and exposed to such skills as the set, bump, dig, spike, block; several ways of serving; and strategy. With another year of physical maturity, most children really begin to blossom as volleyball players during their junior high years.

Therefore, it is very important that children be given the best possible instruction during their elementary school years so that each will be able to master the more challenging skills to come. They should participate in and enjoy everything volleyball has to offer, whether it will be for varsity competition or recreation.

VOLLEYBALL ACTIVITIES FOR GRADES K-3

At the risk of being redundant, this is a reminder. Definite prerequisites to the following volleyball activities are the three-week sessions involving bean bags (see Chapter 4) and balls (see Chapter 6). Make certain that your students follow this sequence, because this chapter is based on the assumption that the children have been exposed to a proper progression of varied bean bag and ball routines involving eye-hand activities.

Since we begin with a few simple throw-bounce-catch activities that lead into a series of progressively more challenging activities, we have not attempted to classify activities for certain grade levels. For example, if this is the first year a third-grade class has participated in a planned and organized physical education program, they may have to spend a lot of their allotted time with the simple throw-bounce-catch activities, whereas another third-grade class that has had planned physical education classes since kindergarten can probably go from circle games all the way through a fair game of "Newcomb."

FACILITIES AND EQUIPMENT NEEDED: It is a poor excuse if you say your school does not have the facilities or the money to offer volleyball. Many elementary schools have excellent volleyball activities going on while using the following free-for-the-asking and homemade materials.

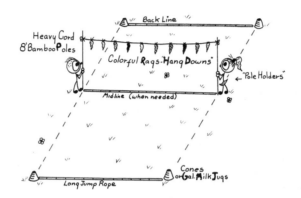

To involve the whole class, you will need two homemade courts:

4 8′ bamboo poles
8 cones or gallon milk jugs
2 8½″ playground balls
25′ of heavy cord
An assortment of colorful rags for "hang downs"

NOTE: In the following volleyball activities, the equipment needed for each activity is listed. When the equipment calls for two courts, they will include the preceding items unless you are fortunate enough to have four roll-away standards and two store-bought nets.

Circle Drills

Equipment: You need 4 playground balls.

Formation: Divide the class into four squads. Place one child in the center of each squad. To get the children used to circle work, have the child in the middle *roll* the ball to each squad member in order, who then rolls the ball right back to the child in the center. Next, place someone else in the middle of the circle and have them *bounce* the ball to each person in order. With the next new person in the middle, *toss* the ball to each person with a gentle underhand toss.

This time, again, have each squad form a circle and give each child a number. Put 1 in the center of the circle with a ball. Child 1 will begin the drill by calling out 2 and then throwing the ball into the air with a high arch. Child 2 will try to catch the ball on the first or second bounce. Child 2 *rolls* the ball back to 1, who then calls 3. Repeat this procedure until all the children have had a chance to catch the ball. Next, put 2 in the center and have him or her follow the same procedure. Repeat until everyone in the class has had a chance to be in the center.

Remember, there will be four squads doing this drill, so you and an aide must position yourselves where you can observe all the action and be where you are needed quickly. Some of the children may have a difficult time with the numbers, so let them use names if they wish. Encourage them to keep their eyes on the ball and to move their bodies into a position to catch the ball.

Now form another circle but have no one in the center this time. Give the ball to one child in each squad, who will throw the ball up *first* and then call a name or number; that person will then try to catch the ball on the first or second bounce. Whether that child is successful or not, she throws the ball up from her place in the circle next time. You will have to make sure that *all* the names (or numbers) are called. Stress a *high* arch when the children throw the balls up—this is very important as it gives the receiver a chance to get in a position to catch the ball.

"Bombs Away—Low Net"

Equipment: You need 2 courts and a playground ball for each child.

Formation: Set up the two courts and divide the class into four teams. Set the low net at about 3′ above the floor or ground. The object of this activity is to see which team in each group has the least number of balls on its side at the end of a 30-second time period. The balls must go over the net and there are no back boundaries. The children catch or chase the balls and quickly return close enough to throw the ball *over* the net into their opponents' area. Stress that the children quickly retrieve the ball and throw it. Also stress that it is much quicker to catch a ball on the *bounce* and then throw, rather than trying to run after it, return, and throw. At the end of 30 seconds, call "And stop" and count the balls to see which side won. Then be sure to rotate the pole holders so that they get a chance to participate.

"Bombs Away—High Net"

Equipment: You need the same equipment as in "Bombs Away—Low Net" except raise the nets to about 6′ above the ground or floor.

Formation: The procedures are the same as in "Low Net" except that the net is higher and, again, all the balls must be thrown *over* the net. Encourage catching the balls on the first bounce and inspire those few who can possibly catch the ball on the fly to do so.

"Over the River"

Equipment: You need 4 long jump ropes for the river boundaries, 2 playground balls, and 4 cones or gallon milk jugs.

Formation: This is a simple throwing-and-retrieving activity. Divide the class into four teams and set them up into two areas as shown in the illustration. Use the long jump ropes for the boundaries. Begin by having the ropes about 4′ apart and gradually increase the width to 5′ then to 6′ then 7′ as the children's throwing ability improves. Have the teams line up single file behind the cones as shown except for 1 in team B who is the first thrower. (In the beginning, the cones can be about 10′ or 15′ from the boundary lines.) Player 1 throws the ball over the river and player 1 on team A quickly retrieves the ball, runs up to the boundary line and throws the ball over the river to 2 on team B who follows the same procedure. After each child has handled the ball, he returns to the back of the line to wait another turn. Encourage students to quickly run up to the boundary line and throw the ball. Also encourage the catchers to watch where the ball is being thrown and to position themselves in front of the ball. As their skills increase, encourage the students to catch the ball either on the first or second bounce. As their throwing skills increase, you may need to move the cones farther back from the boundary line of the river.

Team A(1)
6 5 4 3 2 1 ▲
X X X X X X
| River | 1 ◌ ▲ 2 3 4 5 6 ◌ ◌ ◌ ◌ ◌ Team B(1)

– – – – – – – –

Team A(2)
6 5 4 3 2 1 ▲
X X X X X X
| River | 1 ◌ ▲ 2 3 4 5 6 ◌ ◌ ◌ ◌ ◌ Team B(2)

"No Man's Land"

Equipment: You need 2 playground balls.

Area: Playground or multipurpose room.

Formation: Set up two areas so that everyone will be able to play at the same time. This is a good throwing-and-catching game. The object is to throw across "No Man's Land" and to catch, on a fly, a ball thrown over "No Man's Land" by the opponents.

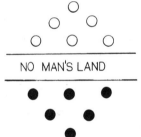

Scoring: A team receives one point for each catch on the fly and one point for each ball that falls into "No Man's Land." The game continues even though there is a score. Have the teams call out their scores as they happen. Set either a time limit or a number of points to win.

Penalty: The ball is given to the other team if a player goes into "No Man's Land" to throw or catch.

"Junior Sky Ball"

Equipment: You need 2 playground balls.

Formation: This is an old favorite with a slight modification for possible use with kindergarten children. Divide the class into four teams and have two formations. The two center people (A and B) each have a ball and stand facing each other. On the signal "Go," each center person throws the ball in a high arch over his head to his team, which is standing behind him. The object of this activity is for someone to catch the ball on the first bounce. If successful, that team gets one point and the person who caught the ball becomes the new center person. If the ball is not caught on the first bounce, the same person remains as the center person and no point is awarded. If the ball is caught on the fly, two points are given and this highly skilled child becomes the new center person. You can set a number of points to win or set a time limit, and the team with the highest number of points wins.

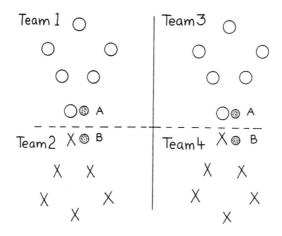

"Regular Sky Ball"

Equipment: You need 2 playground balls.

Formation: This is the same as "Junior Sky Ball" except that it is played by second- and third-graders who have been playing "Junior Sky Ball" for the past few years. In "Regular Sky Ball" the ball must be caught *on the fly.* All other rules are the same except for awarding only one point for all correct catches.

"Rebound—Low Net"

Equipment: You need 2 playground balls and 2 courts.

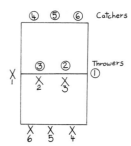

Formation: The throwers try to bounce the ball hard enough into their opponent's court so that the ball will travel over the end line in the air. The catchers, who are positioned outside the end lines, try to catch the ball on the first bounce. If they are successful, they roll the ball up to one of their throwers, who follows the same procedure. If the catchers do not catch the ball, or if one drops it, then it is a point for the other team. The ball then goes over to the throwers of the pointwinning team, and they put the ball back into action. If a thrower does not bounce the ball across the end line, it is a point for the receiving team and one of their throwers puts the ball back into play. REMEMBER: The catchers must catch the ball behind the end line on the first bounce. When a team wins a point, it rotates before resuming play. The team with nine points wins; the teams then change courts.

Beginning "Newcomb"

Equipment: You need 2 courts and 2 playground balls (or volleyballs).

Formation: This is the children's introduction to "Newcomb." Rather than put half the class on one-half of the court and the other half on the other side, set up two courts where you will have 6 or 7 on a team rather than 14 on a team. With two courts going, each child will get almost twice the action that he or she would get from a game using one court.

The object of the game is to have the children throw and catch over a 6' net (or string with hang downs). The thrower always tries to throw the ball (underhand) over the net and into the

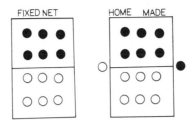

opponent's court where it might not be caught—thus scoring one point. The ball is never thrown over the net from the back row—it must be passed up to the front row where it is then thrown over the net. In the beginning, there is no formal rotation and the service can be from halfway to the net if necessary.

Fouls: One point is given to the opposite team for these fouls—(1) dropping the ball or failing to catch it, (2) not throwing the ball over the net, (3) throwing the ball out of bounds, (4) throwing the ball over the net from the back row.

Scoring: Eleven points is a winner.

Note: You should switch the lines from front to back occasionally to give everyone a chance to play in all the areas. Move the students on to "Newcomb" when they are ready.

"Newcomb"

Equipment: You need 2 courts and 2 playground balls (or volleyballs).

Formation: In this game, the children learn the basic rules and the rotation used in regular volleyball. The illustration shows the six-player rotation with fixed courts and homemade courts (which involve pole holders). Most classes can begin to play "Newcomb" during the third grade if they have had sound instruction in volleyball activities since kindergarten.

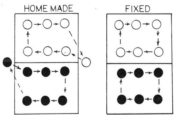

"Newcomb" can be played in the gym, multipurpose room (if the ceiling is high enough), or outside on a regulation court or on grass or on blacktop using the homemade courts. The height of the net can be from 5' to 6' depending on the throwing skill of the children. We highly recommend that you use two courts and have no more than six or seven children on a team.

The basic procedures for "Newcomb" are as follows: The ball is put into play with a throw over the net by the server who is standing in the rear right section of his court. Allow him to move in closer to the net if he has a weak throw. The receiving team is strongly encouraged, after receiving the ball, to pass the ball in *some* situations two times, and in *most* situations three times to each other before throwing the ball back over the net.

♦ *Example A:* Any player on the back line who receives the ball (1) will throw it to one of his players (2) on the front line who will in turn throw it to another front line teammate (3). This player must throw the ball over the net.

♦ *Example B:* If a middle front player (1) receives the ball, she can throw the ball to either

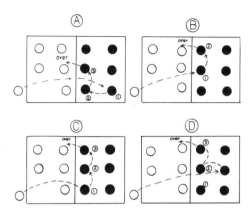

the player on her right or to the player on her left, who must throw the ball over the net. This is an example of when the *second* player throws the ball over the net.

♦ *Example C:* If a front end player (1) catches the ball, he can throw it to player (2) and player (2) can throw to player (3) who is next to him. Player (3) will immediately throw the ball over the net.

♦ *Example D:* If the middle person in the back row receives the ball, he can throw the ball to either players 1, 2, or 3 in the front row. In this case, he throws the ball to 2, who then throws to 3. This player must throw the ball over the net. Player 2 also had the option to throw the ball to 1, who also would have had to throw the ball over the net.

REMEMBER: The front line never throws back to their back line, and the back line never throws the ball over the net unless it is the server who begins the game.

Encourage the children to throw the ball as quickly as they can. Some of the children are so proud that they caught the ball that they want to be sure everyone else has seen what they have done. This slows down the game and allows the other team to get set. You may have to set a time limit for holding the ball.

The pole holders must keep the net pulled tight at all times.

When a person loses the serve, that team rolls the ball to the other team under the net.

After a successful serve, the ball continues in play until there is a miss. If the serving team misses, it loses the serve, and the receiving team becomes the serving team. No points are scored by either team. If the receiving team misses, the serving team scores a point and continues to serve until it misses and the same server continues to serve. Each time a team wins the serve, the whole team rotates, and they play the same position until they lose the serve. Since this is class time, set a time limit and the team with the most points at the end of the time period wins.

Here are some terms you'll use in "Newcomb" (and other volleyball games):

♦ *Serve*—This means to put the ball into play by throwing the ball over the net from behind the baseline. However, if the child cannot throw the ball over from this distance, he or she can move up closer to the net. Always have the server call out the score before serving. Call the score of the serving team first.

♦ *Fair Ball*—This is a ball that clears the net and falls into the opponent's court inside or on the boundary line.

♦ *Misses*—These are dropping or not playing a fair ball, throwing a ball out of bounds unless touched by a member of the other team before it goes out, and touching the net while throwing the ball.

♦ *Side Out*—This occurs when the serving team loses the serve and the ball goes to the other team. Remember, no point is scored at this time.

♦ *Let Ball*—This is a served ball that hits the top of the net and goes over into the opponent's court; play it again. However, if the ball is in play and hits the top of the net and goes over, it is a fair ball and remains in play.

"Stretch"

Equipment: You need 24 old bicycle tires (or hoops), 2 courts, and 2 volleyballs.

Formation: The purpose of this game is to stress position play. If you don't need it, don't play it.

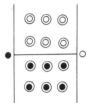

The children stand in the tires or hoops. They cannot stand on or move their tires at any time. If they do, depending on play, it is either a side out or a point for the other team. They can stretch as far as they can forward, sideways, or backward, but they must not step on or move their tires in the process. Otherwise, the regular "Newcomb" rules and rotation are in effect. You may want to adjust the size of your court to fit this activity.

"Ball and Chain"

Equipment: You need 24 bicycle tires (or hoops) and 2 courts.

Formation: This is another position-play activity. It is almost the opposite of "Stretch," although the children line up in the same formation. Standing in their tires, the children can move in any direction as long as they move their tires along with them while using their feet in a shuffling motion. Obviously, this activity works better indoors than outside. Regular "Newcomb" rules and rotation are used. Students must never touch their tires with their hands or step outside their tires. Depending on play, this will result as a side out or score for the other team.

"Four Square Newcomb"

Equipment: You need 2 homemade nets.

Formation: As in "Four Square," there are four separate teams in this game. When serving, teams 1 and 2 may serve only to teams 3 and 4. Also, teams 3 and 4 can serve only to teams 1 and 2. But, after receiving the serve, the receiving team can hit the ball back to any of the other three teams. As in regular "Newcomb," when a fair serve is made and the ball touches the floor in bounds or fails to get out of the receiver's court within the allotted three hits, the serving team scores one point and continues to serve. Remember, when any receiving team hits a ball legally into another team's court, this team immediately becomes the serving team. If the receiving team fails to get the ball successfully out of its court, the new receiving team is awarded one point. The rest of the regular volleyball rules apply.

Sideline "Newcomb"

Equipment: You need 1 court and 1 volleyball or playground ball.

Formation: This is a very handy game if you are pushed for space (indoor or outdoor), if you only have one ball, or if you want a little variety from regular "Newcomb."

Sideline basketball, sideline soccer, and sideline "Newcomb" are similar in that there are sideline players who are somewhat involved in the game and are continuously rotating around and into the playing courts as the game goes on.

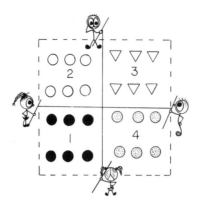

This activity is designed for 24 players, 12 on each team (a few more or less will not matter). The illustration shows that 6 members from each team are in opposite courts. The other team members are called sideline players and are on opposite sides from their teammates where they can play any of their team's out-of-bound throws. Sideline players cannot enter the court area but are free to pass any out-of-bound balls from their team into the opposite team's court if the ball has not touched the ground. Sideline players are not allowed to pass to each other. When a sideline player catches and throws a ball, it is designated a free throw and does *not* count as one of the opposite team's throws.

FIXED NET ROTATION

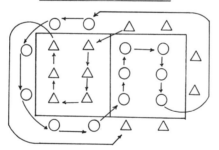

HOME MADE NET ROTATION

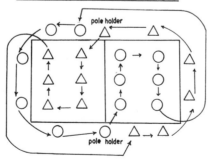

One sideline player from each team enters and one leaves their respective play area on every point scored by either team, or on any side out by either team. The illustration also shows the rotation for both fixed courts and homemade courts that use team members as pole holders.

"Mad Dog 'Newcomb' "

Equipment: You need 2 courts with midlines (4 cones).

Formation: To score points, a team must make five consecutive catches. The players should call out the number of each catch loudly so that everyone on the team knows the situation at all times. Whoever catches the fifth ball (for example, player 3 on team A) yells "5" as loud as possible and at the same time throws the ball into the other court. The ball must land inbounds or it will nullify the five catches. Immediately after making a fair throw into the opponent's court (for example, player 3 who caught the fifth ball), 3 quickly runs out the back of her own court with the rest of her team following in single file. Player 3 and her team must run around the court, passing on the outside of the four cones. Every time 3, with her team behind her in single file, goes by cone E, it is a point for her team.

Meantime, when the opposite team (B) caught 3's throw, the person who caught the ball (for example, 4) runs up to the midline carrying the ball while the rest of his team lines up behind him in single file. Player 4 then passes the ball person to person, over and under, to the last person in line who yells "Turn" loudly. He turns with them and passes the ball back down the line again over and under. When 4 gets the ball again, he yells "Stop" and team A immediately stops running. Team A scores one point for each time 3 has passed cone E. Both teams now rotate in their own courts and continue to play.

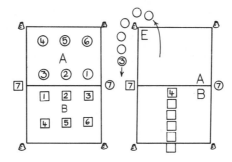

VOLLEYBALL SKILLS PROGRESSIONS FOR GRADES 4-6

At this stage of the volleyball program, most of the fourth-grade classes should be playing a sophisticated game of "Newcomb." Where possible, they are using regular volleyball rules, rotating, playing with six players on a team, playing "three and over," and so on. Children at this age level—and with the short time available for instruction, drills, and playing time—are not quite ready for the more complex skills of the bump, dig, set, spike, blocking, and others. A few of the fifth-graders and some of the sixth-graders, if they have had good sequences and continuity in their volleyball program since kindergarten, should be ready for instruction and drills in these advanced skills.

But, let's be realistic, some of these children, even though they have a good volleyball foundation, are still not quite ready physically and will be slow picking up these new skills. The few more physically precocious children will readily pick them up and will be ready to put their new skills to work. If possible, it is very important at this stage that the highly skilled children have their own game of regular volleyball and that the slower children continue playing "Newcomb" until they are ready to move on. So, you may end up with one court playing regular volleyball while the other court is playing "Newcomb."

IMPORTANT: We are not playing down the slower children; some are just not physically ready at this time. We have seen many of these slower developers as eighth-graders play excellent volleyball on the varsity team alongside teammates who were ready at an earlier age. Remember this and always be patient and understanding. Never ridicule and embarrass the slower children in front of the class or otherwise. They need support and encouragement; their time will come.

Overhead Volley

This is used to play a ball over the head.

♦ *From a Prone Position*—To hit the ball straight up, the elbows should be straight out to the side, forearms straight up. Rotate the forearms until the hands are forward with the thumbs and index fingers forming a triangle. As the ball comes down, extend the arms upward and snap the wrists straight as contact is made with the fleshy part of the fingers and thumbs. Follow through with the fingers pointing up in the direction you want the ball to go. Hit the ball *up,* not forward!

♦ *From a Chair*—Stress arm extension when contacting the ball. Don't forget to form a triangle with the thumbs and index fingers when preparing to contact the ball. Emphasize getting under the ball and hitting the ball *up* in the air rather than forward.

♦ *Standing Position*—Stress moving *under* the ball and giving good arm, leg, and wrist extension when hitting the ball. Follow through. Hit the ball *up,* not forward.

♦ Use the "Keep It Going" drill. Keep the ball up and going using the overhead volley drill.

The Bump

This is used to play a ball below the head with two hands. Its purpose is to get the low ball up high enough for someone to play it.

♦ *From a Sitting Position*—Clasp the hands together, rotate the elbows inward, put one foot slightly forward, keep the elbows locked together, get under the ball, and make contact with the mid-forearms. Don't lift or scoop the ball up—let the ball rebound off the arms.

♦ *From a Standing Position*—When receiving the ball, maintain a low body position. Bend the knees at about 90°, spread the feet a little wider than the shoulders, and have the forward foot pointing in the direction you want the ball to go. Remember, don't scoop the ball—let it rebound off the forearms.

- ♦ Use the "Keep It Going" drill. Keep the ball up and going using this drill.
- ♦ Use the three-on-one drill for quickness. Have three other players throw balls immediately one after another to one player who must react quickly and bump the balls under control.

The Dig

This is used to play a ball that has dropped below the head with one hand (fist). The purpose of the dig is to get a low ball up high enough for someone else to play it. While dropping the body to get under the ball, make a fist and rotate the forearm so that the palm side of the fist is up; contact with the ball is made on the upward turned fist. Do not bring the arm upward with a big swing; make just enough contact so that the ball will be high enough for a teammate to play it. Go slowly and be very careful with the dig drills. Some of the children can become over enthusiastic and try some of the spectacular diving digs they have seen on television. We don't want any bruised knees and bumped heads!

- ♦ *From a Chair*—Have a partner make a high drop as shown in the illustration. In the beginning, most of the children in the chair are going to go after the ball when the ball is too high. It will take practice to wait until the ball is low before going after it—that is what this drill is all about. Later, after they have learned to wait for the low ball, try the same drill without the chair.

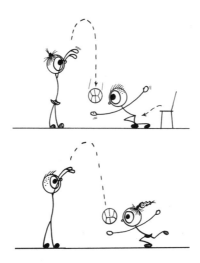

Spiking

The spike is the most devastating play in volleyball, and it is very difficult to return. To execute a good spike, the spiker must have a good *set* by his teammates. This is a difficult skill for this age group to master; nevertheless, we want to spend a short time giving them instructions and time for a few drills.

EXECUTION: The right-handed spiker stands with the left side of his body facing the net. His body should be slightly bent from the waist, both arms back and knees bent with the weight of the body on the balls of the feet. When a teammate sets the ball up, the jump is made. The right arm is raised with the elbow above and behind the right shoulder. The wrist of the right hand is bent and the palm is facing toward the ball. As the ball is brought forward, the body twists left until it is facing the net. The right shoulder rotates down toward the net, the arm moves down and the wrist of the hitting hand snaps through with the hand hitting down on the top nearside of the ball.

♦ The illustration shows a teammate holding the ball in a position for the spiker.

♦ This illustration shows a teammate using an overhead volley to set up the ball for the spiker. Partners can take turns doing both drills.

Blocking

Good blocking is a must if you ever want to stop the spike.

EXECUTION: Timing the block is very important. The blocker needs to be up there when the spiker hits the ball. There is a tendency for the blocker to be over eager and to jump too soon. Keep your eye on the spiker. Jump from both feet with the arms fully extended, palms open and fingers extended right in front of the ball. If the timing is right, the block should cause the ball to go back into the opponent's court or the ball should be slowed down enough so that the offense can handle it. Be sure that the jump is far enough away from the net so that the arms can move forward enough on the block and still not touch the net. Keep your eye on the offense!

Serving

This is a difficult but necessary skill for this age group.

EXECUTION: In the underhand method (right-handed server), the left foot is placed ahead of the other. The ball is held in the palm and fingers of the left hand slightly below the waist. The right hand is held with the fingers closed so that you make a fist with the palm upward. The right arm is swung backward; the knees are bent forward. As the arm is brought down and forward, the body twists back around to the left. The knees are straightened as the ball is hit and the arm follows through forward and upward. Follow through in the direction you want the ball to go.

Overhead Shuffle Drill

Partners practice the overhead pass while they shuffle (slide step) down the length of the net. When they reach the end of the net, they run back to the starting place and continue. (They take the ball with them.)

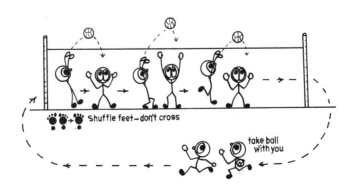

BASIC VOLLEYBALL RULES

The official rule says six people on a team. In elementary physical education, we like to be a little more flexible, especially when we first introduce "Newcomb," where we sometimes have as many as nine people on a team. More than nine tends to be chaotic, with very little action. Later, when we make "Newcomb" a bit more sophisticated, we use only six players to a team, but we have two games going on at the same time so that most of the children in the class are active.

Begin the games with a flip of a coin. The winners of the toss have two choices: (1) to serve or (2) his or her choice of courts.

The player serving must stand behind the right one-third of the end line with both feet. While serving, he or she must not step over the end line.

A team must be serving to score a point and the server continues to serve as long as his or her team wins points. When the server's team loses a point, there is side out, and the serve goes to the other team. Members of the team take turns serving according to rotation.

The server gets one chance to get the ball legally into his or her opponent's court. If the ball tips the net on the way over, the serve is lost—the ball must go completely over the net to be a good serve.

The boundary lines are a part of the court, so balls hitting the line are good and are in play.

A ball is considered "in" if a player touches it even though both the player and the ball were outside.

The ball must be returned over the net after a maximum of three volleys or less. No player may hit the ball two times in succession.

SIDE OUT: This is when the serving team fails to return the ball to the opponent's court successfully or if a member of the serving team has violated a rule.

VIOLATIONS: (1) Stepping *over* the center line; stepping *on* it is not a foul. (2) Palming or lofting the ball. (3) Reaching over the net during play. (4) Touching the net during play. A player may play a ball out of the net as long as he or she does not touch the net.

SCORING: Fifteen (15) points is the game, but the team has to be at least 2 points ahead. If not, the teams continue to play until one of the teams has a 2-point lead.

SCHOOL SITUATION: Due to the limited amount of time, you may want to set 9 or 7 points as a winner.

Basketball ——————————— 19

Many elementary children are loyal and enthusiastic fans of their local junior high and high school basketball teams and may dream of some day playing on these teams. Your students can start aiming for that dream in grades K–3 by experiencing growth and development in the areas described in the list that follows. Developing and improving these areas will also lay a sound foundation for the more complex basketball skills to come. The activities used are listed next to the areas, with the appropriate chapter number of the activity in parentheses. Remember, these areas have a carry over into all sports—not just basketball.

- ◆ *Peripheral vision, awareness*—spatial awareness drill (2)
- ◆ *Moving through general space*—basic locomotor skills in association with the spatial awareness drill (2)
- ◆ *Stamina*—running (2), tires (9)
- ◆ *Agility*—vault bars (3), tires (9), rope jumping (22)
- ◆ *Speed and quickness*—vault bars (3), relays (15), reaction games (24)
- ◆ *Team work*—parachute (10), tug of war (14), relays (15)
- ◆ *Upper body strength*—the bars (3), tug of war (14)
- ◆ *Rhythm*—rope jumping (22), dances (23)
- ◆ *Eye-hand coordination*—bean bags (4), balls (6)
- ◆ *Ball-handling skills*—balls (6)
- ◆ *Sportsmanship*—all competitive activities, especially "Four Square" (13)

In grades 4–6, emphasis is put on the skills of passing, shooting, and dribbling. Lead-up games to basketball are introduced so that the children can learn a few basketball rules and put the new skills they have learned to use in game situations. NOTE: Do *not* teach passing, shooting, and dribbling in relay-type drills; in the heat of the excitement and pressure, the children tend to get sloppy and won't take time to think the skill through.

If a child is really interested in playing basketball, encourage that child to become involved with an after-school basketball program for his or her age group. The local YMCA, recreation department, and some churches/other organizations have organized programs in which the child will get more coaching and be able to participate in scheduled and officiated games.

The following are a few examples of ball routines taken from Chapter 6, "Balls," for grades K–3 that can be used successfully with grades 4–6 in a gym or multipurpose room or outside on a black top surface. Each student will need a playground ball. The class has to spread out in empty places.

1. While standing in their personal space facing you, have the children use one hand only

and bounce the ball while looking at you. Now have them use the other hand. *Do not look at the ball.*

2. *Without looking at the ball,* can the students dribble into empty spaces without bumping into anyone else while walking? Running? Can they do the same thing with the other hand?

3. While standing in their personal space—and keeping their knees slightly bent, hips back and head up—can they dribble the ball into the same spot without looking at it? Can they circle around the ball as they dribble by using a sliding motion with their feet? *They must not cross their feet as they go around.* Try going the other direction, then alternate going one direction then the other. Are they doing this without looking at the ball?

4. By using the same routine as explained in example 3, can they protect the ball from an opponent who comes up behind them and tries to reach in and steal the ball? Have the students form pairs and take turns protecting and trying to steal the ball. Remember, they are to move in a circular motion in their own space. As their opponent tries to come around them, circle the opponent using the sliding steps; this keeps their hips into the opponent. Keep the head up at all times so that they can pass off or break.

5. While standing in their own personal space, have them throw the ball straight up over their head. They should not wait for the ball to come down to them—go up and get it. If their timing is good, their arms will be straight and their feet off the floor when they catch it. To use this drill to practice *rebounding,* the children need to do the following. When they catch the ball, bring it no lower than their chin—stick elbows straight out to the sides, crouch over the ball with the knees bent, trunk bent over to protect the ball. The head should be up looking for an opening to move out or to find someone to pass to. Practice this a lot with the children so that they automatically do all these things without having to think about them.

6. Have the students get into pairs, with each pair needing one basketball. Partners should stand approximately 8' apart and practice the chest pass, the bounce pass, and the overhead pass.

7. Have partners face each other. Both of them should move to the right and make a circle by moving the feet in a sliding motion. *Do not cross feet.* When they are able to do this, pass the ball back and forth while they circle and use a chest pass. Students should be aware of having to lead their partner slightly with the ball. Circle and pass both ways. Then try circling and passing with a bounce pass.

These are only a few examples. Have the children come up with new ideas and combinations that involve basketball skills.

BASIC BASKETBALL SKILLS

Chest Pass

The ball is held in both hands, the fingers spread on the sides of the ball slightly to the rear, and the thumbs pointed toward the inside. The ball is held at chest height, knees slightly flexed and the body slightly bent forward. The elbows are kept close to the body and the ball is released by extending the arms forcefully while snapping the wrists and stepping in the direction of the pass. Follow through!

Overhead Pass

The ball is held overhead with both hands, thumbs under the ball and fingers spread on the sides of the ball. The passer steps forward toward the receiver and transfers her body weight to the front foot. At the same time, she forcefully straightens the elbows, and snaps the wrists, thumbs, and fingers in the direction of the intended receiver.

Bounce Pass

This pass is executed in the same manner as the two-handed chest pass except that the ball is bounced into the hands of the receiver. The ball should strike the floor 4′ or 5′ from the receiver and bounce belt high.

Dribbling

Dribble low for maximum protection. The wrist and the fingers should be kept relaxed because the ball is controlled by these parts. The fingers control the direction of the ball and the wrist supplies the force. The eyes and head should be kept up at all times. A good rule to remember is never dribble the ball when a pass can be completed successfully.

Defense

The defensive player should stand about 3′ away from his opponent (who has the ball) with both hands ready to move in order to block a pass, to distract, or to block a shot. His feet should be comfortably spread, with his weight evenly distributed on both feet so that he can move quickly in any direction.

Two-Hand Set Shot

The hands should be placed lightly and evenly on the ball with the thumbs behind the ball. The fingers should not be spread too widely; just lay the hands normally on the ball. The thumbs should be a few inches apart. (The smaller the hands, the closer the thumbs.) The ball should be raised to eye level so that the eyes should be looking directly over the ball to the basket. Keep elbows in close to the body, legs slightly bent with the weight leaning slightly forward on the balls of the feet. The right or left foot should be slightly forward. Without lowering arms from their position, drop the ball slightly so that your fingers are pointing straight ahead. You've just unlocked your wrists. The knees should be slightly bent and, as you come up, push the ball in an upward arch toward the basket. Your momentum should carry you a few inches off the floor; follow through straight forward toward the basket.

Lay-up Shot

The player frequently receives the ball on the run and usually on a hop-catch-step-and-shoot sequence of movement. The ball is pushed up with both hands, with a follow-through and final release by one hand. The takeoff from the floor is from the opposite foot; for example, if the final movement is done by the right hand, the takeoff will be from the left foot. When approaching from the side, the ball is laid against the backboard, usually at a place 12″ to 18″ above the rim and 6″ to 8″ to the side nearest the player. This spot will depend upon the height of the jump by the shooter and the angle to the right or left according to the approach to the basket. The success of the shot depends upon the control of the jump, the finger release of the ball, and lots of practice that finally makes this move come natural.

BASKETBALL LEAD-UP GAMES

"Corner Spry"

This is an old favorite. It is a good drill for giving everyone involved a lot of practice time with the three basketball passes they'll be working on. CAUTION: In the beginning, use this activity as a *drill only*—not as a relay race. Beginners, under pressure and in the excitement of the relay, will forget about using the proper form and make hurried and sloppy passes. They may set up bad habit patterns that will be hard to correct later on. So, in the early grades, use "Corner Spry" as a drill only. If students in grades 4–6 have already developed good form in their passes, try it in a relay situation. If they get sloppy, go back to drills.

Equipment: You need 3 playground balls.

Formation: Three squads are needed. To begin the drill, player 1 has the ball. He passes the ball to 2 who returns it to 1. Player 1 then passes to 3 who returns it. Player 1 continues this same routine until the ball gets to 8. When 8 catches the ball, she does *not* return it to 1. Instead, she yells "Corner spry!" and everyone changes positions (8 moves to 1's space, 1 goes to 2's space, etc.). As soon as everyone has rotated, 8 passes to 1, and so on. This drill continues until everyone is back into his or her original position. Use the three basketball passes (the chest pass, the bounce pass, and the overhead pass). Don't try to mix them up; use one type of pass for a complete rotation.

"Pass and Squat"

This is another relay, but use it as a drill until the children have developed good passing techniques. The chest pass and the overhead pass work well in this drill.

Equipment: You need 5 playground balls.

Formation: Divide the class into approximately five teams of five children in each according to class size. Player 1 on each team stands facing her team, about 4′ from 2. (See the illustration.) On the signal to begin, 1 passes the ball to 2, 2 passes the ball back to 1 and 2 quickly squats down. Player 1 passes the ball to 3, who immediately passes the ball back to 1, and so on. This routine continues until 5 (or the last person) gets the ball. He does *not* return the ball to 1. Instead, he yells "Turn," and everyone who was in a squatting position stands and turns to face 5 who immediately passes the ball to 4, 4 passes the ball back to 5 and squats, 5 passes to 3, and so on. This continues until the ball gets back to 1.

The drill can stop here or it can continue. To continue the drill, when 1 gets the ball, he yells "Change!" He hands the ball to 2 who steps up to 1's place, while everyone else moves forward one place as 1 moves to the back of the line to 5's place. Continue this routine until the teams are back into their original position. This is a good passing-and-catching drill that involves throwing different distances.

"Rotation Ball"

This is an exciting passing-and-running game. Work on the students' passing techniques before playing this game.

Equipment: You need 2 playground balls, 2 bases (carpet squares), and 14 bicycle tires or hula hoops.

Formation: See the illustration. Three different formations are shown, so adjust to the size of your class. Also place the position of the bicycle tires closer or farther away from each other according to the ability of the class. Set up two games—four teams of six or seven players on each team.

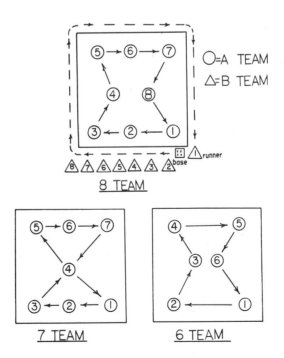

On the signal "Go" (follow the arrows), team A's player 1 passes the ball to 2, 1 follows the ball and is ready to step into 2's tire as soon as 2 passes the ball and moves out to 3's tire. Each player rotates to the spot where he or she passed the ball. This continues until 7 (or the last person) gets the ball; when 7 gets the ball, he keeps it and runs up to 1's tire.

Simultaneously, as 1 passes the ball to 2, the first player on team B runs around the formation (see the solid line) in an attempt to return home before team A can complete the passing rotation. If successful, one point is scored; otherwise, that player is out. After three outs, the teams change.

You will need to set up two of these areas as close to each other as possible so that you can stand in between and direct the games.

"Basketball Keep Away"

This is an excellent lead-up game to basketball. It involves passing, catching, and maneuvering to get open to pass or receive the ball. It is also an excellent team game, but you will need some way to identify the players. If you have bibs in two different colors, you are in business; if not, try head bands. They should be at least 2″ wide and tied around the head, with each team wearing a different color. There has to be a way to identify your teammates quickly, or the game is chaos and very frustrating.

Equipment: You need one playground ball or basketball.

Area: Gym or playground.

Formation: Divide the class into two teams. To begin, toss the ball into the group. The object of the game is for the team that has the ball to continue passing to their teammates as long as they can while the other team is trying to intercept the ball. When a team intercepts the ball, they keep it and pass it around to their own teammates. There is no scoring; the game is continuous.

Variation: If the class wants to keep score, members of the same team can call out the number of continuous successful catches every time they catch the ball. When the ball is intercepted, the team that had the ball must begin with a new count the next time they get the ball. The team that runs up the higher number of catches wins.

"End Ball"

This game gives the children practice in passing, catching while someone is guarding them, and following the discipline of staying in their own territory.

Equipment: You need 1 playground ball or basketball.

Formation: Divide the class into two teams with 9 to 14 members on each team. Position the players as follows. The end zone players place themselves in the end zone *opposite* from their own guards and forwards. The forwards play near the center line in their half and the guards play near the end zone in their half.

The object of the game is for the forwards to throw the ball over the heads of the opposing team to one of their end zone players.

Begin the game with a center jump between two opposing forwards on the center line. The team that gets the ball tries to throw the ball up to their forwards so that they can throw the ball to one of their teammates in the end zone. To score, the end zone player who catches the ball must catch it while keeping both feet inside the end zone. Players cannot travel with the ball (may take one step), and it must not be held more than 5 seconds. The guards and forwards may pass the ball among themselves before passing to their end zone. So that

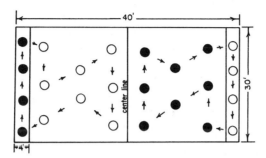

all the players get to play each position, both teams will quickly rotate one position (follow the arrows in the illustration) before play is resumed by a throw from the end zone that just scored.

Fouls: The following fouls result in a loss of the ball to the other team:

1. Holding the ball more than 5 seconds.
2. Stepping over the center line or end line into the opponent's territory.
3. Taking more than one step while holding the ball.
4. Pushing or holding another player.

Scoring: Each time a ball is caught legally in the end zone, the team scores one point.

Out of Bounds: The ball belongs to the team that did not throw it out. The closest player retrieves the ball and returns it to the guard on the proper team.

"Boundary Ball"

Equipment: You need 2 playground balls.

Formation: Divide the class into two teams. Each team occupies one-half of the court. The captain on each team has a ball. On the signal to begin, the captains start the game by trying to throw the ball so that it *rolls* or *bounces* across the opponent's goal line. If the ball goes over the goal line on the *fly,* it does not count. Members of each team are busy trying to keep balls thrown by the other side from crossing their goal line. All team members move around freely in their own territory, but they must not step across the center line into their opponent's territory. When a player catches a ball, he must throw it himself; he *cannot* pass it to a teammate. Players must run up to the center line when they throw it. REMEMBER: Balls that cross the goal line on a fly do not count; if the ball passes beyond the boundary lines, the player nearest the ball retrieves it, runs to his goal line, and puts it into play by throwing it to a teammate. Set a time period.

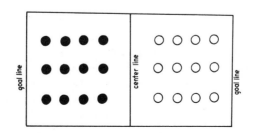

Scoring: One point is scored if the ball legally crosses the goal line. One point is awarded the opposing team if a player steps on or runs over the center line.

"Captain Ball"

This game involves throwing, catching, and guarding.

Equipment: You need 1 playground ball and 22 bicycle tires.

Formation: This game calls for 11 players on each team. The players occupying the center circles are called *captains*. The captains and the circle players take their field positions with their guards lined up across the center line facing each other.

Object of Game: The object is for the guards to get possession of the ball on the toss up and to throw the ball to one of the circle players on their team (across the center line). If their circle player successfully catches the ball, he can either throw to the captain (which is one point) or pass it to the next circle who, in turn, will pass it to the next circle, and so on. If the ball makes a complete circuit of all the circle players, it results in three points. REMEMBER: The opposing guards will be trying to intercept the ball all this time!

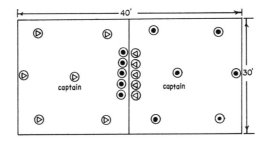

The game starts with a center jump using a guard from each team. The captains and the circle players are assigned specific circles, and they must keep *one* foot in the circle at all times. If they catch the ball with *both* feet out of the circle, the ball is taken out of bounds by an opposing guard.

Out of Bounds: A ball going out of bounds on either side is given to a guard on that side.

Fouls:

1. Traveling (more than one step) or kicking the ball.
2. Holding arms over space in a circle.
3. Stepping into a circle by a guard and stepping out of a circle with more than one foot by a circle player.

Penalty: The ball is given to one of the forwards who gets an unguarded free throw to the guarded captain. One point is scored if he or she is successful; if not, the ball is in play.

Three on Three

Equipment: You need 2 basketballs (or playground balls).

Area: Indoor basketball court or on black top area outdoors

Formation: Have two formations as shown in the illustration—one at each end of the court. As shown, three offensive players are facing the basketball goal. Three defensive players are facing the first three offensive players. This activity stresses basketball rules. The middle player (A) on each offensive team will have the ball. On the signal to begin, the middle player will move forward to begin play. If there is a score or the defense creates a turn over, the scrimmage is over. The offensive unit now becomes the new defensive threesome and the old defensive group goes to the back of the offensive line. The ball is given to the middle person in the next offensive threesome and play is ready to begin again. Have a time limit on the scrimmages so that everyone will get several chances to play, both on offense and on defense. Each group should keep its own score.

Sideline Basketball

Before playing sideline basketball, the class should be well drilled in all the skills and be familiar with the basic rules of basketball. Without these prerequisites, this game will result in chaos and frustration for everyone involved.

Equipment: You need 1 basketball.

Area: Indoor or outdoor basketball court.

Formation: Divide the class into two teams and arrange the teams as shown in the illustration. In the center of the court are six players: three from each team *facing* their own team members and their own goal. The game is started with a center jump and the object is to try to move the ball down the court by dribbling and passing and to score a basket (worth two points).

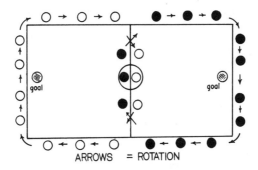

ARROWS = ROTATION

There can be a 2-minute time limit. If neither team scores in that time, both teams rotate counterclockwise with three new players in the center of the court from each team. Also, if either team scores, there is a rotation. The players on the sideline cannot cross over the sideline and come on to the court. Their job is to field all balls that go out of bounds and to pass them back to their teammates. *They cannot shoot baskets from their sideline position,* but the players on the court can pass the ball back and forth to their teammates on the sidelines if they need to.

Softball _____ 20

Softball is a game of many skills, but when used in physical education, it is almost classified as a passive activity because of the short time allotted to the physical education periods.

In many elementary schools, the physical education periods are 30 minutes. If a class plays softball for the full 30 minutes, each child would spend the greater part of the period waiting in the field for a ball to come his or her way or would be in home waiting for a turn to bat. To weaken the situation more, the teacher usually does the pitching (the most active part of the game) for both sides. Therefore, it is regrettable that softball is the only outdoor activity for many elementary schools. There are obviously many problems with this. Children at this age need a variety of vigorous activities, and softball falls far short of this. Also, the majority of classroom teachers know very little about the skills involved, so there is little teaching taking place.

Softball has great appeal for children and can play an important part in their physical education program. Therefore, have a specific time period set into your physical education curriculum for it; do *not* allot softball activities any more time than the other activities.

In grades K–3, lead into softball with simple activities that involve throwing, catching, batting, fielding, and base running in order to build a foundation for the refinement of these skills in the more complicated drills and activities in grades 4–6.

SOFTBALL DRILLS AND GAMES

Touch Base Drill

Equipment: You need 4 carpet squares for bases.

Formation: This is a quick drill that can be good training for tagging the bases. Line up the class as shown in the illustration. Runner 1 leads off and the rest of the class follows at

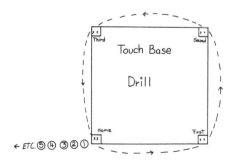

about 5' to 6' intervals. Don't let students get too close to the person in front or they will be stepping on heels. *Absolutely no passing is allowed!* The run is an easy jog with the focus on tagging all the bases as they go by. Three or four trips around the bases are enough. This is a drill and not a substitute for the regular warm-up run.

Throwing

Underhand: The ball is held in the hand with the palm up and with the weight on the right foot. While keeping the arm in close to the body, swing the arm backward then forward. At the same time, step forward with the left foot while releasing the ball at hip level. Follow through with the throwing arm. (Left-handed children should use opposite hand and feet positions.)

Overhand: Hold the ball with the palm down and with the fingers spread around the ball. Face the target with feet parallel, body balanced, and eyes on the target. Bring the arm back with the elbow bent and shift weight to the right foot. Swing the arm forward using the hand, wrist, and shoulder. Turn to throw the ball as the weight is shifted to the left foot. Follow through with the arm and body. (Left-handed children should use opposite hand and feet positions.)

Catching, Fielding, and Batting

Catching: Keep eyes on the incoming ball and at the same time move the body in line with the incoming ball. Keep the hands relaxed and slightly cupped. As contact is made with the ball, give with the hands and close them firmly around the ball. Balls caught above the waist should be caught with the fingers up and the thumbs in line. Balls caught below the waist are caught with the fingers pointed down and with the little fingers in line with each other.

Fielding: Keep eyes on the ball and move the body in line with the ball. Stand with feet comfortably spread to permit movement in any direction. As ground balls often bounce, the fielder can step forward with fingers pointed down and field the ball just in front of the toes.

Batting: Stand with the body facing home plate and parallel to the pitcher. Grip the bat with both hands close to the end of the bat and with the right hand on top and the left hand on the bottom. The feet should be comfortably spread with the weight evenly distributed between the two feet. Keep the knees slightly bent and the elbows away from the body. The bat should be tilted up and back *over* the right shoulder, not resting on it. Swing the bat parallel to the ground with the arms extended so that the ball is hit in front of home plate as the weight is shifted to the left foot. The follow through is done with a roll-over of the wrists as the bat completes the swing to the left side of the body. (Left-handed children should use opposite hand and feet positions.)

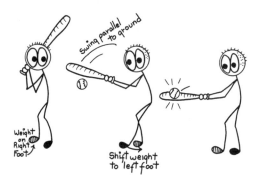

Slow Roll Rotation

Equipment: You need 4 playground balls (or *soft* softballs).

Formation: This drill can be used to teach the children to keep their eyes on a rolling ball and to move in any direction needed to place their body in front of the incoming ball. Stress fielding the ball with the fingers pointed down. Later, this same formation can be used for catching underhand and overhand throws. To get more participation, divide the class into four squads of approximately six children in each squad. Number them off as shown in the illustration. Player 1 stands in front of the squad and rolls a slow ground ball to 6, who will field the ball and roll it back to 1. This same procedure continues until the ball is fielded by 2 who, after fielding the ball, keeps it and moves up and takes 1's place. Player 1 takes a new position beside 6. Continue until everyone has had a chance to be in front of the squad.

"Over the River"

Equipment: You need 4 jump ropes for river boundaries, 4 cones or milk jugs, and 2 playground balls.

Formation: This activity involves throwing and catching skills in a controlled situation. In the beginning, the two-hand underhand toss is recommended. The catcher is encouraged to keep her eye on the ball and to position herself to catch the ball on the first bounce whenever possible. The distance across the river must be set according to the ability of the class; you want them to be successful yet challenged.

This is a drill, not a contest, so no score is kept at this time. Divide the class into four squads as shown in the illustration. The first squads to throw are squads B(1) and B(2). The throwers (1's) move up to the river bank and toss the balls *across* the river toward their receivers A(1) and A(2), who remain behind their markers until the balls are thrown. Next, the receivers become the throwers, and the throwers become the receivers. When the 1's have finished, they go to the back of their squads and the 2's continue the same procedure. Follow this same routine until all the children have had a chance to catch and throw.

"One on One—Two Teams"

Equipment: You need 2 long jump ropes for midlines, 4 cones or milk jugs, 2 *soft* softballs, and 4 carpet squares.

Formation: This is a simple activity involving the skills of throwing, fielding, and base running. There will be two games going on at the same time back-to-back for better control. The object of the game is to throw well and to score runs. To begin, player 1 from teams A(1) and A(2) throw first and player 1 from teams B(1) and B(2) are in the field between the cones. The throwers must stand behind home base and throw the ball into the field between the two cones located in front of their teams. The thrower is out if the ball is thrown outside the cones. After throwing a fair ball, the thrower attempts to run out and touch the base (located in front of his team) and return and touch home base without being tagged with the ball by the fielder. If he can do this, he scores one run for his team and he goes to the end of his team's line and takes 6's place after everyone has moved down one position. All six throwers from teams A(1) and A(2) follow this same procedure before becoming fielders. At the same time, the fielders from teams B(1) and B(2) have been rotating positions after fielding at the same time as the throwers. After the inning, the throwers become the fielders and the fielders become the throwers, and play is resumed.

The distance between the bases will depend on the ability of the children. Make scoring possible, but keep it challenging.

"One on One—Four Teams"

Equipment: You need 8 carpet squares, 8 cones or milk jugs, 4 *soft* softballs, and 4 long jump ropes for boundary lines.

Note: Have your children play "One on One—Two Teams" before trying this one.

Formation: This activity looks complicated, but it is basically the same game as "One on One—Two Teams." This time, there are four smaller teams instead of the two larger teams. This formation gives the children more activity in the allotted time. You also have an excellent vantage spot from which to direct play.

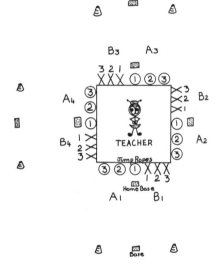

As shown in the illustration, the A teams have a thrower up first and the B teams have a fielder in the field first. Follow the same rules and procedures as listed previously for "One on One—Two Teams."

Touch Base Relay

Equipment: You need 4 carpet squares for bases and (optional) 24 bicycle tires or hula hoops.

Formation: Divide the class into four teams and line them up as shown in the illustration. The object of this relay is to be the first team to have everyone touch all four bases. On the signal "Go," runner 1 in each team leads off. Let's follow runner 1 in team A. Runner 1 circles his own bases and touches bases at B, C, and D, then his own A as he circles his squad and touches off the next runner (2). As each runner leaves, everyone in the squad moves up one place. After touching the next runner, the runner goes to the back of the line (6).

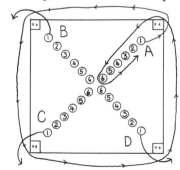

Grounders

Equipment: You need 4 *soft* softballs and jump ropes for boundary lines.

Formation: Divide the class into four teams. Give each team a letter (A, B, C, D). Set up two areas like the one shown in the illustration. Place team A on one side of the boundary line and team B behind the boundary line on the other side. Do the same thing with teams C and D in the other area. To begin the activity, give teams A and B a ball, and teams C and D a ball. The object is to throw a ground ball, *which must hit the ground* between the two boundary lines, through the other team. The receiving team must field the ball before it goes through them. If the ball goes through the receiving team, the throwing team scores one point. If the receiving team successfully fields the ball, then they immediately throw a ground ball right back and try to score. Make sure certain individuals do not try to do all the fielding and throwing.

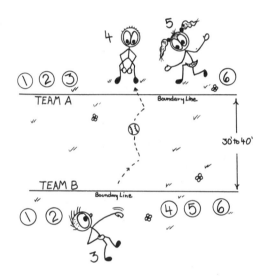

Fly Balls

Equipment: You need 2 playground balls and 12 bicycle tires or hula hoops.

Formation: This is a simple drill of throwing and catching. Divide the class into four squads and set up two areas like the one shown in the illustration. In both areas, put one squad on the outside with each child standing in a tire or hoop. Both squads will be numbered off 1–6. The squads in the bicycle tires will be the throwers and the squads on the inside of the circle will be the catchers. Give each thrower a chance to throw the ball, using a two-hand underhand toss. For example, when 2 is throwing, he calls his own number and the receiver with that same number will try to catch the ball on the first bounce. His squad mates must make room for him to catch the ball. Successful or not, the receiver *rolls* the ball to the next thrower (3). Continue until all the throwers have had a chance to throw the ball. Then both teams change places—the throwers become the receivers, and the receivers become the throwers.

Some first-graders, more second-graders, and most of the third-graders should be able to catch a gentle fly ball. When ready to try this, the thrower will have to give some loft to the ball so that the catcher can have time to move under the ball to make the catch. Keep the eyes on the ball!

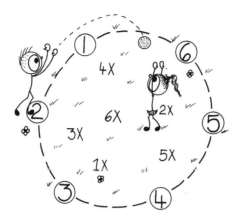

Around the Bases

Equipment: You need 16 carpet squares for bases and 4 *soft* softballs.

Formation: Begin with 15 steps between the bases; then make the distance longer or shorter when needed. When setting your distance between the bases, remember that students need to experience success, but they also need to be challenged if they are to grow.

Since these are drills and not relays, do *not* encourage the squads to see who can finish first. Rather, encourage them to follow the directions carefully and to execute the throwing and catching skills the best they can.

For more individual activity and participation, you will need to set up four squads of approximately six children in each squad, and each one should be set up as shown in the illustration.

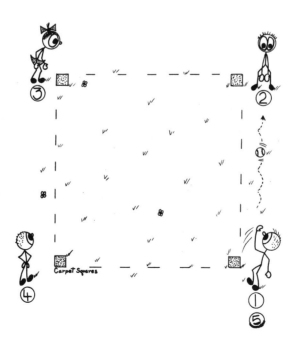

Player 1 rolls the ball to 2 and immediately follows the ball. Player 2 fields the ball, pivots and rolls the ball to 3, and follows the ball. Player 3 pivots and rolls the ball to 4 and follows the ball. Player 4 pivots and rolls the ball to 5 who has stepped up into 1's vacant place. Player 4 follows the ball and lines up behind 6. Continue this routine as long as needed.

If space permits, set up the four areas as shown in the illustration here so that you can be in a good position to observe, control, and encourage the children. Stop the activity anytime there is need to demonstrate the proper execution of skills.

Progressions: As the children improve in skills, use the same procedures listed above and let them throw

- ◆ Underhand bouncing grounders.
- ◆ Overhand bouncing grounders.
- ◆ Underhand throw to the next base (in the air all the way).
- ◆ Overhand throw to the next base (in the air all the way).

As the children's skills improve, you will need to move the bases a little farther apart for some of the progressions. The entire class will not progress at the same rate, so you may want to put your more skilled children into their own squads to keep challenging them with new progressions. At the same time, keep those children together who are progressing more slowly. Keep them doing the simple routines so that they can progress at their own rate and still feel success.

Batting Rotation

Equipment: You need 8 cones (stacking 2 cones on top of each other will make the needed 4 batting T's shown in B), 4 carpet squares for bases (A), 4 softball bats, and 4 *soft* softballs.

Formation: If there is enough space, set up your squads in a box formation as in "Around the Bases" so that you can be positioned in a good vantage point.

By setting up four squads of approximately six children in each, everyone will be able to get more batting practice along with more fielding practice.

This first activity is a rotating drill. Set up each squad as shown in the illustration. To

ease confusion, each squad member is given a number and will follow the batting order shown. Player 1 gets three swings at the ball. Whoever fields the ball *rolls* the ball back to 2, who places the ball back on the T for 1. After 1's third swing, the squad rotates. *Everyone* rotates one position (1 to 6, 6 to 5, 5 to 4, 4 to 3, 3 to 2, 2 to 1). Continue this procedure until everyone is back into their original positions. Continue as long as needed.

Later, to make a game out of this drill, set up a base (A) at an appropriate distance from the T (B) for each squad's skill level. Again, 1 gets three swings. If she hits the ball, she first places the bat inside the bicycle tire or hula hoop (C) and then tries to touch base and return and touch the T before the child who fielded the ball can *tag* her with the ball. Each time she returns safely back to the T, she scores one point. If she fails to put her bat into the tire or hoop, she is out. At the end of three swings, regardless of which fielder caught the ball, the squad rotates the same way as listed.

Line-up

Equipment: You need 2 playground balls and 4 carpet squares or rubber mats for bases.

Formation: In order to have your entire class active, you will need to divide your class into four teams of approximately seven players on each, and have two games going on at the same time. Place the bases about 20′ apart, one in the field and one for home base. Begin with one team spread out in the field and the other lined up behind and to the side of home base (A). The first player from the home team throws the ball from home base into the field and attempts to run to the other base and to touch home before the fielding team can line up behind the first one who picks up the ball (B). If the runner is successful, a point is scored; otherwise, the runner is out. After three outs, teams change.

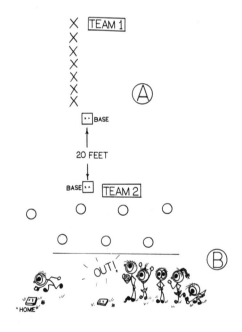

Note: This is an excellent game for cold weather. It teaches the players in the field to realize that pushing and shoving to get in line only give the runner more time to score. If *outs* are made too easily, move the bases closer together. If *runs* are made too easily, move the bases farther apart.

"One o' Cat"

Equipment: For three games, you need 3 softballs, 3 softball bats, and 9 carpet squares for bases.

Formation: To have all the students involved in this game, set up three teams of about nine players on each. Basic softball rules apply. When the batter hits the ball, he runs to first base and returns to home base. If he can successfully do this without being put out, he remains at bat. If he is put out, he becomes the *last fielder,* as shown in the illustration, and all players advance one position as shown, working toward pitcher, catcher, batter, and so on.

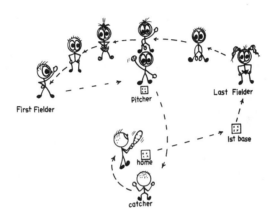

"Beatball"

Equipment: For two games, you need 2 softballs and 8 carpet squares for bases.

Formation: Arrange the bases as in softball in both playing areas. You need to set up four teams of about seven students on each. Team A is at bat. Team B has one or two players on each base and a pitcher. If there are two basemen, they alternate playing the bases and backing up each other. Play begins when the pitcher pitches the ball to the catcher who throws it to the first baseman who must tag the base with her foot before throwing the ball to the second baseman, and so on, until the ball reaches home plate. Simultaneously, the first runner from team A runs the bases, touching each base in order, in an effort to beat the ball home. If he is successful, a run is scored; otherwise, he is out. After three outs, the teams change positions and the game continues.

"Throw and Run"

This is an excellent lead-up game that gives you a practical way of teaching the game and rules of softball by eliminating the time-consuming "pitcher-batter" duel. There is one big problem, however; many classes have at least 28 children. This game calls for 18 children (9 on each team), which leaves approximately 10 children out. To change this situation, set up two playing areas and have 18 of the children play "Throw and Run" and the other 9 or 10 play "One o' Cat." The following day, one of the teams playing "Throw and Run" can rotate with the group who played "One o' Cat" the day before. This will give everyone a chance to play "Throw and Run."

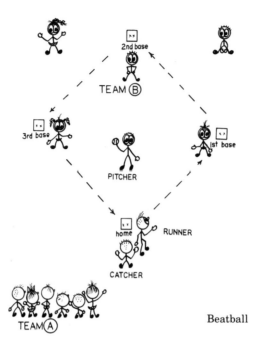

Beatball

Equipment for "Throw and Run": You need 1 *soft* softball and 4 carpet squares for bases.

Equipment for "One o' Cat": You need 1 *soft* softball, 1 softball bat, and 3 carpet squares for bases.

Formation: "Throw and Run" is played very much like softball except for the following exceptions. With one team in the field at their regular positions, the pitcher throws the ball to the batter who, instead of hitting the ball, catches it and *immediately* throws it out into the field. The ball is now treated as a batted ball and regular softball rules apply. However, a foul ball is out.

Variations:

1. Underleg throw—Instead of having the batter throw directly, have him lift a leg and throw a ball into the field under it.
2. Beat ball throw—Instead of playing regular softball rules, the fielders throw the ball directly to the catcher. In the meantime, the batter runs around the bases. He gets one point for each base he touches before the catcher gets the ball and calls out "Stop!" There are no outs, and each batter gets a turn before changing sides to the field. A fly ball caught would mean no score. Similarly, a foul ball would score no points but can count as a strike.

"Mad Dog Softball (I)"

Equipment: You need 1 batting T (either store-bought or homemade using 2 cones), 1 *soft* softball, 2 cones (bases B and C), and 1 bicycle tire.

Formation: Divide the class into two teams. Then number each team off (1, 2, 3, 4, etc.). This becomes their batting order. Put one team in the field and the other at home. The home team gets three times at bat. If they miss the ball or if they hit the T, this is a strike; three strikes and they're out. They are also out if, after hitting the ball, they sling the bat (a very dangerous action). After hitting the ball, they must place their bat in the bicycle tire or hula hoop (A); then the batter's whole team joins in behind the batter and follows him around cones B and C. Every time the batter goes around cone B, he scores a run.

In the meantime, the team in the field is converging as fast as they can on the person who caught the ball (D). Immediately, the team in the field lines up single file behind the person who caught the ball. The ball is then passed, from front to back, between the legs of every person on the fielding team (E). When the last person gets the ball, she runs to the front of the line and yells "Stop!" This signals the home team to stop running around the cones and to add the runs made to their score. After three batters have had their time at bat, they reverse with the home team—the home team goes to the field and the field team goes to home.

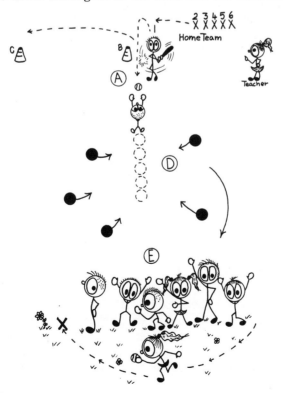

"Mad Dog Softball (II)"

Equipment: You need 1 batting T, 1 *soft* softball, 2 cones (bases E and F), 14 bicycle tires or hula hoops (one for each child in the field), and 1 bicycle tire or hoop (to put the bat in after a hit).

Formation: This version is similar to "Mad Dog Softball (I)" except for the throwing and catching involved.

Divide the class into two teams—batting team and fielding team. The batting team will line up as shown in D in the illustration. Students count off for their batting order. When 1 hits the ball into the field, he will first put his bat into the bicycle tire (C), then he will circle cones E and F with the rest of the batting team following him. Everytime 1 circles the cones, you count one run. The batting team continues to circle the cones until the fielding team completes their routine and calls "Stop." If the batter fails to put his bat in the bicycle tire, he is out and no runs can be scored. Three batters get to bat; then they change sides with the fielding team.

The fielding team will scatter as shown. Suppose that the batter hits the ball high into center field and it is caught by player G. Player G immediately runs and stands inside tire A, and the rest of the fielding team fills in the other tires as quickly as they can. As soon as someone is in the *adjacent* tire, the person in tire A throws either underhand or overhand according to the skill level of the class. If anyone drops the ball, he must run to get it and be back into the tire before he can throw it to the next person. *Every person* on the fielding team must catch and throw the ball. When the last person in line (B) catches the ball, she yells "Stop!" and the batting team must stop running around the cones.

"Mad Dog Softball (III)"

Equipment: You need 1 batting T, 1 *soft* softball, 4 carpet squares as bases, 14 bicycle tires or hula hoops (one for each child in the field), and 1 bicycle tire or hoop (to put the bat in after a hit).

Formation: This third revision was suggested by a student from East Flat Rock Elementary School. He asked why don't students run around the bases after hitting the ball as in regular softball. It would cut down the scoring and involve just as much running. The game was tried with grades 3 and 4 and it worked fine!

This is the same format as "Mad Dog Softball (II)" except that when the batter hits the ball off the T (A) and puts his bat in the tire (B), he runs and touches each base while the rest of his team following him does the same. Each time he goes by home base (A), he scores a run. It is an out if the batter does not put his bat into the tire at B. The batting team gets three at-bats; then the fielding team becomes the batting team. Be sure to number the batting team for their batting order—this will save a lot of fussing.

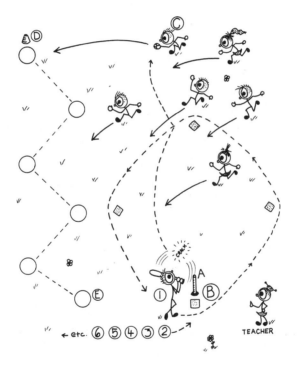

The fielding is the same as in "Mad Dog Softball (II)," but use the tires or hoops in a zigzag formation. Adjust the distance between the tires to the skill of your class. When the ball is hit, the person who stops the ball (C in this case) runs with the ball to the tire at D (the last tire should be marked with a cone). When player C gets into his tire, he throws the ball to the next tire shown in the illustration. If the ball is dropped, it must be picked up by the person who dropped it, and this person *must* get back into his tire before he can throw it to the next person. The ball must be thrown and caught by every person on the fielding team. When the ball reaches the last tire (E), this person yells "Stop!" as loudly as he can; this stops the batting team from scoring any more points.

Students will become winded when they first begin to play this game, but it is good exercise and reinforces their throwing, catching, batting, and running skills.

BASIC SOFTBALL RULES

See the following illustration for a diagram of the nine players on a softball team. Their names and approximate positions in the field are given.

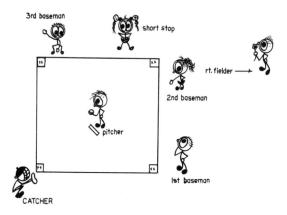

Playing Area

The baseline for intermediate grades should not be over 45' and the pitching distance should be 35' or less.

Pitching

1. Pitching is underhand.
2. While holding the ball in both hands, the pitcher faces the batter with both of his feet on the pitching rubber.
3. The pitcher is allowed one step toward the batter and must deliver the ball while taking that step.
4. The pitcher must wait until the batter is ready before he pitches the ball.
5. A *strike* is called if the ball is over the plate and is between the knees and shoulders of the batter. A *ball* is a pitch that goes outside these areas.
6. *Three strikes* make the batter out. *Four balls* allow the batter to walk to first base.

Scoring

To score a run, the runner must make the circuit of all the bases before her team has made three outs.

Batting

Use a softball bat only. Players must hit in order or they are out. A bunt foul on the third strike is out. If the batter is hit by a pitched ball, he goes to first base.

Base Running

Base runners must touch all bases. The runner cannot leave his base until the ball leaves the pitcher's hand; if he does, he is out. The runner may advance one base on an overthrow that goes into foul territory and out of play. If the catcher overthrows the second baseman and the ball is rolling into center field, the runner may advance as far as he can. A runner hit by a batted ball when he is off base is out. A runner has 3' on each side of the baseline in which to avoid being tagged by the ball.

Fly Ball

If a foul or fair ball is caught on the fly, the batter is out.

Foul Ball

A foul ball is a hit ball that crosses outside the foul lines between home and first base and between home and third base. If the ball goes *over* these bases, it is a fair ball. Any fly ball hit outside of the baselines beyond third base and first base is a foul ball.

Getting to First Base

The batter is safe if, after hitting the ball, she can touch first base before the fielding team can throw the ball to the first baseman. Also, the first baseman must have a foot on first base when the ball is caught *before the runner gets there* if the runner is to be put out.

Safety

1. *The danger of throwing the bat after getting a hit.* This is obviously very dangerous and is a real problem with this age group in the beginning. In the excitement of getting a hit, it is difficult for some of the children to remember the safety rules regardless of how thoroughly they were presented. SOME SUGGESTIONS:
   a. Have them put their bat into a hula hoop or bicycle tire before they take off for first base. (Some may even forget to do this!)
   b. Take their bat with them to first base.
      Regardless of what method you use, always call them *out* if they throw their bat.
2. *The danger of members of the fielding team running into each other when trying to catch a fly ball.* The players should never cross over into another player's area of responsibility to catch a fly ball. If the ball is in a borderline area, then the person closest to the ball should loudly call "I've got it!" several times.
3. *The danger of being a catcher.* If this person is expected to stand close behind the batter to catch the ball, she *must* wear a catcher's mask.
4. IMPORTANT: Be sure to use a *soft* softball for this age group.

Classroom Activities————21

All physical education and classroom teachers, regardless of their school's facilities, are going to find eventually that there will be days when the gym or multipurpose room is not available for some reason (roof is leaking, a magic show, painting, etc.) and that they are going to have to do activities in the classroom. It is best to prepare for the inevitable by thoroughly explaining the situation to the students in advance and having the class, along with yourself, set up procedures and rules for safe, orderly, and—we hope—productive classroom activities.

SUGGESTIONS: If possible, try to select classroom activities that will maintain some continuity with your regularly scheduled physical education program. For instance, there are some excellent rhythm records available (see Chapter 23, "Rhythms"), and many of these can be used with the children standing, moving around the room, or sitting at their desks. If the classroom can be "flattened" (desks moved back against the wall to create an open space) and mats brought in, there could be some tumbling activities. Remove the mats and try folk dances, lummie sticks, and so on. Also, if you have a large classroom and the open space after flattening your classroom is large enough, the activities using the small bicycle tires (20″ × 1.75″) work very well as individual stations for activities and relays. There is, however, one problem with the tires of which you and your students need to be aware—there is the possibility of catching a toe in the tire and tripping. Students will have to be reminded to pick up their feet as they do when they are using the big tires.

No matter how hard you try and how much cooperation you get from your students, many of the classroom activities will be noisy and will disturb the classrooms located close by. You should alert these teachers of your intentions, or better yet, see if they could possibly schedule their classroom activities at the same time.

There are many books and sources of classroom activities available. Read through them carefully. It will be obvious that some will not appeal to your particular class at all. However, if you find some that look interesting, but you can see a problem or two in it, change what needs to be changed to suit your situation. REMEMBER: The best classroom activities are usually the ones that you and your students have designed according to the environment of your own classroom and the equipment and supplies you have readily available.

Select and design activities that keep most of the children active and involved at the same time. Now and then after a particularly active session, you may want to throw in a quiet or passive activity to calm and cool down the students.

One of your first sessions for classroom activities could be used for instructing the children on how to set up the classroom for the different types of activities as safely and quietly as possible. This would save time and a lot of hassle in the future.

SAFETY:

1. Usually the noise factor and dangerous situations go hand in hand.
2. Set up boundary lines away from walls, windows, and other possible dangerous areas. Caution the children continuously about safety hazards that cannot be removed.
3. During relays held between the rows of desks, have all the children keep their feet *out of the aisles and under their desks.*
4. Use Nerf™ balls, sponge balls, fleece balls, bean bags, and panty hose balls when possible. Use playground balls for ball handling and passing relays with classes that have had thorough instruction previously in "Ball Activities" (see Chapter 6). Otherwise, use one of the softer balls just listed.
5. Watch for children overheating in the winter. Many classrooms are kept far too hot.
6. Keep any pencils or crayons off the floor.
7. Remind the children of the possibility of catching a toe in the small bicycle tires when they are used.
8. Build goodwill among your students by joining in on some of the activities when possible.
9. Don't overdo a good activity; stop and go to another activity before students tire of it.

"3-2-2-1 WARM-UP"

As you can see, this activity takes a large space after the classroom has been "flattened." You will need at least a 15′ square and even then it is going to be crowded. It is called 3-2-2-1 because of the position of the cones in the square. Set the cones or gallon milk jugs as shown in the illustration and line up the children. Have them walk it first; then they can do an easy run or the other locomotor moves (skip, hop, jump, leap, slide, gallop, etc.). Have each child watch the person in front at all times. *They must not touch, pass, or push the person in front of them.*

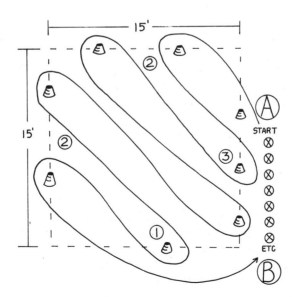

RELAYS

Over-and-Under Relay

Active-Passive

Equipment: You need balls, bean bags, or any other safe objects that may be passed from one person to another.

Formation: Set up teams of five or six members each standing in a row beside their desks. At the signal "Go," the leader passes the ball or object to the person behind him. That person passes the ball over his head and so on to the last person, who runs to the head of the line and starts the ball again. This continues until the original first person returns to the head of the line. The team that finishes first wins.

"Pass-the-Tire Relay"

Active-Passive

Equipment: You need 1 bicycle tire (or hula hoop) for each team.

Formation: Students stand in files by rows with backs to desks while holding hands. There are five to six children in each row. Each team lines up as shown in the illustration. To begin, player 1 has a tire (or hoop) hanging on her extended free arm. The object is to see what team can get the tire down to the last person's free extended arm without anyone else letting go of another's hand. The first team to do this wins. When the students become good enough, let the tire go down and back.

"Over-the-Head Relay"

Active-Passive

Noise Factor: Very noisy unless controlled.

Equipment: You need a bean bag (or eraser or Nerf™ ball) for each row.

Formation: The children are in relay teams sitting at their desks in rows. If possible, set up an even number of children in the rows of desks. Using 28 as an average number of children, you may have to have three rows of six children and two rows of five children. In the two rows of five children, have the last child in each of these two rows run two times. The first time they run will be when the bean bag gets back to them the first time; then they will run again when they have worked back to the last position.

To begin the relay, each child in the front desk will have a bean bag. On the signal "Go," he passes the bean bag *overhead* to the person behind him with both hands. Do *not* throw it back. The next children do the same thing. When the last person receives the bean bag, she stands to the *left* of her desk and runs to the *front* of the *first* desk and yells "Change!" Each person in the row quickly gets into the seat *behind* and the person with the bean bag gets into the empty front seat and goes through the same routine. The first team to get everyone in their original position wins. Make sure they do not change desks until the runner calls "Change" from the front of the head desk. Make sure, too, that the floor is clear of all books, pencils, and crayons.

"Bean Bag Toss"

Active-Passive

Equipment: You need one bean bag for each student.

Formation: There are five or six students in each row sitting on the floor beside their desks. The players are seated in a single-line formation with the bean bags placed in a pile in front of the first player in each line. On the signal "Go," the first player reaches into the pile of bean bags and passes each one back over her head—one at a time. When the last person in each row receives a bean bag, he places them in a pile behind him. When he has received the last bean bag, he yells "Turn!" and everyone on his team reverses his sitting position so that he is facing the other direction. The last person immediately begins to pass the bean bags—one at a time—back to the front. The front person puts each bean bag behind her in a pile. When she has put the last bean bag in the pile, she quickly stands up and raises both hands. *Students must not yell!* Other classes are in session, so students must be considerate. You can have the students repeat the routine two or three times without stopping after they get it down pat.

"Bean Bag Pitch Relay"

Active-Passive

Noise Factor: Medium.

Equipment: You need a bean bag for each row and a wastebasket or box for each row.

Formation: Have the students file by rows, with the first person in each row standing behind a line made of masking tape. Line up the rows beside their desks facing the front of the room. There is a wastebasket or box about 5' or 6' in front of player 1. On the signal "Go," 1 tosses the bean bag at the box or wastebasket. If she misses the box or wastebasket, she retrieves the bean bag and returns  to her place and continues to throw until she throws the bean bag into the wastebasket. Then she retrieves the bean bag and runs to the end of the line. She immediately passes the bean bag to the front, person to person. Player 2 has moved forward to the front of the line and, as soon as he gets the bean bag, he tosses it at the box or wastebasket. Follow the routine until the last person (5 or 6) has successfully thrown the bean bag into the wastebasket.

To eliminate despair, frustration and slowing down of the relay, you may want to say that if a child misses *three tosses,* he or she may retrieve the bean bag on the third miss and run to the end of the line and continue the relay.

Variation

Equipment: You need 3 homemade balls for each student and 1 wastebasket or box in front of each team.

Formation: Same as "Bean Bag Pitch Relay." First, have available a large pile of old newspapers. Give each child three 6″ strips of masking tape. Challenge them to roll or wad the newspapers up tightly and carefully wrap the three strips of masking tape around them tightly, making as round a ball as they can. Have each child make three balls. Now have the class line up as before. On the signal "Go," the 1's toss one ball at a time at the wastebasket.

If they miss, let them be. The object is to get the three balls into the basket *one at a time*. When the 1's have tossed their last balls, they leave them where they are and run to the back of their lines. As soon as 1 leaves, 2 moves into his spot and takes three tosses at the basket. Continue this routine until every team has finished. When scoring, give a point for each ball in the basket plus three points for finishing first, two points for second, and three for third. (You can use the same option for ''three misses'' as described earlier with bean bags.)

"Pass and Squat"

Active-Passive

Noise Factor: Medium.

Equipment: You need a Nerf™ ball (or bean bag or playground ball) for each team.

Formation: The children stand by their desks in rows. Divide the class into five or six teams according to the size of the class. If possible, the first person on each team stands facing his team at about 4′ or 5′ from the second person. On the signal ''Go,'' 1 tosses the ball to 2, who passes the ball right back to 1 and squats quickly; 1 then tosses to 3 who also tosses back to 1 and quickly squats. Continue this routine until the last person gets the ball. As soon as the last person gets the ball, she yells ''Turn!'' Everyone on her team turns and stands facing the last person. She immediately tosses to the first person facing her, who returns the ball to the tosser and squats. Follow this routine until the ball is passed back to 1. The first team to get the ball back to 1 wins.

"Chest Pass—Down and Back"

Active-Passive

Noise Factor: Could become quite noisy if not controlled.

Equipment: You need 2 playground balls (or 2 large Nerf™ balls) and 28 bicycle tires (or hula hoops) if you have them.

Formation: See the illustration. Divide the class into two teams and place each child in a bicycle tire if possible. Place tires and desks as shown in the illustration. On the signal ''Go,'' 1 chest passes to 2, 2 to 3, and so on. When 14 gets the ball, she passes right back to 13, 13 to 12, and so on. The first team to get the ball back to 1 wins. You can have the students make two or three trips down and back. If anyone drops a ball, he must retrieve the ball himself and get back into his tire before he passes the ball.

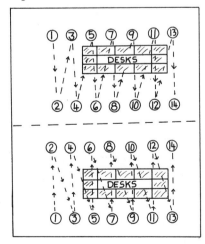

"Bounce Pass Relay"

Active-Passive

Noise Factor: Medium.

Equipment: You need 4 playground balls and 28 small bicycle tires (or hula hoops) if possible.

Formation: See the illustration. On the signal "Go," player 1 bounces the ball to 2, and so on. When 7 gets the ball, he yells "Change!" and everyone changes as shown. When 7 gets to 1's old spot, he immediately bounces the ball to 2, and so on. Continue until everyone on the team is in his or her original position.

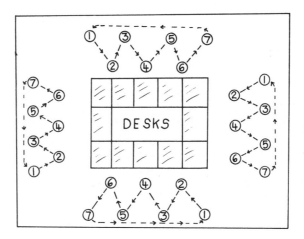

"Pivot and Hand Off"

Active-Passive

Noise Factor: Medium.

Equipment: You need 2 playground balls (or 2 large Nerf™ balls), 2 wastebaskets, and 28 bicycle tires if possible.

Formation: Divide the room into two sections and push the desks into the center of each section as shown in the illustration. On the signal "Go," player 1 pivots and hands the ball to 2, and so on. When 14 gets the ball, she shoots at the wastebasket goal—one shot only. Immediately after 14 shoots, everyone else moves up one space (14 to 1, 2 to 3, etc.). As soon as 14 retrieves the ball, she steps into 1's space, pivots, hands off to 2, and so on. Continue this routine until everyone is back into his or her original position. Score only the baskets made.

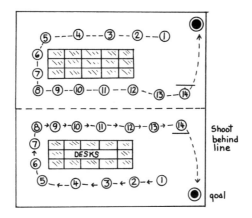

"Pivot-Pass-Pivot"

Active-Passive

Noise Factor: Medium.

Equipment: You need 2 playground balls (or 2 Nerf™ balls) and 2 wastebaskets for goals.

Formation: See the illustration. Divide the class into two teams and have them stand beside their desks as shown. On the signal "Go," 1 makes a soft chest pass to 2, and so on. When 15 gets the ball, he passes right back to 14 who pivots and passes to 13, and so on. When the ball gets back to 1, she shoots for the basket—one shot only. If time permits, you can make this a continuous relay by having everyone move up one spot after 1 shoots for a goal. For instance, 1 moves to 2, 2 to 3, and so on. As the shifting begins, 14 (or the last person) immediately moves to the 1 spot via the corner where 3 is shown in the illustration. He retrieves the ball and begins the relay immediately.

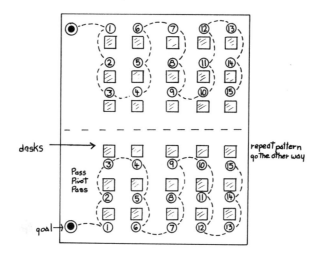

"Corner Pass Relay"

Active-Passive

Noise Factor: Medium.

Equipment: Depending on the skill level of the class, you need 4 Nerf™ balls (or 4 fleece balls or 4 playground balls) and a wastebasket for the goal.

Formation: Set up four teams (A, B, C, D) in the corners of the room as shown in the illustration. Players A, B, C, and D stand in the center of the room with their backs to the wastebasket and face their teams. On the signal "Go," players A, B, C, and D will underhand toss or chest pass the ball to 1 who will toss or pass it right back to player A, B, C and D, who will immediately pass the ball to 2, and so on. Continue this same routine to each player on the team. When 6 catches the ball, he yells "Change!" Everyone moves down one space and the 6's move out to the middle of the room and become the new A, B, C, and D's. If anyone drops a ball, he must retrieve it and get back into his original position before he can throw the ball again. Continue this routine until all four teams are back into their original position. The first team back wins.

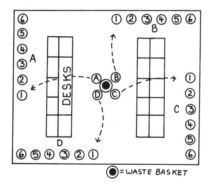

DRILLS

Reaction Drill

Active

Noise Factor: Medium.

Equipment: None.

Formation: Students stand beside their desks. The Reaction Drill is similar to the football "grass drill" that is used to develop quickness and agility. It is fun, effective, and a vigorous activity that requires no equipment and is done in the child's personal space (staying in one spot while doing nonlocomotor activities). Although this drill can be used in the gym, in the multipurpose room, or on the playground, it is especially valuable as a classroom activity because the children can stand beside their desks and perform most of these activities safely.

You can make these activities as vigorous as needed. Have the students go from one position to another, as shown in the illustration.

Reaction Drill

Active

Noise Factor: Medium.

Equipment: None.

Formation: See the Reaction Drill. After the students have learned all the positions in the Reaction Drill, they can go into the sequences shown in the illustration. Shown here are only a few examples of sequences. Encourage the children to design new sequences, try them all, and be sure to give credit and praise to all who contribute.

GAMES AND ACTIVITIES

Front, Back, Right, Left

Active

Noise Factor: Very noisy unless controlled.

Equipment: None.

Formation: have the children sit at their desks. This is a favorite game where the entire class is active at the same time. To be able to play this activity, the children should be able to exit right and left from their desks. Some desks have a bar across the right or left side that would, of course, make this activity impossible.

If, after the children are seated, there are any vacant desks, they should be removed or have books put on top of them to indicate that they are not to be used. Therefore, everyone will have a desk except for one or two children (extras) who will be actively trying to get a seat. You will be giving the commands "Front," "Back, "Left," and "Right." On command, each child will try to move quickly one seat in the direction called. While the class is changing seats, the one or two extra students who have no seats will be trying to anticipate the call and beat someone else to a vacant seat.

If the command is "Front," then the children sitting in the front desks will have to turn and run to the rear seat in their row. If the command is "Back," those in the back row will have to go to the front. If the command "Left" or "Right" is given, the children in these outside rows must move around to *their corresponding seat* on the other side of the room.

If any child moves in the wrong direction, one of the extra players takes his or her seat and that child now becomes an extra.

In the beginning it may be a good idea to have the children walk through this activity until they can do it with some control and order.

Circle Activities

Active

Noise Factor: Medium—play music softly so that the students can still hear the commands.

Equipment: You need 4 cones or gallon milk jugs and a record player.

Formation: If there is room for the students to form a circle after moving the desks against the wall, you will find Circle Activities a very versatile activity for grades K–3. You can make the activities as challenging or as simple as needed for the particular grade. In the beginning, you can give the commands to the kindergarten classes; in later grades, you may want to let the children take turns being the leader and giving the commands.

Suggested Commands:

1. Walk, march time, swing arms.
2. Walk faster, stretch legs ("giant" steps).
3. Hop on one foot, then the other foot.
4. Walk with stiff knees.
5. Walk on the toes.
6. Walk on the heels.
7. Stop and do five or more sit-ups; get up and resume walking as soon as everyone has finished.
8. Walk like a prancing horse, raising the lead knee as high as possible.
9. Stop and do five or more modified push ups (see B in the illustration); get up and resume walking as soon as everyone has finished.
10. Grasp ankles and continue walking.
11. Frog jump (squat down and spring forward).
12. Stop and do five or more "striders" (see "C" in the illustration); get up and resume walking as soon as everyone has finished.
13. Walk on the heel of one foot and the toe of the other foot; reverse.

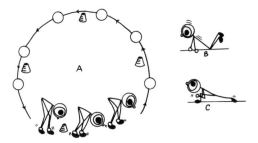

Encourage the children to think of more ways to travel around the circle.

"Leap the Brook"

Active

Noise Factor: Medium.

Equipment: You need 2 rubber-backed carpet squares.

Formation: Have the students form a circle. Put down the two carpet squares about 2′ apart in the beginning so that everyone can successfully leap from one square to the other. The carpet squares represent the banks of the brook and anyone who misses gets his or her feet "wet." After everyone has had a chance to leap the original distance, move the carpet squares about 2″ or 3″ farther apart and let them leap again. Do not make them sit down if they miss;  these are the children who need this practice the most. Encourage the students to really try hard, to stretch and reach with that lead leg. Continue to move the carpet squares a few inches apart after each complete rotation. This is fun and challenging, but do not overdo it. Stop while the children are still having fun.

"Shipwreck"

Active

Noise Factor: Will be noisy unless controlled.

Equipment: You need a tire or hula hoop for every two children in the class and a record player with appropriate music.

Formation: Have two children stand in each tire or hula hoop. The tires or hula hoops are randomly spread throughout the room. When the music begins, every child travels from tire to tire in all directions. Try not to bump or touch anyone else when traveling in this very close space. While the children are traveling, you should remove one or two tires at a time. When the music stops, everyone tries to get into a tire or hula hoop with the other children. Continue this same routine until the tires or hula hoops can hold no more children. Encourage the children to see how many of their classmates they can fit inside a tire without someone stepping or falling out.

"Newspaper"

Active-Passive

Noise Factor: Negligible.

Equipment: You need 28 or enough old *front* pages of newspapers for each child to have one. (You will have to plan in advance for this.)

Formation: Children stand in the aisle by their desks. Have them print their name in large letters on the bottom of their newspaper with a crayon.

Have them look over their newspaper carefully and circle any items of importance. For instance, the date, weather, headlines, or news stories may be of interest. Let them share any appropriate and interesting items from their paper with the class. *Caution them to be very careful and not tear their newspaper.*

Using both hands, hold the newspaper between the thumbs and forefingers. Move the paper to arm's length in front of the body, then raise the arms overhead. Lower slowly to arm's length in front of the body again, then bring the paper back to the body so that it is touching the chest. Can we do this together? Let's try. Front, up, front, back. Good. Again. . . . Continue doing this together.

This time, hold the newspaper at arm's length in front of the body. Can you let go of the paper and watch it hit the floor? How did it fall? Did it drop fast or slow, did it float down, did it go forward or backward? Do this several times and see if it does anything different each time.

Now, holding the paper in the same way, can you drop it and carefully catch it before it hits the floor? Remember, this is your own paper—try not to tear it when catching it. Try this several times.

Try doing the same routine while holding the paper overhead with the arms straight up. Did the paper fall differently from this new height? Was it easier to catch?

This time, while holding the paper in close to your body, stoop down; then rise and *bring the paper up over your head to a straight arm position as you come up.* The arms should be straight when your arms are straight. Let's do this together. Down, up, down, and so on. Continue five or six times.

Now, when you reach the *up* position, release the paper and watch it travel to the floor. Do this several times. Did it travel to the floor different ways each time? Can you catch it before it hits the floor?

How many of you have not torn your newspaper so far? Good!

We are going to make a long tube out of our paper, so roll one of the long edges of the paper in toward the other long edge. A good tube will be about ¾″ in diameter. When you have done this, you will be given a small piece of masking tape to hold the tube together.

Can you hold the *bottom* of the tube in one hand so that it is standing straight up? Now open your hand and let the tube slide through your hand. Can you close your hand and stop the tube near the top? The closer to the top, the better. Try this a few times with *each* hand.

Hold your arms straight out in front of you *with your palms down.* The tube should be horizontal and resting at about the elbows. Slowly lower both arms so that the tube will roll off the fingertips. Can you catch the tube before it hits the floor? Work on this.

Hold the tube in the same way as earlier, except this time, have the *palms up.* Lower the arms again slowly and let the tube roll off as you did before. Can you turn your hands and catch the tube palms down before it hits the floor? Work on this one a little bit.

Now hold the tube in your right hand, arm straight up over the right shoulder. Can you let the tube drop out of your hand straight down and reach across with the left hand and catch it? Practice this a few times and do the same thing with the left hand dropping the tube and the right hand reaching across to catch it.

Who can balance the tube on his or her right hand? How long? Can you also do it with your left hand?

Everyone take the tape off your tube and flatten the paper out. We are now going to fold the paper carefully into the smallest square that we can get it. Now place the square on the floor and place the *sole* of your foot on it and see if you can *carefully* spin all the way around on it. Can you do the same thing with the other foot? This time, place the *heel* of one foot on the square and try to spin all the way around. Can you do that same thing with the other foot? *Be careful—don't swing your arms around and hit your classmates!*

By using your feet only, can you work the square between your feet and jump the square into your hands? Good. Can you drop the square between your feet and do it again?

Unfold the square a couple of folds only, so that it will fit across the instep of one foot like a small tent. Can you hold that foot out in front of you and turn your body around in a circle with the other foot without bouncing the square off your foot? Hop smoothly. Good. Now try it with the other foot.

Now unfold all the paper. It will be quite wrinkled, but that is all right. Hold one corner of the paper in the right hand and stick that arm straight up in the air. With no help from the other hand, can you roll your paper into a ball while keeping the right hand straight up in the air? Good. Straighten the paper out and roll it up with the other hand while following the same procedure.

This time, leave the paper rolled up like a ball. Can you toss it in the air and catch it with both hands? Can you toss it up and catch it with one hand? Repeat and catch it with the other hand. How many times can you bat the ball into the air with one hand without dropping it? How about with the other hand?

Hold the ball over your head with one hand and drop it. Can you catch it before it hits the floor with the same hand? Do the same thing with the other hand.

Now, with the ball in one hand straight above the head, drop it and reach across the body with one hand and catch it. Can you do the same thing with the other hand?

Good. Now, look at your hands. That is printer's ink. Throw your paper ball into the wastebasket and wash your hands thoroughly before doing anything else!

"Find the Leader"

Active-Passive

Noise Factor: Medium.

Equipment: None.

Formation: The class stands in as large a circle as possible except for "It" who stands in the middle of the circle. One person is selected as "It" and leaves the room for a moment while a group leader is chosen. "It" then stands in the middle of the circle while the members of the circle go through constantly changing activities. The group leader changes the activities by action, not by words. "It" is constantly looking at everyone in the circle and tries to pick out the group leader. If "It" is successful, the group leader becomes the next "It," and the previous "It" takes a place in the circle. You may want to go to a time limit in some situations.

"Fox and Goose"

Active-Passive

Noise Factor: Medium.

Equipment: You need 2 different objects to pass around the circle (one is to be the "fox" and the other is the "goose," for example, a bean bag and a Nerf™ ball, or an eraser and a yarn ball).

Formation: The class is in as large a circle as possible. One of the objects (the goose) is passed person to person around the circle. When the goose is halfway around, start the next object (the fox). Keep both objects going around the circle. If one is dropped, have that person pick it up and quickly resume passing. If the fox catches the goose, the fox wins; if the goose catches the fox, the goose wins.

"Busy Bee"

Active-Passive

Noise Factor: Can be noisy unless controlled.

Equipment: None.

Formation: Partners are scattered around the room. Select one child as "It" who has no partner and stands among the partners. The partners will react to your commands of "Front to front" and "Back to back." But when you say "Busy Bee," *everyone*—including "It"—will change to a new partner. The new "It" will be the child who fails to find a new partner. Continue.

"The Poor House"

Active-Passive

Noise Factor: Can be noisy unless controlled.

Equipment: You need hula hoops or bicycle tires.

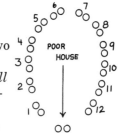

Formation: Assign partners, who will stand side by side, holding hands, in the bicycle tires that are arranged in horseshoe formation. Two bicycle tires are placed at the open end of the horseshoe. These tires represent the poor house. *Remember, the partners must hold hands at all times.* The partners are given a number. (See the illustration.) The partners in the poor house call out two numbers, and these partners try to change places before the poor house partners successfully get one of the vacated places. They now take over that number and the partners who were "beaten" become the new partners in the poor house. If the poor house partners call "House on fire," *all* partners must exchange places. (As you already know, you will have a hard time getting some of the boys and girls to hold hands!)

"Simon Says"

Active-Passive

Noise Factor: Negligible.

Equipment: None.

Formation: The students stand by their desks. This is an old favorite for sharpening listening and reaction skills. You should be the leader until the children show that they can be effective leaders themselves.

The leader gives a command that is to be executed by everyone only if it is introduced by "Simon Says." The rules state that anyone who executes a command that is not introduced by "Simon Says" must sit down, but it may be that you will want to think about this a minute. Usually the ones who "mess up" in the beginning are the ones who need this sort of challenge the most. How about giving a point each time to those who mess up? At the end of a specified time period, select those who have the fewest points as winners.

Classroom Dodge Ball

Active-Passive

Noise Factor: Can be loud unless controlled.

Equipment: You need 2 Nerf™ balls (or 2 sponge balls or 2 fleece balls or 2 yarn balls).

Formation: Divide the class into two teams: one team is on the outer edge of the classroom while the other team is scattered through the aisles and seats. The object of the game is to see how many players the team on the outer edge of the classroom can hit with a ball in a 1-minute period. At the end of 1 minute, both groups change places and repeat the procedure. The team with more hits wins.

A hit is scored from a fly ball only; a bounce does not count. You cannot hit two people with one thrown ball. If a ball hits any part of the body or clothing, it is called a hit. The players on the inside must quickly return any loose balls on the inside by a toss to the outside team. A player does not leave the game when he or she is hit. (It takes a special class to play this game without fussing!)

"Bicycle Race"

Active-Passive

Noise Factor: Medium.

Equipment: None.

Formation: Children in the inside rows that have desks on each side of them will stand. Children in the outside rows remain seated. Begin by having each child in the inside rows place one hand on her desk and the other hand on the desk across from hers. On the signal "Go," each child imitates riding a bicycle with her legs while supporting her weight with her hands. The winner is the child who can ride the longest without touching the floor with her feet. (They must keep peddling with their legs!) Select the winner from each row. Now, have the children in the outside rows change with an inside row and choose the winners from this group. You may want to play a passive activity at this point to give the winners a rest; then let the winners compete to find the class champion. IMPORTANT: Make sure the desks will not tip over with the child's weight on it!

"And the Boiler Burst"

Active-Passive

Noise Factor: Can be momentarily explosive.

Equipment: None.

Formation: Everyone is in his or her seat, except for the storyteller (one of the children). Vacant desks should have books on them to indicate that they are not being used. The storyteller stands in front of the room and begins a story that he has made up. At a dramatic moment in the story, he suddenly and loudly says, "And the boiler burst!" All the children at this moment must exchange seats, and the storyteller who, up to this point has no seat, tries to get one of the momentarily empty seats. If he is successful, the person who is left without a seat becomes the new storyteller.

"Alphabet Action"

Active-Passive

Noise Factor: Medium.

Equipment: None.

Formation: First, arrange the entire class in a circle; then assign each child a letter of the alphabet, except for the leader who is chosen from the class. The leader stands in the middle of the circle and calls out two letters of the alphabet. The children who have been assigned these letters quickly try to exchange places with each other. The leader then tries to get into one of their places before they get there. If the leader is successful in doing this, the person who is left out becomes the new leader and the activity continues.

"Kim's Games"

Passive

Noise Factor: Quiet.

Equipment: You need a collection of 15 to 20 small objects and a box or a towel.

Formation: Children are seated at their desks. This game is similar to that used by the U.S. Marines to sharpen powers of observation. Place 8 to 10 small objects (pencil, nickle, paper clip, bottle cap, acorn, leaf, key, etc.) under a box or a towel where the children cannot see them. Then lift the box or towel for a period of 10 seconds for the entire class to see. At the end of 10 seconds, cover the objects and ask for a volunteer to name all the objects. On the next round, you can remove some of the old objects and add new ones before playing again.

"Who's Disappeared?"

Passive

Noise Factor: Quiet.

Equipment: None.

Formation: Children are seated at their desks. This is a challenging passive activity that can be played after an active game to settle down the class. The game challenges the students' concentration and memory skills. One member of the class is "It." He is put into a corner with his face to the wall and he must keep his eyes closed. One or two other members of the class are told to step outside of the room while the rest of the students quietly change seats. Then "It" is told to turn around and try to discover who has disappeared. If he is able to identify the missing children, another "It" is chosen and the game continues.

FOUR-ITEM CLASSROOM FITNESS CIRCUIT

Noise Factor: Medium.

Equipment: You need 3 jump ropes.

Formation: See the illustration. Divide the classroom into four areas, and, if the room is large enough, place three or more couples in each area. One partner in each couple will be the "Counter" and the other partner will be the "Performer." The events are timed for 30 seconds. At the end of each time period, the couples swap jobs—the performer becomes the counter, and so on. When the couples have performed in their particular area, there is a rotation—group 1 will go to 2, 2 to 3, 3 to 4, and 4 to 1. This procedure is followed until everyone has been a counter and performer in each of the four areas.

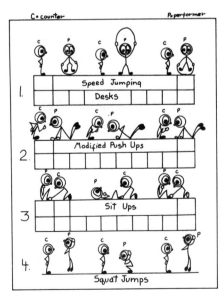

- Station 1, *Speed Jumping*—How many times can you jump in 30 seconds?
- Station 2, *Modified Push-ups*—Encourage the students to do regular push-ups if possible. If not, have them do modified push-ups (on their knees) with their backs straight. How many can you do in 30 seconds?
- Station 3, *Sit-ups*—Cross the arms across the chest. Curl up so that the elbows touch the legs; do not reach out with elbows. How many can you do in 30 seconds?
- Station 4, *Squat Jump*—With hands on head and fingers locked, drop to a ¾ squat (not a full squat). Then spring into the air and back down to ¾ squat. Continue. How many can you do in 30 seconds?

FITNESS CIRCUIT FOR A LARGE CLASSROOM

Noise Factor: Medium to loud.

Equipment: You need 8 hula hoops or bicycle tires, 28 bean bags (14 for shuttle run and 14 for bean bag toss), 2 short jump ropes, 6 chairs, and 2 reeds or broom handles.

Formation: This circuit is drawn up for 28 children, but can easily handle less. There are seven stations as shown in the illustration. Each person has a partner, with each taking turns being the performer and the counter. All the events go on at the same time for 30 seconds. Then the performer becomes the counter, and the counter becomes the performer. After both partners have performed at their station, they rotate to the next station. The same procedure follows until each person has participated in all seven activities.

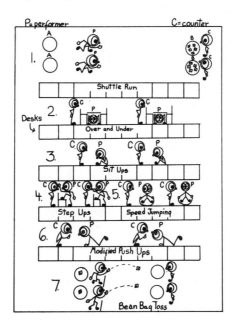

- Station 1, **Shuttle Run**—On the signal "Go," start from the inside of hula hoop A and run to hula hoop B. How many bean bags can you move from hula hoop B to hula hoop A in 30 seconds?
- Station 2, **Over and Under**—Have two chairs face each other with a reed going from one to the other as shown. On the signal "Go," how many times can you step over and crawl under the reed in 30 seconds?

♦ Station 3, *Sit-ups*—With arms crossed on chest and knees up as shown, how many sit-ups can you do in 30 seconds?

♦ Station 4, *Step-ups*—The performer stands in front of the chair as shown. To do one step-up, the performer steps on the chair with one foot, brings the other one up beside it, and steps down with the original foot followed by the other one. How many complete step-ups can you do in 30 seconds?

♦ Station 5, *Speed Jumping*—This is very simple. How many times can you jump in 30 seconds?

♦ Station 6, *Modified Push-ups*—These push-ups do not take as much strength as the regular push-up. They are done just like a regular push-up except that the knees—instead of the toes—are on the floor. Keep the back straight and touch the chest to the floor. How many correct modified push-ups can you do in 30 seconds?

♦ Station 7, *Bean Bag Toss*—How many bean bags can you toss into the hula hoop in 30 seconds? The bean bag must land *inside* the hoop.

CLASSROOM "SKILLS FITNESS" CIRCUIT

Noise Factor: Medium loud.

Equipment: You need 2 hula hoops, 2 playground balls, 6 carpet squares, 2 wastebaskets, 2 boxes of bean bags, 4 pylons, 2 reeds or broomsticks, 4 Nerf™ balls, and 2 target faces (6″ circles).

Formation: There will be four children at each station—two are performers and two are counters. The performers do the activity in their station for 30 seconds while the counters count. At the end of 30 seconds, they reverse roles and the performers become counters and the counters become performers. They have 15 seconds to rotate and get set to perform. After all four children have performed in their area, they will—on signal—move counterclockwise to the next station. They will also have 15 seconds to move to the next station and get ready to perform the new activity in this area. Continue this circuit until all the children have performed at each of the seven stations. This circuit takes approximately 12 minutes to complete.

♦ Station 1, ***Bean Bag Toss***—How many bean bags can you toss into the wastebasket in 30 seconds? (Throw one at a time!)

♦ Station 2, ***Sit-ups***—How many sit-ups can you do in 30 seconds?

♦ Station 3, ***Ball Dribble***—How many times can you bounce the playground ball in the hoop in 30 seconds?

♦ Station 4, ***Jump Stick***—How many times can you jump back and forth over the stick without knocking the stick over in 30 seconds?

♦ Station 5, ***Wall Bounce***—How many times can you bounce the Nerf™ ball off the wall and catch it in 30 seconds?

♦ Station 6, ***Target Ball***—How many times can you hit the target (black area) with the Nerf™ ball in 30 seconds?

♦ Station 7, ***Push-ups***—How many push-ups can you do correctly in 30 seconds? If you cannot do regular push-ups, how many modified push-ups (back straight, knees on floor) can you do in 30 seconds?

Rope Jumping ——————————— 22

This chapter will discuss both short rope jumping and long rope jumping.

SHORT ROPE JUMPING *

What a great activity! Not only is rope jumping's contribution to physical fitness well founded, it is also inexpensive and offers a strong activity that requires little space. When it is done to music, rope jumping is another great rhythm activity, too. The progression in rope jumping—from simple to complex—holds a challenge for all children. Rope jumping is big on the lifetime sports list, too, so we can begin it very early and continue it for most of our lives.

THE SHORT ROPE: There are many good jump ropes on the market today. Some have plastic sections, some are solid plastic, there are the ever-popular cotton ropes, and so on. Try a variety of these ropes before making your final decision to purchase a particular kind.

Some schools find it cheaper to buy the yellow plastic (not nylon), tight weave, ⅜″ diameter rope that is available from most hardware stores. The ends of the rope can be melted very simply with a candle so that they will not unravel.

Rope size for elementary schools has always been a problem. If you buy ropes to fit the shorter children, then the taller children will not be able to use them. But if you buy or cut your ropes in 9′ lengths, both the shorter and taller children can use them. The shorter children will have to be shown how to wrap the rope around their hands several times so that they can jump with them.

TERMS: The following terms are used with rope jumping:

1. *Rebound*—The rebound is the little hop or jump that is done in place as the rope passes overhead. The more experienced jumpers only bend their knees slightly and their feet will seldom leave the floor. The rebound is used only in *slow* time, and the purpose is to carry the rhythm between steps.
2. *Slow Time*—In slow time, the child jumps or hops over the rope, then rebounds as the rope goes overhead. Continue.
3. *Fast Time*—In fast time, you turn twice as fast as in slow time, take out the rebound, and jump or hop over the rope. Continue.

---

* Some of the terminology and steps have been excerpted in part from Paul Smith's pamphlet, "Rope Skipping Fundamentals" (Seattle: Washington Public Schools), with his permission.

PROGRESSIONS: Some of the following short rope activities will be very challenging for the children in the beginning, so it is usually a good idea to let them practice the footwork without the rope until they get the moves down pat. Then let them work on the moves with the rope.

As usual, some of the children will pick up the new skills faster than others, but be patient because once the slower learners finally pick up the new moves, they usually perform as well as the more skilled jumpers.

Short Rope Jumping Routines

Whenever possible, play appropriate "rope jumping" music when the children are practicing. It not only makes the activity more enjoyable, but also emphasizes the fact that rope jumping is an outstanding rhythm activity.

- ◆ **"Two Feet/Slow Time"**—Stand with your feet close together. Jump no higher than 3″ or 4″ when the rope passes under your feet. In slow time, the jump is followed by a rebound as the rope goes overhead. The rebound is simply a very small jump in place on both feet in order to carry out the rhythm between jumps.
- ◆ **"Alternate Feet/Slow Time"**—As the rope goes overhead, shift your weight to one foot and hold the other foot off the floor. Jump as the rope passes under the foot and rebound with the same foot as the rope goes overhead. Repeat the same procedure with the opposite foot.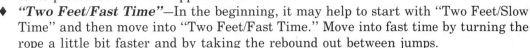
- ◆ **"Two Feet/Fast Time"**—In the beginning, it may help to start with "Two Feet/Slow Time" and then move into "Two Feet/Fast Time." Move into fast time by turning the rope a little bit faster and by taking the rebound out between jumps.
- ◆ **"Alternate Feet/Fast Time"**—Follow the same procedure as for "Two Feet/Fast Time." Move into "Alternate Feet/Fast Time" by turning the rope a little faster and by *taking out the rebound* between jumps. (This particular skill is usually the most difficult to teach. It will take concentration and practice for some of the children.)
- ◆ **"Forward Swing"**—This is almost the same as "Alternate Feet/Slow Time," except that you swing the forward foot gracefully out front each time.
- ◆ **"Side Swing"**—Swing the free leg out to the side each time with the knee straight while the opposite knee is rebounding. Alternate legs each time. (Keeping a knee straight takes a lot of practice.)
- ◆ **"Rocker Step"**—Keep the same leg forward (for instance, R) and the same leg back (for instance, L) when doing this routine. As the rope passes under the left foot, the weight is shifted from left to right with a rebound, while the rope is above the head. On the next turn of the rope, the weight is shifted from the forward foot (R) to the back foot (L), repeating the rebound on the back foot.
- ◆ **"Strider"**—Begin in the stride position as you did in the "Rocker Step." Have your weight equally distributed on both feet. As the rope passes under the feet, reverse foot position. Rebound each time and continue.
- ◆ **"Side Shuffle"**—Begin with both feet together. As the rope passes under the feet, push off with the right foot, side stepping to the left. Land with your weight on the left foot and touch the right toe beside the left foot. Repeat in the opposite direction as the rope passes under the feet again. Continue.

♦ **"Heel Toe"**—Begin with both feet together. As the rope passes under the feet, jump with your weight, landing on your right foot. At the same time, touch your left heel forward and rebound in the same position. On the next turn of the rope, jump and land on the left foot and touch your right toe beside your left heel. Rebound in this same position. Repeat, using the opposite foot.

♦ **"Heel Click"**—Learn how to do this without the rope at first. Warm up with some "Side Swings"; then try the following. Begin with the feet together. Follow the same procedure as in the "Side Swing" except that when the right foot swings sideways instead of rebounding when the rope is above your head, raise the left foot to click the heel of the right foot. Repeat this same routine on the left side.

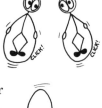

♦ **"Crossing Arms"**—When the rope is above the head and just beginning the down swing, bring the right arm over the left arm and the left under the right. Jump the rope with arms crossed. *Keep turning the rope.* Jumping can be continued in this sequence or the arms can be crossed or uncrossed on alternate turns of the rope.

LONG ROPE JUMPING

One of the big problems in long rope jumping is developing good reliable turners within the class. It is just as important that the children learn how to turn the rope as it is to learn the many long rope routines.

Many lower elementary grades have an aide to assist the teacher. In most classes, too, you may have at least two precocious children. You can use one of these children as a turner on your rope, and the aide can use the other child as a turner on another rope. This will get two ropes going with an instructor at each rope. You will probably be able to divide the groups again, with you and the aide taking two more children to train while the original two children turn a rope of their own. This will result in three long ropes in action with shorter waiting lines. *Make it a privilege to be a turner.*

As soon as possible, have every child who can turn the rope trained so that the class can rotate between turning and jumping. Ideally, you want to be free from turning duties so that you can move among the three groups to supervise, encourage, and teach.

There are other methods of teaching the children to turn the rope, so experiment and pick the method that suits you and your class the best. *Classes that have only one jump rope going have long waiting lines, which can result in boredom and discipline problems.*

THE LONG ROPE: The length of the long ropes can be the same for both the shorter and taller children. The lengths usually used are from 16' to 24'. Again, as in short ropes, there are many good ropes on the market. One that is readily available is the yellow plastic, ⅜" diameter tight-weave rope, as described in the short rope section of this chapter.

Long Rope Jumping Routines

♦ **"Front Door"** (running through)—First, the jumper should watch the rope as it turns to see which way it is turning and also to pick up the rhythm of the turning rope. The front door comes *down* in front of the jumper's face, hits the floor, and turns away and up again. So, when the rope swings downward, the jumper should be ready to *chase* it through as it hits the ground. Keep running through so that it will not catch up with the runner as it swings up behind him.

♦ *"Back Door"* (running through)—The back door will be just the opposite of the front door. The jumper will have the rope turning *up* in front of him. Again, he should keep his eyes on the rope as it is turning and pick up the rhythm as it turns. Be ready to start the run through as the rope passes *upward* by his face. This time as he is running through, he will meet the rope coming down and toward him when he is about halfway through so he will have to *leap over* the rope as he continues his run through.

♦ *Jumping* (slow time/fast time)—This time, the jumper will jump in either by the back door or the front door to the center of the rope and jump as the rope passes under her feet. If the rope is turning slow time, she will jump either two feet/slow or alternate feet/slow as she did in the short rope routine. If the rope is turning fast time (two times faster than slow time), the jumper can jump either two feet/fast or alternate feet/fast.

♦ *Combinations*—After a child has practiced the short rope and the long rope routines, she may want to take a short rope into the longer rope with her.

♦ *Combination Plus*—Follow the same procedure as listed for Combinations except include any other jumpers who may want to join in.

♦ *"Double Dutch"*—You may have some third-graders who can handle this spectacular and challenging routine if they have had good long rope instruction and participation beginning in kindergarten and continuing through the first and second grades.

The following are long rope skills needed for "Double Dutch":

a. Able to jump in the front door
b. Able to jump in the back door
c. Able to jump fast time, both two feet/fast, and alternate feet/fast

When a child is getting ready to "jump in" "Double Dutch," he should stand near the shoulder of either one of the turners and enter from that angle.
The following are suggested techniques for "jumping in" "Double Dutch":

a. While the two ropes are turning, ignore the front door rope and enter the back door rope.
b. After successfully jumping in, the jumper will have to jump fast time because there are two ropes turning.
c. The jumper's foot action should be alternate feet/fast time. Also remember to keep the elbows in close to the sides and to face one of the turners while jumping. (It may be easier for some of the children to jump two feet/fast time in the beginning before moving to alternate feet/fast time.)

♦ *"Egg Beater"*—This is another spectacular activity that is fun and challenging for both the turners and the jumpers. There are two ropes that will be turned across each other by four turners. Begin with both ropes on the ground with one on top of the other. Then both ropes turn at the same time with one rope being turned *clockwise,* and the other rope turning *counterclockwise.* Both ropes should rise and fall at the same time. Whether they jump in front door or back door depends on which of the four sides the child jumps in.

♦ ***"Egg Beater Combination"***—Follow the same procedure listed for "Egg Beater," except include any other jumpers who may want to join in with or without short ropes.

Long Rope Jumping Formations

Have two or more of these formations going on at the same time. The children can *run through* these formations or *jump in* and jump.

♦ ***"Front Door"***—The jumpers can run through, circle around the turners, and get back in line again.

♦ ***"Back Door"***—The jumpers can run through, circle around the turners, and get back in line again.

♦ ***Single Rope***—The jumpers can run through the front door, turn, and run back through the back door.

♦ ***Single Rope/Opposite Lines***—While one line is running through the front door, the other line is running through the back door.

♦ ***Two Ropes***—One rope is turning front door, and the other rope is turning back door. When everyone has gone through one way, they can turn and go through the other way.

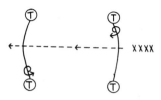

♦ ***"Double Dutch"***—Notice the angle of entry.

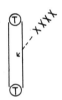

♦ ***"Egg Beater"***—In a single line, *run through* or *jump in,* and jump.

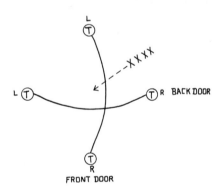

♦ ***"Two-Line Egg Beater"***—A runs through the first rope front door. B runs through the first rope back door and the second rope front door. Continue.

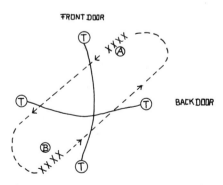

RHYMES FOR JUMPING ROPE

One, two, buckle my shoe;
Three, four, shut the door;
Five, six, pick up sticks;
Seven, eight, lay them straight;
Nine, ten, big fat hen;
Eleven, twelve, bake her well.
(Count 1, 2, 3 . . . .)

Come to my party,
Don't be late.
Eat all you want,
But don't eat the plate.

I wish I had a nickle,
I wish I had a dime.
I wish I had a lolly pop
To last me all the time.

Had a little radio,
Put it in free.
Only station I could get
Was W-B-Z.
(Hot pepper until jumper misses.)

Bubble gum, bubble gum,
Chew and blow.
Bubble gum, bubble gum,
Scrape your toe.
Bubble gum, bubble gum,
Tastes so sweet.
Get that bubble gum off your feet.
(Run out.)

Momma, momma, I am sick.
Call the doctor quick, quick, quick.
How many pills must I take?
(Count 1, 2, 3 . . . until jumper misses.)

Pretty Patty dressed in lace,
Went upstairs to powder her face.
How many boxes did she use?
1, 2, 3, 4, 5, 6, 7, 8, 9, 10.

Engine, engine, number nine,
Running on Chicago line.
See it sparkle, see it shine.
Engine, engine, number nine.

First the heel, then the toe;
A skip and a hop and over you go!

I asked my father for fifty cents
To see the elephant jump the fence.
He jumped so high he reached the sky,
And didn't get back until the Fourth of July.

Cinderella dressed in yellow
Went upstairs to kiss her fellow.
How many kisses did she get?
(Count 1, 2, 3 . . . until jumper misses.)

Cinderella dressed in green
Went upstairs to get ice cream.
How many spoonfuls did she eat?
(Count 1, 2, 3 . . . until jumper misses.)

Cinderella dressed in black
Went upstairs and sat on a tack.
How many stitches did she need?
(Count 1, 2, 3 . . . until jumper misses.)

Cinderella dressed in red
Went downstairs to bake some bread.
How many loaves did she bake?
(Count 1, 2, 3 . . . until jumper misses.)

When I move out,
Let Cindy move in.
When Cindy moves out,
Let Sally move in.
When Sally moves out,
Let Joe move in.
When Joe moves out,
Let Tad move in.
(etc.)

Johnny on the ocean,
Johnny on the sea,
Johnny broke a tea kettle
And blamed it on me.
I told Ma,
Ma told Pa,
Johnny got a licking
With a ha, ha, ha!

Mable, Mable,
Set the table,
And don't forget
The red hot pepper!
(Hot pepper until jumper misses.)

Rhythms —————————— 23

The following rhythms are described in simple-to-understand terms so that you will be able to present the activities easily to the children. The children will succeed and enjoy your efforts!

DAYBREAK

This first rhythm is easy to do and can be adapted to your particular situation if necessary. It was actually invented by children.

The original music used was the song "Daybreak" on the Barry Manilow album *Live* (Arista Label #8500). Let's begin with the way it was originally performed and then suggest some alternatives. Talk with the children about the shape of a square. Draw some on the chalkboard and put some large ones on the floor if you have enough room. Now, standing at the lower left-hand corner, begin the rhythm. If there is room, draw many squares on the floor and have the children divided up with a few at each square.

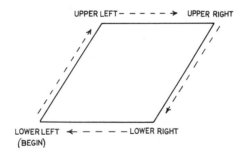

Walk forward three steps and stop on the fourth count at the upper left corner. For the next four counts, raise the arms sideward until both arms are above your heads. (This is part of the "daybreak" idea.)

Then go sideward to the right for four counts; side, close, side, close. You should be at the upper right corner now. Touch one toe two times behind the other foot and two times in front of the other foot.

Then go back for three steps and stop on the fourth count. Now you should be at the lower right corner.

Use the next four counts to touch one foot behind the other, to the side of the other, and

199

then to the front of the other. On the fourth count, put the feet together.

Now go to the left for four counts: slide, close, slide, close. You should be at the lower left corner, which is where you began.

At this point, use three counts to squat and jump straight up on the fourth count. This, again, emphasizes the "daybreak" theme.

As you can tell, you have completed a square. It is just a matter of continuing the square pattern until the children become tired.

Do not make too much fuss over the shape of a square for the younger children. Any four-count music will do. The children will gladly bring their favorites. If you find the majority having difficulty, some record players will permit you to slow the tempo which will allow more children to succeed. Other suggestions include walking instead of the side-close-side-close sequence.

CROSSOVER

If the music is right, this can be a very vigorous rhythm! Divide the class into four small groups. You will need the four corners of a large square. Give each group a number from 1 through 4, and assign each group a corner in consecutive order. (You should be able to stand in the center of the square and count clockwise each group in a corner, starting with 1, then 2 to your right, 3 to your right again, and then to 4.)

Group 1 will always begin first. After a few times, you can renumber the groups so others will have a chance to be first. Or you may prefer to wait until another day and then have another group be first.

Before the music begins, select two or three students in group 1 to be ready to lead their group. If you are so inclined, you may take the lead for 1 a few times. After a few leaders are selected from group 1, begin the music. Each group always travels in the same direction—straight across to the opposite corner. Therefore, groups 1 and 3 will reverse places, and groups 2 and 4 will reverse places.

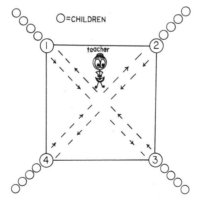

As soon as group 1 is out of the way, group 2 begins. Then group 3 begins as soon as group 2 is out of the way.

One leader in group 1 leads her group across the area doing a physical skill. This can be any acceptable skill everyone in the class can perform. Some suggestions you may want to include are the eight basic locomotor skills: walking, running, hopping, jumping, skipping, galloping, sliding, and leaping. Variations may be made, such as turning while doing a basic locomotor movement. The children may add going backward, or doing everything very high or very low.

After each group has crossed the area to their temporary corner, either the same leader from group 1 or a different leader again initiates another physical skill as she goes across the floor back to the original corner. After all of the groups have returned to their original corner, group 1 (with either the same or a new leader) begins another skill and the pattern is repeated.

As you can see, the music selection will influence how vigorous the activity becomes and what skills are selected. Floor-level skills or crawling on the front or on the back are good for the younger children.

BASKETBALL

You will want to use some current music for this one, something with the four-count easy-to-find rhythm. The children may be in a mass formation, columns and rows, large or small circles, or squads. (If the children enjoy basketball, you may want to tell them about how this rhythm helps basketball players.)

The skills are simple: run forward for eight counts, run backward for eight counts, run to the right for eight counts, run to the left for eight counts, and pivot to the right a quarter turn for the next four counts. Everyone will then be facing the same wall, which should be a quarter turn to the right from the wall the children were originally facing.

You may want to do this a few times using the right pivot and then introduce pivoting to the left and do a few in that direction. As the children improve, or if you feel they are ready, you may try doing four (or any other number of your choice) pivots to the right and then four to the left and continue alternating every four times.

This is a simple fun rhythm, but the pivot is sometimes a neglected skill in many physical education classes. Always precede the pivots with the four running sequences.

SLAP, CLAP, SLAP, JUMP

You need a lively four-count rhythm for this one. The children can be in a mass formation, rows and columns, squads, or one large or many small circles. There are four parts (four skills): slap knees, clap hands, slap knees, and—on the fourth count—jump vertically. That's all there is to it!

If you want variety, you might try a half turn during the jump or a full turn during the jump. Additional variations might include a hop, a leap, touching the floor before jumping, or touching the floor after jumping while still trying to stay with the music.

"SALUTE THE CAPTAIN"

This rhythm can be vigorous depending upon the chosen music. Select any theme and adapt the movements. The "Captain" in this example is a Navy captain. You could use an Army captain, a Navy admiral, or whatever else you and the children choose. It would help to read and study about the chosen theme. Many groups choose a circus theme or an athletic event. Before adding music, it is a good idea to present various physical movements and have everyone practice.

The following are some ideas you may use with the "Salute the Captain" idea:

Run in place.
Pull up the anchor.
Raise the flag.
Hit the deck. (fall on stomach)
Salute the Captain.

Fire the cannon.
Scrub the floor.
Row the ship. (sit on floor)
Wash the dishes.

Each child will do the skills alone as you (or a selected leader after some practice) calls out the skill to be done. You (or leader) call out another skill after the music has allowed the group to perform the current skill. A great amount of variety is important. As you can tell from the list above, the participants will be reaching up, falling down, pulling with their arms, and generally using their entire body. You and/or the children should certainly try to add to this list. The biggest problem is trying to do too much in a short amount of time. This is also a good warm-up before going on to something else.

"MOUSE TRAP"

Select music of your (or the children's) choice. Everyone forms a circle (or you may want to use a few smaller circles). Select two children to form a bridge at some place in the circle. Everyone else in the circle travels clockwise (or counterclockwise) around the circle. Every time anyone arrives at the human bridge, they must go through the bridge (under the upheld arms of the two children forming the bridge). The bridge people try to catch anyone in the bridge. The *only* time a child may be caught is when the music *stops*. Someone must stay with the music and stop the music at random. Each time someone is caught, he stands in the center of the circle until someone else is caught. Everytime there are two people in the center, they form another bridge somewhere else in the circle. It is not necessary—and not a good idea—to continue until a last person is caught. By stopping early, everyone wins and there is less pressure to win.

"FOLLOW THE LEADER"

The formation may be one large circle or several small circles. It also works well using a scattered mass in the room. Select someone to be the first leader, who invents a skill to go with the music. After everyone has had an opportunity to participate, the leader invents another skill. Each leader may invent four skills and then choose someone else to take her place. Usually, no one is allowed another turn as leader until everyone has had a first turn.

If you use several small groups or circles, each group could operate independently of the others, or all groups do whatever the chosen leader presents. Another variation is to form several lines and travel about the room doing skills the leader has selected. Another variation is to allow the children to have a partner and they work together doing the selected skills.

"SUNSHINE ON MY SHOULDERS"

The best song for this rhythm is "Sunshine on My Shoulders" by John Denver. However, you may use any song that distinctly separates the musical portions from the vocal. During the vocal portions, the children move about the room thinking and getting ready for the musical portions. During the musical parts, everyone must freeze in a shape of their choice. They must stay frozen during all of the instrumental. Then they again move about the room during the vocal, getting ready to freeze into another shape of their choice during the musical. This theme also works well with partners or small groups (from three to five children).

Once in a while, allow each group to present to the other groups one of their formations.

You should encourage cooperation, use various levels (floor, medium, high), and use as much space as possible and still work as a group.

"BIRDIE SONG"

This rhythm requires "Birdie Song," a record that can be obtained from Elmer Sheffield, Jr., 3765 Lakeview Drive, Tallahassee, Florida 32304. One side of the 45 rpm record includes directions along with the music. The other side is instrumental only. The jacket also includes the directions, so it becomes very easy to present. This is a simple, fun activity that every age may enjoy.

The first skill is to use your hands to imitate a bird saying "Cheep, cheep, cheep." Then put your arms in a flapping position and flap your "wings" three times. Then wiggle (bend knees) three times, and then clap your hands three times.

The music changes and you may select various ideas during this time. One suggestion is to allow the children to roam around the room until the music tells them to begin the three "cheeps" again. Or they may find a partner and join elbows and circle each other. The record jacket suggests making a right-hand star for eight steps, reverse with a left-hand star, and repeat with the right and then the left again. You and/or the children may certainly use other ideas, too, if desired.

"TENNESSEE WIG-WALK"

This next one was originally made up by Ambrose Brazelton, a retired P.E. teacher from Columbus, Ohio, to accompany the song "Tennessee Wig-Walk." However, you may use any four-count song you or the children choose. Everyone can either be seated or standing, and the rhythm works very well in the classroom with students at their chairs or desks.

Clap hands two times, slap knees two times, place one hand above the other, and move them each in a circular motion one above the other for two counts. Then put the bottom hand above the top hand and repeat the circular motion for two counts. Hold one hand open, make a fist with the other hand, and hit the open hand with the fist hand two times. Then reverse the hands and hit for two counts. Touch one elbow with the other hand two times and touch the other elbow with the other hand two times. Repeat the entire sequence as long as desired.

"PLAYGROUND IN MY MIND"

This one was also invented by Ambrose Brazelton and originally done to the song "Playground in My Mind." It will also work with most four-count rhythms. The children may be sitting or standing.

Raise one arm and make four large circles with the arm (the same motion used to lasso a horse), then repeat the motion with the other arm. Use one arm to hitchhike (four times) and repeat with the other arm. Use one hand to wave to all the cars as they pass by. Then use the other hand to wave to the passing cars. Use two counts to show the victory sign over one shoulder and then repeat the victory sign over the other shoulder. The victory sign may be two fingers pointing up while the hand goes up. The last part takes four counts to do one time. Catch a ball with one hand, put the ball in the other hand, throw the ball into the air, and kick the ball on the fourth count. Repeat the entire sequence as many times as desired.

"OVERHEAD PROJECTOR"

This may not be a good title, but it does tell you what equipment is needed! Your overhead projector can be put on the floor or on a cart at least 10′ to 15′ from a plain wall. Sometimes it is necessary to cover the electrical cord if the children must go over the cord to participate. The projected light should be large enough to provide a shadow on the wall for one, two, four, or eight children, depending upon your situation and ability level.

Select lively music and have the children form a large single circle so that part of the circle goes between the projector and the plain wall. An easy way to help the children form a circle is to use masking tape on the floor to provide some guide marks in the shape of a circle. After making the circle, draw a beginning line and an ending line at least 10′ to 15′ before entering the lighted wall area and about 10′ to 15′ after leaving the lighted wall area. This space will be for people in front of the overhead projector and no one else.

Now that you have established boundaries, begin the lively music and allow each child to perform in front of the overhead projector. They should perform a physical motion of their choice and leave the area when you tell the next child to begin. The children remain in their circle and, as time permits, take a second or third turn. If you select different types of music on different days, the children will enjoy making up movements and receive quite a bit of physical activity. You may have the children form groups of two and, using the same idea, let each group make up and perform its activity. Another day, you might have the children divide up into groups of three, four, five, or whatever other number and perform their activity.

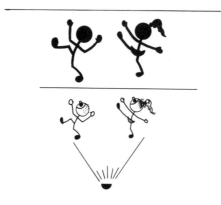

SOUNDS

Most people will try to have three sounds when they first do this rhythm. Find something that will give a *long* sound, something that will give a *short* sound, and something that will give a sound between the long and short sounds. Examples include a whistle for a long sound, bolts in a can for the short sound, and a tamborine for the middle sound. More ideas include clapping two boards together, a horn, bells, and drums.

Take one sound and introduce it to the children. If you choose the long sound first, emphasize the length and have the children make up a physical skill to represent the long sound.

Their long sound skill (movement) should last during the entire sound.

Next, introduce the short sound. Allow time for the children to invent their short sound movement. After everyone has had time to invent and practice their long and short sound movements, introduce the middle-length sound. It is certainly acceptable for the children to help each other invent movements and for many to use the same movements.

While this idea is new to the children, you may want to manipulate all three sounds. The main idea is to present the sounds one at a time but not in the same sequence over and over. After the children have had a few opportunities to participate (every so often throughout the term), you might select three children and ask them to each be responsible for one sound. Allow them to practice presenting their sound and then proceed as before with the three children presenting their sound using different patterns. From then on, select different children to make the sounds and, as things improve, you may want to add a fourth sound. By the time everyone has had a turn using a sound, you will have thought about other devices for different sounds and the process continues.

NUMBERS

This is a fun activity while reviewing numbers and learning various body parts. Form one large circle or several small circles. Practice walking around the circle clockwise or counterclockwise (reverse directions from day to day). Select lively music and begin walking around the circle. When the music stops, call a number. Everyone places as many body parts on the floor as the number called indicates. This may be repeated as many times as desired, changing the number called each time. After some practice, other locomotor movements may be used besides walking (running, skipping, hopping, jumping, sliding, galloping, leaping).

As the children become more comfortable with the activity, you may want to have the children select partners and continue the same pattern. When the children are ready, try numbers up to 24, especially after the children can handle 10 or 12 individually. If you notice a few children using just their fingers, go back to smaller numbers.

LUMMI STICKS

This is a manipulative rhythm. For the younger children, use paper lummi sticks instead of the wood dowel type. Making the lummi sticks and using them are all part of the fun. Roll four complete sheets of newspaper for one lummi stick. Each child needs two sticks to participate. The sticks should be glued, taped, or otherwise fastened so the paper does not unroll during use. It is fun to paint, color, and decorate the sticks to add something to the newspaper's usual black and white.

Some teachers like to have the children in one large circle, others like a few smaller circles, and still others have the children sit and face a partner. The description here will have the children sit and face a partner. Some basic movements are holding one stick in each hand and tapping one end of the sticks on the floor. The command for tapping on the floor is "Down." After a few minutes of the "Down" hit, play any four-count music and practice the "Down" tap and the "Together" position (gently touching the two sticks together). The first sequence is to alternate (keeping time with the music) "Down, together, down, together," and so on. After some success with the "Down, together, down, together" pattern, add the "right hit" skill. This means each child uses the lummi stick in her right hand and gently touches the corresponding stick (hand) of the partner. The right hands (holding a stick) cross over and touch sticks.

The students can now do a real lummi stick routine. Begin the music and have the children start when you say "Down." The four-part sequence should be called out by you: "Down, together, right hit, together." Continue with "Down, together, right hit, together" as long as desired. You have probably guessed something about the next sequence: it is "Down, together, left hit, together." Practice the two patterns with different music and watch everyone smile! This next sequence is a combination of the first two: "Down, together, hit right, hit left." All three patterns use four-count music and may be repeated over and over.

Written one line at a time, the three patterns look like this:

Down, together, right hit, together.
Down, together, left hit, together.
Down, together, right hit, left hit.

Other patterns include "Down, together, touch right, together." "Touch right" means touch both sticks to the floor on the right side of the legs. As you can guess, the next sequence is "Down, together, touch left, together." (At this point, you might want to have your students perform at a parent-teacher meeting.)

You may now want to add another pattern: "Down, together, touch right shoulder, together." The "Touch right shoulder" command means use the right-handed stick and touch the right shoulder. Follow with "Down, together, touch left shoulder, together." Put the last two together and you have "Down, together, touch right, touch left." Put everything together and you have

Down, together, right hit, together.
Down, together, left hit, together.
Down, together, right hit, left hit.
Down, together, touch right, together.
Down, together, touch left, together.
Down, together, touch right shoulder, together.
Down, together, touch left shoulder, together.
Down, together, touch right, touch left.

Another pattern is "Down, together, touch shoulders, together." "Touch shoulders" means touch the right shoulder with the right stick and touch the left shoulder with the left stick. (By now, you are ready for your second parent-teacher meeting!)

A few more patterns are

Down, together, raise, together ("Raise" means just that—raise both sticks overhead)
Down, together, cross, together ("Cross" means cross the sticks in front of the body)
Down, together, side touch, together ("Side touch" means touch the sticks to the floor on their respective sides of the body)

Let your students think of other lummi stick movements and incorporate these into the performances.

"PUNCHENELLA"

Form one circle and practice this rhyme a few times:

What can you do, Punchenella, little fella?
What can you do, Punchenella, little dear?
We can do it, too, Punchenella, little fella!
We can do it, too, Punchenella, little dear!
Who is coming next, Punchenella, little fella?
Who is coming next, Punchenella, little dear?

When you feel most of the class is ready, select one child to stand in the center of the circle. Everyone begins the rhyme. While the first two lines are sung, the child in the center begins a physical movement (you might help the first few children think of something physical). While the third and fourth lines are sung, everyone—including the child in the center—does the physical motion. During the last two lines, the child in the center selects someone else to take her place. The new child should be ready to begin another physical motion by the time the first word of the first line is sung.

"RIDDLE, RIDDLE, RIDDLE, REE"

The children may either sit or stand in a circle. Ask one child to be in the center of the circle. The rhyme is

Riddle, riddle, riddle, ree,
Do what I do after me.

During the rhyme, the child in the center does a physical motion. After the rhyme, everyone does the same motion. Then the child selects someone else to take his place in the center. A good four-count record/tape is needed to keep the rhyme going. The music can play continuously, and you may want to decide how long each motion should last after the rhyme. You might also try using several small groups instead of one large group; this will allow more children the opportunity to be in the center.

"SHOW US WHAT YOU FOUND"

Form a large circle and have one child in the center. While everyone sings the following rhyme, the child in the center does a physical movement:

Put a movement to a sound,
Show us what you found.

Using a four-count record/tape for this rhythm, everyone does the motion. After a short time, the child in the center selects someone else to take her place and the rhyme begins again. Allow the record/tape to keep playing.

"IN A CABIN IN THE WOODS"

Everyone sits and faces the leader/teacher. The ditty, "In a Cabin in the Woods," is about a man and a rabbit and how the man saves the rabbit from a hunter. Here are the words and corresponding movements. The pace of the song is determined by each line:

In a cabin in the woods (*everyone uses one hand to draw a square/rectangle cabin in the air*)
Little man by the window stood (*use one hand to shade the eyes while looking out a window*)
Saw a rabbit hopping by (*use victory sign—two fingers—to show the rabbit hopping by*)
Knocking at his door. (*knock with fist*)
Help me, help me, help me, the rabbit cried (*throw hands up in air with each "help me"*)
Or the hunter will shoot me dead! (*point as if holding a rifle*)
Little rabbit come inside (*motion the rabbit to come inside*)
Safely to abide. (*stroke forearm*)

"ITSY BITSY SPIDER"

This is also a pleasant, easy-to-learn ditty. The idea of the rhyme is to never give up—just as the spider never gave up.

Have the children practice making the spider move up and down the water spout—use both hands and touch the thumb of one hand to the forefinger of the other hand. As the spider goes up the water spout, the forefinger and thumb alternately touch. Any motion will do to illustrate the rain water and spider washing down the spout. Show the sun by raising both arms and swinging them from side to side. Again, show the spider going back up the water spout.

The words are:

Itsy bitsy spider went up the
    water spout.
Down came the rain and washed
    the spider out.
Out came the sun and dried up
    all the rain,
And the itsy bitsy spider went
    up the spout again.

"I'M JUST A CLOWN"

"I'm Just a Clown" will work better if you use the Statler record 229B with the movements. However, many teachers have the entire class sing with the movements and do not use the record. All movements (the hands, feet, tightrope, parasol, nose, etc.) are imitations. Let the children be creative in their movements.

The verse follows:

I'm just a clown who dances up and down. I make the people laugh when the circus comes
    to town.
I get into mischief, sometimes it's true. It makes me want to cry, I feel so blue.
My hopes are high and I aim to please; like the daring man on the flying trapeze.
The tightrope walker, he sure is great. I think he's the one I will imitate.
See the grease paint on my face, and my big red nose.

See my two hands, they're not so small, but neither are my toes.
So I'll walk across that rope with my little parasol; I hope these feet won't make me fall.
Whoops, I did it, I bounced right down. But what can you expect, I'm just a clown!

"PUNCH AND JUMP"

"Punch and Jump" uses a song from side one of the *Fun Dances for Children* album. Everyone begins in a standing position. The following motions were invented by a group of children:

Punch right fist forward.
Punch left fist forward and over right.
Jump to the left.
Bend elbows and knees in right angles.
Twirl arms (at the elbow) two counts.
Return arms and legs to right angle positions.
Jump to the right.

The entire sequence requires eight counts. It is a good idea to begin with a slow eight-count song.

"CHICKEN SCRATCH"

This rhythm can be adapted to various songs depending upon the ability of your children. You need an eight-count song with distinct sounds. (We've used the 45 rpm speed song "Little Black Book" by Jimmy Dean.)

With the right hand held head high, make a pecking motion to peck down to the floor to an 8-count song. Then use the left hand head high and peck down to the floor. Now use both hands head high and peck down to the floor. Raise the heels of both feet, place thumbs in armpits, and "scratch" with feet four times (this equals 8 counts). Walk 4 counts in a small circle to the right and then walk 4 counts in a small circle to the left. For the last 16 counts, everyone does his or her own thing and prepares to begin with the right hand doing the pecks from the head down to the floor.

"CALIFORNIA STRUT"

Adapted for children, this is a simple routine and will use any eight-count song. Begin with a slow song and then change the song as the children improve:

Walk forward four counts.
Walk backward four counts.
Use the next four counts to turn a circle to the right.
Use the next four counts to turn a circle to the left.
Repeat as often as desired.

"TUXEDO JUNCTION"

"Tuxedo Junction" is best if you have a tape or record of the song "Tuxedo Junction." You should sit facing the group. Sing the words and make the motions with your fingers. The children follow your lead:

Show me one.
  Say, this is fun!
Show me two.
  That's what you do.
Show me three.
  Well, yes sir-ee!
Come on, let's count some more.

Show me four.
  Just four, no more.
Show me five.
  Well, sakes alive!
Show me six,
  And none of your tricks!
Come on, let's count some more.

Show me seven.
  This game is heaven.
Show me eight.
  Now don't be late!
Show me nine.
  You're doing fine.
Show me ten.
  Let's play again!

Repeat the activity, and this time mix up the actions to be sure the children are listening and really know their numbers.

"STAYIN' ALIVE"

This rhythm is vigorous. (The "Stayin' Alive" song is by the Bee Gees.) You may prefer doing part of the routine during one session and another part the next day. Eventually, the children will be able to do the entire routine if small portions are added over a period of several weeks. You might want to begin the movements after the musical introduction.

Jump forward for 2 counts, then backward for 2 counts. Then jump to the right side for 2 counts, and then to the left for 2 counts. Do 8 straddle jumps for 16 counts (2 counts for each straddle jump.) Place hands on the floor and extend one leg back. For 16 counts, alternate extending the legs back and forward. Immediately stand and reach (stretch) both hands forward and back to the chest for 8 counts. Then stretch both hands to the right and back to the chest for 8 counts. Then stretch both hands to the left and back to the chest for 8 counts. Then stretch both hands overhead and back to the chest for 8 counts.

Repeat the entire routine depending upon the children's ability.

Games —————————————— 24

As mentioned in Chapter 2, games are not scheduled during the year as major activities themselves but as supplements to other scheduled activities. This does not imply that games have a minor contribution to make to your program; on the contrary, children should be provided opportunities to pursue wholesome activities in group, team, and mass situations. This age group needs the experience of working together, helping others to succeed, and learning to appreciate the efforts of others. Games have a significant part to play in the physical education programs for elementary and secondary children.

There are many outstanding games books full of exciting activities available on the market today. Therefore, the purpose of this chapter is to help you in your selection of *active* or *passive* games from other sources when they are not labeled as such and to help you use games when needed to present a varied and active program to your children.

IMPORTANT: Make sure all shoes are tied before the children start playing any of these games!

"SQUIRRELS IN THE TREES"

Active-Passive

Equipment: None.

Formation: This is a great favorite! Have the children form a large circle, and then have them count off by three's. The 1's and 2's becomes the trees: they turn, face each other, and hold hands. The 3's are the squirrels: they step inside the trees. There will be a 1 and possibly a 2 who do not have a 3 for the squirrel, so these students become squirrels and stand in the center of the circle.

On the signal "Change," all the squirrels must change trees; they cannot go back to their old tree. In the meantime, the squirrels in the center try to get into a tree while everyone is changing. This means that there will be one or two squirrels each time who do not have a tree.

Stress on the signal "Change" that the trees raise their branches high (lift their arms) so that the squirrels can get in and out easily. Also stress, especially with the kindergarten children, that on the signal "Change," the trees do not run! Some will do it anyway in the beginning.

Swap the trees and the squirrels periodically so that everyone gets a chance to play both positions.

"RUN FOR YOUR SUPPER"

Passive

Equipment: You need 4 cones or gallon milk jugs.

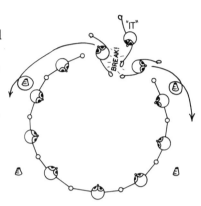

Formation: Have the class form a large circle and hold hands as shown in the illustration. Four cones are placed around the circle. One person is "It" and walks around the outside of the circle . "It" selects two joined hands and breaks them apart with his hand. Both the people in the circle whose hands were slapped quickly pull out of the circle and run around it in opposite directions. The person on the left will run to the left, and the person on the right will run to the right. The children *must circle each cone* as they run around the circle. If the other person is circling one cone when the other child gets there, she must wait until he finishes circling before circling it herself.

As soon as the two players leave the circle, "It" immediately steps into one of the vacant places. This leaves only one empty space now, so the two runners are racing around the circle to see who can get there first and get the empty space. The person who does not get the last empty space becomes the new "It."

"CATCH THE CABOOSE"

Active

Equipment: You need 14 strips of 1½" × 3" cloth (or 14 old stockings).

Formation: This is a vigorous game and should not be played too long at one time. Have the children get into groups of three. If you have one or two extra children, they may each join separate groups so that one or two groups will have four children. Each group needs a piece of cloth. Have the children stand one behind the other in their groups. Except for the child in front, the other two grasp the hips of the one in front. The back child in each group tucks the hose into his back waist with most of the cloth still showing. You must have boundaries, but do *not* use walls as boundaries.

On your signal, all groups try to steal the cloth from as many other groups as possible. The team losing its cloth may go to a box and obtain another cloth and rejoin the game. Each group may want to hold the ones they steal or put them in one spot each time they obtain another cloth.

You will find the team being chased going out of bounds. One suggestion is to give their cloth to the team that caused them to go out of bounds. Another suggestion is to warn the offending team a few times and then give their cloth to the chasing team. The idea is participation and (except for safety) not worry too much about going out of bounds. After a short time, stop the activity for a rest and then begin again. Don't bother with determining a winner; it is better to go to another activity and minimize winning, therefore minimizing losing.

Variation 1: A variation of "Catch the Caboose" is to have everyone face a partner. Each person has a hose tucked in his belt at the back. On the signal "Go" (or when the music begins), the two children facing each other try to pull out the other person's cloth. Do not allow too much time during one session. On your command "Stop" (or when the music stops), have everyone find a new partner and repeat the activity.

Variation 2: Another variation of "Catch the Caboose" is for everyone to have a cloth tucked in his belt at the back. On the signal "Go" (or when the music begins), everyone tries to pull as many cloth lengths as they can. When someone loses his cloth, he may run to a box, replace the cloth, and continue the activity. Again, when you signal "Stop" (or when the music stops), the activity is over for the moment.

"NUMBERS CHANGE"

Active-Passive

Equipment: You need 1 playground ball and 20 bicycle tires (or hula hoops).

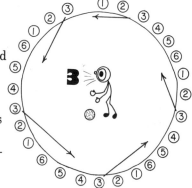

Formation: Have the class form a large circle so that when they hold their arms straight out, only their fingertips touch. Then have them drop their hands, take one giant step backward, face the center of the circle, and stand still until you give a bicycle tire or hula hoop to each person in the circle. Have the children put the tires on the ground and stand in them. Going around the circle to the left, have everyone count off by six. Now put one person as "It" in the center of the circle, with a playground ball at his feet. "It" calls any number between 1 and 6. For example, suppose "It" calls "3." All 3's must immediately change places by running inside the circle. If "It" can hit one of these 3's *below the waist* with the ball, he takes that player's place and the person hit becomes the new "It." *Stress to "It" that he cannot pick up the ball until after he has called out a number.*

"WHISTLE MIXER"

Active

Equipment: None.

Formation: This activity is better using a whistle, but calling out numbers will do if you do not like to use a whistle or do not have one. Everyone assembles in the middle of the area. Explain to the children that you will blow a whistle a certain number of times. They are to form groups after listening to the number of times you blow the whistle. Thus, if you blow 3 times, they should form into groups of 3; if you blow 11 times, they form groups of 11.

As the groups are formed, you should count each group. Usually, there are one or more children unable to be in a group depending upon the number of times you blow the whistle. Have these children stand with you until all groups have been counted. The children not in a group are then asked to do a simple short activity together, such as sing a short verse, do a short dance, or spell the same word. Make sure these children succeed and that they do not take too long. Then blow the whistle again and repeat the process. (If you do not use a whistle, you may call out a number such as "four" and the children form groups of four. The same process of having the extra children perform for a brief moment is still part of the activity.)

As you can tell, blowing a whistle requires everyone to listen as compared to calling out a number. You may want to try both ideas. The fewer number of children in the group, the smaller the numbers you will be able to use. If you have 25 children in the group, your largest number may be 10. However, if you have 80 children in a group, you could use numbers as high as 25. Blowing a whistle 25 times might also be fun.

Variation 1: For very young children, you may want to actually count each number out loud until you reach the number of your choice. An example would be to count to nine, but call out each number until you reach nine: "One, two, three, four, five, six, seven, eight, nine."

Variation 2: Tell the children how they must travel about the room as they form their groups. For example, say that everyone must skip about as they form their groups. The next time they must hop about as they form their groups.

"CIRCLE PASS"

Active-Passive

Equipment: You need 3 or 4 different kinds of balls (or objects, such as bean bags and erasers).

Formation: Divide the class into two even teams and put them into two circles as shown. Select a leader in each team and give her a ball or an object. On the signal "Go," the leaders start the balls or objects around their circles, going around their circles person to person in one direction. At any time, you can insert other balls or objects into each circle so that there can be three or four balls and objects going around the circles at the same time in the same direction. Whenever a child drops a ball or an object, he must retrieve it, return to his spot in the circle, and continue. A point will be scored against his team each time this happens. After a period of time, the signal is given to "Stop." After totaling the number of points against each team, a winner is declared.

"TWO DEEP"

Active-Passive

Equipment: None.

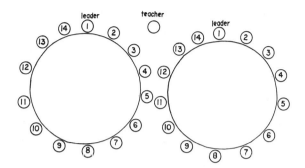

Formation: Have the class—except for two players who are a chaser and a runner—form a large circle with arms straight out and a fingertip away from the children next to them. The chaser and the runner are standing on the outside of the circle.

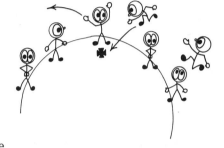

On the signal "Go," the chaser chases the runner in an effort to tag him. To keep from being caught, the runner can stop in front of anyone in the circle. Immediately this person becomes the runner. If the chaser tags the runner, then the roles reverse and the runner becomes the chaser and the game continues. Running can take place both inside and close to the outside of the circle.

Encourage the runners to change often, as this gives the children a chance to participate and makes the game more exciting.

"RACETRACK"

Passive

Equipment: None.

Formation: Have the children form one large circle or a few small circles. If you (or the children) select automobiles as the theme, go around the circle and give each child an automobile name such as Ford, Chevrolet, Jeep, Plymouth, and so on. If you use four different names, you end up with four groups of children. Sometimes use a different theme such as frogs, toads, salamanders, lizards, and crayfish, in which case there are five groups of children.

After everyone has a name, you will call out one name. Everyone with that name backs out of the circle and runs to their right (or left) all at the same time. Each child runs around the outside of the circle and back to his original spot. As soon as one group has returned to its place, call another name. Do not call the names in a particular order but also make sure all groups receive about the same number of opportunities to run around the circle. After a few minutes, you may tell everyone to skip around the circle, then run backward, slide side-ward, gallop, leap, and so on. Try to avoid deciding which group or which child was the fastest.

PARTNER HUNT

Active

Equipment: You need a record player with appropriate music if in the multipurpose room; no equipment if outside.

Formation: Have the children arrange themselves in a double circle, one circle inside the other. The inside circle should have one more person than the outside circle. In the beginning, have the inside circle face the outside circle as partners. Remember, there will be one inside person who has no partner. When the signal is given, the circles skip to their right. This means that the circles will be moving in opposite directions. On the signal "Stop," both circles stop and face each other to establish partners quickly. When following this routine, there will always be one inside person who has no partner. Use the basic loco-motor skills. Have the children hop, jump, skip, slide, gallop, walk, and run.

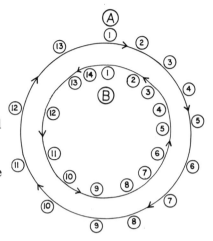

"COWBOYS, BEARS, REDSKINS, RAIDERS"

Active-Passive

Equipment: You need 25 bicycle tires (or hula hoops).

Formation: See the illustration. Make the formation as large as you can. The larger the formation, the more running involved. Put the bicycle tires (or hula hoops) down as shown, and place the children in position. All of the children in position 1 are Cowboys; 2, Bears; 3, Redskins; and 4, Raiders. The "holdouts" are in the middle of the formation and must keep one foot inside the tire at A until they are activated. For example, if you call "Cowboys," all 1's change positions with another Cowboy from another squad. In the meantime, the holdouts (who are also activated on the signal "Cowboys") are trying to get into one of the empty Cowboy spaces. Those left out go to A and await the next signal.

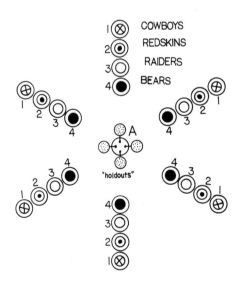

"BONUS BALL"

Passive

Equipment: You need 6 to 8 yarn balls and 20 to 30 old tennis balls.

Formation: "Bonus Ball" has many variations ranging from simple to complex. The beginning pattern is to divide the class into small groups and have each group form a line one behind the other with the first child standing at the beginning line. This activity works better if the groups are in the center of a room facing a wall, but not too close to the wall. Any kind of ball may be used if each group has the same kind of ball.

Let's begin by using colorful yarn balls and then change to other types of balls, such as tennis balls. Hand the first child in each line a yarn ball. Tell every child in each group to learn to identify his group's yarn ball. Now collect the yarn ball from each group. Next, throw all the yarn balls toward the wall, but not so close that the children run into the wall. As soon as the balls are thrown, the first child in each line runs to the thrown balls, finds the ball for his group, and runs back to the beginning line. That child goes to the end of his line, you collect the yarn balls again, and throw them again. The new first child runs to find the correct ball and returns to the starting line. This child goes to the end of her line and the process is repeated.

If you want to add another element, throw one more ball than there are groups. Now the first or next child in line runs to find the correct ball and takes it back to his or her line and then runs back to the area where the balls were thrown and tries to return with the extra ball. All the runners are also trying to return their group's ball and then find the *bonus* ball.

If possible, avoid keeping score. Just keep the activity going and fun will prevail.

Variation 1: An interesting variation is to use old tennis balls and mark numbers or letters on them. Provide each group with one tennis ball. Throw or roll the tennis balls as before. The child must find the ball with the correct number or letter on it and return to the group. You may also add an additional ball and proceed as before.

Variation 2: Throw or roll a variety of many balls and the next child must collect—one at a time—as many balls as possible.

"CROWS AND CRANES"

Active

Equipment: None.

Formation: "Crows and Cranes" is a good spontaneous activity in early childhood. Draw a line on the floor down the center of the available space. (There may already be a line on some of your paved outdoor areas and on your indoor areas.)

Have about half the children on one side of the line and the other half on the other side. The two groups should face each other and be no closer to the dividing line than 2' on each side of the line. This will put the children about 4' apart. Call one group the Cranes; the other group, the Crows. Review the names of each group so the children know the name of their group.

One way to begin the activity is to call out the name of one group. As you call out the name, drag the beginning letters—Crrrrooows or Crrraaanes—so the children will have to listen carefully to the full word. The group whose name is called must chase and try to tag as many of the other group as possible. Behind each group is a "safe" line. This line should not be too far away. The children being chased are safe if they cross the safe line before being tagged. As soon as the chasing is over, the children go back to their original side and you call out one of the names.

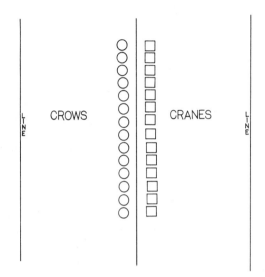

It is good to avoid alternating the names so that you can surprise both groups. Some teachers tell the children tagged that they must join the other group. This is *not* recommended for young children because they may not be ready to learn the other name quickly and will panic when uncertain. Also, this procedure causes some to lose, and there is no reason anyone should lose in this situation.

"STOP BALL"

Active-Passive

Equipment: You need 2 playground balls.

Formation: Divide the class into two teams. Then have each team form a circle, with the outside of the foot touching the outside of the feet of the children next to them. The children should stoop over with hands on knees. In the middle of each circle is the "roller," who has a playground ball. On the signal "Go," the rollers try to roll the ball through the legs of the children in the circle. The children in the circle block the ball with their *hands,* not

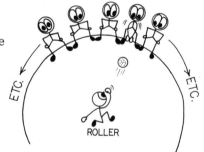

their feet, but they cannot move their hands from their knees until the ball is rolled toward them. When they block the ball, they push it back to the roller so that he can continue. If the ball goes between the feet of the player, that person becomes the new roller. Encourage the roller to use quick changes of direction to mask his intent. Remember, all players must keep their hands on their knees until the ball is rolled toward them.

"MAIL MOVERS"

Passive

Equipment: None.

Formation: "Mail Movers" requires four groups sitting in a square formation similar to "Crab Soccer." The lines should be close to the same length but not necessarily equal. Give each line the name of a city, such as St. Louis, Chicago, Asheville, New York. You may want to use cities close to and including your own area. You may also use states, countries, animals, birds, or any other category your children need for some memory drill.

Begin by calling out, "Move the mail from St. Louis to New York." The children in those two lines get up and walk to the line that is also getting up and the two lines change places. It is a good idea to stress walking. As soon as the move is completed, call out two more lines. All the lines should be receiving turns but not in any particular order. (If you are using metals, you could say "Ship" the iron and gold, and those two lines would change places. If you are learning about animals, tell the children to "Move the goats and horses." This is a good activity to reinforce necessary concepts for any area of the curriculum.)

As the children understand the activity and you feel they are ready, select a child to call out what lines are to change places. An additional element may be included when you feel the children are ready. Instead of walking from one place to another, tell the children to use both feet and both hands to travel. Other suggestions include two feet and one hand, two hands and one foot, face the ceiling as you travel, face the ceiling and only use two hands and one foot, face the ceiling and only use two feet and one hand, and so on.

"MASS CONFUSION"

Active

Equipment: You need a good supply of *soft* items that can be safely thrown.

Formation: This game is fun and vigorous, but it does require a supply of soft items that can be thrown, such as yarn balls, Nerf™ balls, panty hose balls, sock balls, pieces of foam, and so on. Either mark a line on the floor dividing the area into two halves or use an existing line. Select half the group to be on each side of the line. Put approximately half the throwing items on the floor on each side of the line. The object of the game is to have as many items on the other side of the line as possible when play is stopped.

On your command "Go," all the children pick up a throwing item and toss it across the dividing line. No one may cross the middle dividing line. Allow the children to continue throwing as you watch for signs of fatigue. This activity will work better indoors but can be played outside. When played outside, more running is involved. When you decide fatigue is noticeable, call "Stop," and have everyone sit down and stop throwing. Instead of trying to decide which side has the fewer number of objects, just go on to another activity or repeat this one. No one loses. The children will realize very quickly it is better to throw away from the children on the other side rather than at them such as in a dodge ball game. This activity has all the good features of dodge ball and none of the bad features, such as being hit!

"COMBAT"

Active-Passive

Equipment: You need a 30′ circle (or 28 bicycle tires or hula hoops) and 2 playground balls.

Formation: Divide the class into two teams and put 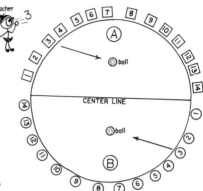 them into a circle as shown. A 30′ circle with a center line in the multipurpose room or outside on a black top surface works fine. If you do not have a circle, bicycle tires or hula hoops put out in a circle formation will also work well. You can use a couple of long jump ropes for the center line.

Team A will be in half the circle, and team B will be in the other half of the circle. Each team will have a playground ball sitting in front. Each person on both teams numbers off 1 through 14 (if there are 28 players). If there is an uneven number in the class, which is usually the case, you may have 14 on one team and 13 on the other. On the team with 13, give one of the players two numbers, which works well in most cases.

To begin the game, loudly call a number, such as 3. The children with that number from both teams quickly run out and pick up the ball that is located in front of their team. The object is to hit the other person below the shoulder with the ball before he hits the other player. The one who hits first wins a point for his team, and both players return to their circles so that another number can be called. Remember, both players *must* stay *behind* their center line at all times. If they step *over* or *on* it, they are out and the other team wins a point.

Now, if 3 from team A throws the first ball and misses, any player in the circle on team B can catch the ball and hold it so that he can give it to his 3 if he throws his ball and misses, too. Both teams can do this, so if all the players are alert, they should always have a ball for their player if he throws and misses. This makes the game very exciting.

Encourage the children to take advantage of the center line. If their opponent throws and misses, then they should immediately go all the way to the center line and throw rather than throw from the back of their circle.

Also, tell the children that they can try to make the thrower miss by retreating to the edge of the circle or close to the bicycle tires, feinting one way then the other, jumping in the air if the ball comes at his feet, and so on.

"PARTNER TAG"

Passive

Equipment: None.

Formation: This is similar in some respects to "Two Deep" except for being a little more advanced and requiring more attention and concentration.

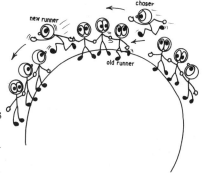

Again, have the class form a large circle. Next, have the class count off in 3's. Each group of three will hook their arms. Again, you need a chaser and a runner who are standing on the outside of the circle. On the signal "Go," the chaser runs after the runner and tries to tag him. If the runner sees that he is about to be tagged, he can hook arms with any of the groups of three. The child at the opposite end of this threesome immediately becomes the new runner and takes off running. If the runner is tagged by the chaser, the roles reverse, and the runner becomes the new chaser and the game continues.

Again, some of the runners will have to be encouraged not to run too long and to hook up sooner as this will give more children a chance to participate and make the game more exciting. You will also have to encourage them to be alert at all times and to be ready to run quickly when their group is hooked on to.

"AMOEBA TAG"

Active

Equipment: None.

Formation: This activity requires running room and boundaries. A large rectangle is desirable with boundaries away from walls, chairs, radiators, and other hazardous items. Explain in a few words something about the amoeba. The main point is the way the amoeba divides during reproduction. After the children understand the idea of division, go on to explain how this game is played using the even division concept.

"Amoeba Tag" begins with one child selected as "It," who tries to tag another child. When a child is tagged, "It" and the tagged child hold hands and begin trying to tag other children. The outside hands of both may be used to tag other children. As children are tagged, they join the "It" group and hold hands as they run. The "It" group must hold hands while trying to tag other children. When the " It" group reaches four children or six children, they split (just like the amoeba) and the new groups are free to begin tagging other children. As more "It" groups are formed, there is less chance to escape being tagged. When someone goes out of bounds, that player joins an "It" group.

It may be best to stop the activity when only a few children remain untagged and begin again with a new "It" person. This is a vigorous activity and should only be allowed for a few minutes.

"CRAB SOCCER"

Active-Passive

Equipment: You need soft volleyball or playground balls (or large yarn balls or Nerf™ balls).

Formation: Modified "Crab Soccer" begins with everyone sitting on the floor in a square formation. Divide the class into four groups and have each group become one side of a square as everyone sits on the floor. Begin with one soft type of ball large enough to be kicked. Toss the ball into the square so that someone may kick it. The object of the game is to kick that ball over the heads of another line. When the ball goes over the head and behind a line of children, put the ball back in play with another toss. When you see that the children are ready, have two balls going at the same time. When one goes over a line of children, toss it back into the square.

To help you live through this activity, you may want to select one child from each line to stand behind her line and toss the ball back into the square. When the group can handle two balls, add one more. When they can handle three, add one more. You must adjust the size of the square to suit your children. However, make sure the square remains intact during the activity.

"OCTOPUS"

Active

Equipment: None.

Formation: This activity requires boundaries located away from hazardous items. The usual large rectangle is still the best shape. Have all participants line up at one end of the rectangle, and select one child to be the "octopus." The chosen "octopus" stands in the center of the rectangle facing the rest of the class. On a signal from you, everyone tries to run to the opposite line without being tagged by the "octopus." Again, there are side boundaries that should not be crossed.

The "octopus" tries to tag as many children as possible before they reach the opposite line. All children tagged must stop where they are and remain on that spot for the remainder of the game. Everyone not tagged should be on the opposite line waiting for the signal to run across to the opposite line (the beginning line). Everyone who is tagged becomes an "octopus helper." These helpers may not run around, but may pivot on one foot while trying to tag children running across the area. A good strategy for the "octopus" is to force the children running across the area to run near an "octopus helper" who may pivot and stretch while attempting to tag a runner. It eventually becomes impossible to make it across without being tagged. It is not necessary to continue the game until everyone has been tagged. When it becomes obvious no one can make it across, begin another game.

"FIRE STATION"

Active-Passive

Equipment: None.

Formation: Divide your class into groups. The more groups you have, the more participation. Select a beginning line and have each group of children line up one behind the other with the first child facing the beginning line. Select a turnaround line parallel to the beginning line and not too far from the beginning line. How far away the turnaround line is from the beginning line is determined by how far you want the children to travel. Give each group a number: Fire Station 1, Fire Station 2, Fire Station 3, and so on.

A good way to begin is to require everyone to walk to the turnaround line and back to the beginning line, so that they all know what to do. Then begin the activity by calling out, for example, "Fire Station 3. That group walks to the turnaround line and back; the entire group goes together. Then call out another fire station and that group walks to the turnaround line and back to the starting line. Continue to call out different fire stations without using a set pattern.

After the children understand the activity and are ready for a change, tell them to walk backward as they travel. Then change the method of locomotion to a slide, gallop, hop, leap, crawl, crab walk, or whatever other skills you feel the children should practice. You may include running if you feel the children can run safely. This activity provides an opportunity for all children to participate and minimizes winning and losing.

"CALL BALL"

Passive

Equipment: You need 2 playground balls.

Formation: Divide the class into two teams, then have each team form a large circle so that each child is about a double arm's length from his or her neighbors. One child stands in the center of each circle with a ball. The other players count off. Play is started when the child in the center carefully throws the ball into the air and at the same time calls out the number of one of the children in his circle. That child quickly runs out to the center of the circle and tries to catch the ball *on the first bounce.* If she is successful, she becomes the new center player. If she does not catch it, the old center player continues.

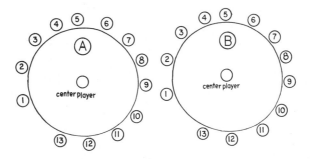

Later, if they show a lot of improvement, the circles can be made smaller and the children can try to catch the ball before it hits the ground. This will work only if the center player can toss the ball high enough.

"BALLOON VOLLEYBALL"

Active-Passive

Equipment: You need 4 or 5 large round balloons.

Formation: This is an excellent activity for young children. Draw a line down the center of the classroom or multipurpose room. Select 4 children to take their chairs (or desks) and face the center line. Then select an equal number to take their chairs (desks) and face the original

4 on the other side of the line. Right now, you should have 4 children on each side of the line, and they should be facing each other. Now select 4 more children for each side of the line to sit with their backs to the original four. You should have 16 children now, 4 on each side of the center line facing each other and 4 on each side with their backs to the children on their side. The next line of children (on each side) will take their chairs and face the children whose backs are to the center line. Be sure to include all the children in the class.

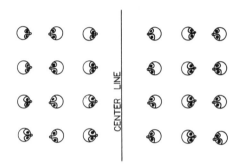

Each side of the center line should have three groups of children (lines). Three lines of children face the same direction and three lines of children face the opposite direction. If you stand at the center line, everyone facing toward your right is on the same team and everyone facing toward your left is on the same team.

Inflate at least four large round balloons. Begin with one balloon and toss it high over the center line. The team facing to your right tries to hit the balloon over the heads of the children facing them. The team facing to your left tires to hit the balloon over the heads of the children facing them. As the balloon falls out of reach for the children, either you toss it back in play or ask the closest child to toss the balloon back in play. When you know the children are ready, toss a second balloon over the center line and allow play to continue. Using at least two balloons keeps the activity exciting and you busy! Depending upon the size of the group, you may want to try three or even four balloons at the same time. Keeping score is not important, but if you want to, a point is scored each time a balloon hits the floor beyond the back lines.

The only rule (and difficult to enforce) is that no one may leave his or her sitting position to hit a balloon. If the children are sitting on the floor (and this may be a better way to play the game), the same rule applies.

"JUMP THE SHOE"

Active

Equipment: You need 1 long jump rope and an old shoe.

Formation: "Jump the Shoe" requires a long rope with a shoe tied to one end. The children form a circle around you and try to jump over the circling object. Begin turning the rope around with a short radius until the children understand that the idea is to jump over the shoe as it comes to them. Gradually increase the radius and the children try to jump over the shoe (or rope) as it passes under them. When the rope stops at someone, begin again with a short radius and gradually cause the shoe to move farther and farther away from the center. Some children will prefer backing away until they are comfortable and will then move forward and try to jump the shoe.

"DETECTIVE"

Active

Equipment: You need a piece of chalk (or other small object).

Formation: This game can be played in the classroom or multipurpose room. The only equipment needed is a small piece of chalk or other small object. Select one child to leave the room. You (or a child) hide the small object in a fair place—not some place the child cannot reach. Then the child is called back to the room. Instead of using loud noises to help the child find the object, the children use physical motions of the arms and legs to help the child find the object. Everyone remains in their seats or desks and uses arms and legs to indicate how close the child is to finding the object. The closer the child is, the more vigorous the motions; as the child moves away, the quieter everyone becomes. When the object is located, that child (or you) selects someone else to become the new "detective."

Track ———————————— 25

Children love to run and jump, so it will not take a lot of work to get them motivated for track. The following skills can be covered easily in squads, practicing them on a rotating basis. You might want to put these skills to use during a spring field day.

THE STANDING START

This is the most realistic and popular way to start on the elementary level because most children at this age level will be running in sneakers or tennis shoes. The runner puts one foot slightly in front of the other and leans slightly from the waist. On the signal "Go," the runner pushes off the back foot and is on his or her way.

THE CROUCH START

The crouch start is a bit more complicated than the standing start. The crouch start must be adapted to each child because of different body measurements. (1) Place the toe of the forward foot about 4″ to 8″ from the starting line. Then place the knee of the other leg on the ground so that the knee is even with the instep or ankle of the forward leg. The fingers are spread on the starting line with the weight on the tips of the fingers. (2) On the signal "Get set," the knee of the rear leg is lifted as the back is raised so that it is level with the ground. The weight is evenly distributed between the hands and the feet, and the eyes are focused at a spot 6′ to 8′ in front of the runner. (3) On the signal "Go," the runner drives hard with both legs as the back leg straightens and the front leg comes forward. It is important that the runner rises gradually from the start rather than stand up straight too soon.

HIGH JUMP

IMPORTANT: There should always be a soft surface for the children to land on when doing high jumps. To do a simple roll, approach the bar at an angle of approximately 45°. (1) Take off on the inside foot and, at the same time, swing the outside leg forward and upward. (2) This will put the body parallel to the bar when crossing. (3) The jumper will do a slight roll as she is crossing the bar. Then she lands on her right foot and hands.

STANDING BROAD JUMP

The standing broad jump is performed by first toeing the line with both feet. (1) Crouch low with knees bent and arms back of the hips. Then (2) jump forward and upward, and (3) land on both feet.

PASSING THE BATON

In official meets, the baton must be passed within a 20-yard space. The *visual exchange* is recommended on the elementary level. When the approaching runner is approximately 7 yards away, the receiver should begin running, looking back with her right arm extended backward, hand open with the palm up to receive the baton. The runner carries the baton in his left hand.

RUNNING LONG JUMP

The short run to the takeoff takes a lot of practice if the takeoff leg is to hit the board in natural stride. IMPORTANT: If the running long jump is used, there should be a jumping pit provided with soft material for children to land in.

The jumper needs (1) a short run of 16 to 20 strides and should be aimed so that the toes of the takeoff foot hit the board in natural stride. (2) While in the air, either the *hitch kick* can be used (where the legs cycle in the air), or the *tuck jump* (where the body is tucked as if sitting in a chair) can be used. (3) As the heels hit the pit, thrust the arms forward so that the body falls forward.

How to Make Equipment——26

Here are directions for making many of the courts and equipment described in this book.

FOUR SQUARE COURTS

Putting down neat and attractive Four Square courts is really not difficult. You need a black top area large enough to put down at least *four* Four Square courts. The equipment needed will be listed as we go along. It is easier if you can get someone to help you, but if you have to do it by yourself, an ice pick can help you. An ice pick will stick into the black top and will do a good job of anchoring one end of your measuring tape or chalk line.

Decide what size courts you want to put down. If your area is small, you may have to go with four 10′ × 10′ courts; if your black top is larger, you may want to put in four 16′ × 16′ courts. Children in grades K–3 seem to like the larger courts better, whereas students in grades 4–6 prefer the smaller courts because they are faster.

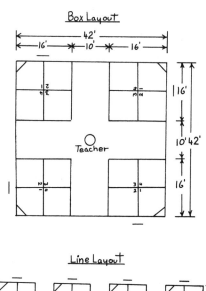

228

Try to get as much room between the courts as possible—ideally 10'. But if your area is small, you may have to settle for 6'. If the courts are too close together, games can be interrupted by loose balls from adjacent courts.

A good Four Square court layout is the *box layout,* as shown in the illustration. In this situation, you can stand in the center and be in an excellent position to direct the action. But if your black top area is long and slender, you may have to go for a *line layout.*

Whatever formation you decide to use, lay it out with a chalk line. The equipment and supplies needed to do this are

- Chalk line
- Container of powdered chalk
- Ice pick
- Tape measure
- Broom
- 2 or 3 pieces of chalk for making midline measuring points

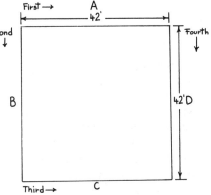

To give an example, this illustration shows the steps involved in chalking out a box layout. First, lay out line A with your chalk line. This line, which includes two 16' × 16' courts and a 10' space between, is 42' long. Therefore, since this is a box layout, all four of the other lines (A, B, C, D) will be the same length (42'). Second, the next line to chalk in is line B. It is very important to get a 90° angle on this first corner. If you don't, the whole square will be out of line. There are many sophisticated ways of getting this angle, but you can easily use either a carpenter's square or simply a large cardboard box (the type that the school's paper towels come in).

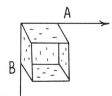

Place the box carefully on the corner of lines A and B, and carefully line up line B on this. Third, measure line C 42' from the end of line B. Fourth, begin your measurement of line D 42' from the end of line A down to the end of line C. This will assure the correct angle at the corner of lines C and D.

Now that you have your box, chalking in the four Four Square courts is easy. Simply measure off the courts as shown in this illustration. This way, you will have all four courts laid out at the same time. Just disregard the chalk lines in the 10' areas. They will soon wash and wear away.

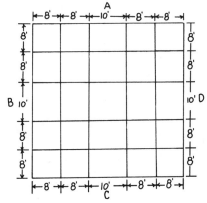

Now you are ready to paint your lines. Two methods of painting your lines are by hand or with a machine. If you do it by hand, it will take longer, but you will get a neater job. If you use the line painting machine (sometimes called a striping machine), you will finish faster, but your courts will usually not be as neat as those done by hand.

If you put the lines down with a line painting machine, you will need

♦ The machine
♦ A supply of spray traffic paint or spray tennis court paint

On some machines, you can adjust the width of the lines to be painted. If you do the lines by hand, you will need the following materials:

♦ A dozen or more rolls of ¾″ masking tape
♦ Several cheap 2″ wide paintbrushes
♦ Thinner, if oil-based traffic paint is used
♦ 2 or 3 no. 10 tin cans
♦ Rags
♦ 1 gallon of traffic or outdoor tennis court paint

First, sweep over the chalk lines with a broom to get rid of sand, rocks, and so on. Then, on the *outside lines* of the Four Square courts, lay your masking tape on *the bottom edge* of the chalk line (see A in the illustration).

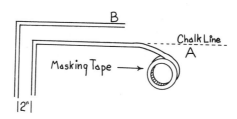

Next, lay another line of tape approximately 2″ above as shown in B.

The *inside lines* will be done differently. This time, you will straddle the inside lines as shown so that there will be approximately 2″ between the tape.

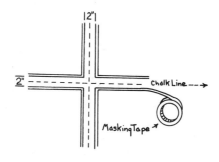

Carefully paint inside the tape. When dry, remove the tape. Remember, you will have to put in your server's triangle, the line for the extra players to stand behind, and the court numbers. Since Four Square rules differ from area to area, you will have to finish your courts to suit your own rules.

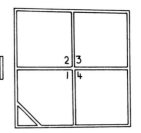

THE BARS

Use 1½" black pipe for all pieces of apparatus except for the hand holds on the monkey bars; use ¾" black pipe for these.

Add 3' to each vertical section that goes into the ground. These should be put in with concrete.

You will need two vaulting bars, which should be 30' apart as shown in the illustration. All joints should be welded and all sharp edges filed off.

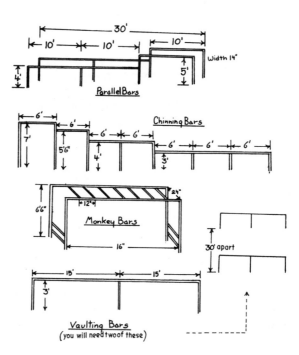

WALL TRAVERSE

Get the feel and challenge of rock climbing in a safe, controlled situation. Since this is strictly a "traverse" and is located close to the floor, no belay ropes, helmets, and other expensive equipment are needed. Use either the metal angle irons or the oak blocks shown in the illustration. This is an excellent item to use in your indoor circuits.

ANGLE IRON

OAK BLOCK

THE RAMP

You might paint the surface of the ramp with sand paint for better traction.

BATTING T

Using two cones, stuff the top cone with newspaper for the desired height.

BOUNDING BOARD

For longer life, use the bounding board only with grades K–2.

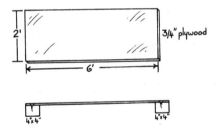

FOOTPRINTS

Make copies of the foot pattern on page 235 and cut them out. Use as is for the right feet; turn over the cutout patterns for the left feet.

HOOP HOLDER

Put the hoop in the holder with one part on the high side for better balance.

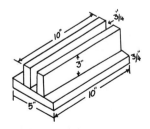

MILK JUG MARKERS

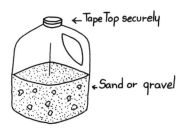

SOCK BALLS

Use old nylons, panty hose, or socks. (1) Stuff the sock with paper and tie the end with a knot. (2) Twist, then pull down. (3) Keep twisting, then pull up. (4) Continue twisting and pulling up until you have a ball.

TURNING BAR

Drill a hole through the pipe and the bottom brace. Insert a bolt to keep the bar from turning.

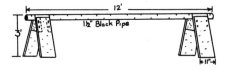

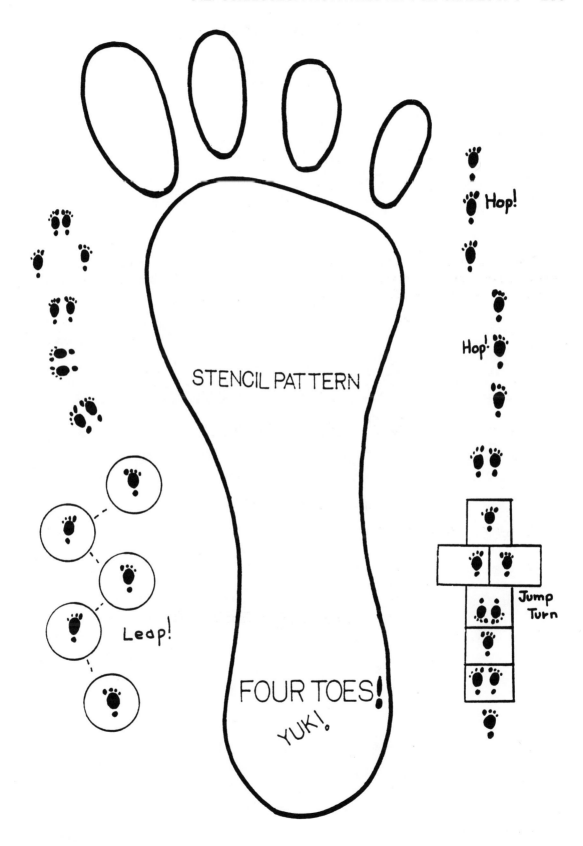

STENCIL PATTERN

Hop!

Hop!

Leap!

FOUR TOES!

YUK!.

Jump Turn

BENCH

Use *dry* wood for the bench construction. Sand the wood and varnish it.

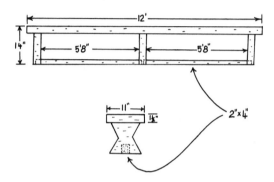

HULA HOOPS

You can get all the materials you need to make hula hoops at your local hardware store. You need

♦ ½" × 8′ plastic water pipe (see A in the illustration)
♦ ½" plastic pipe fittings to hold pipe ends together (see B)
♦ Plastic tape

When you have inserted both ends of the pipe over the fitting, squeeze until both ends of the pipe are touching. Then cover the ends with plastic tape. If you have difficulty getting the pipe ends to go over the fitting, soak the pipe ends in hot water for a few minutes.

BALANCE BEAM

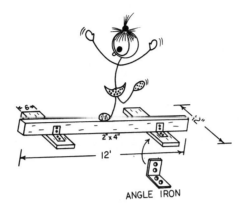

For a wider balance beam, nail two 2″ × 4″s together.